Ken Hom's
CHINESE COOKERY

Ken Hom's
CHINESE
COOKERY

Edited by Jenny Stevens

Guild Publishing
London

The spellings of Chinese words and place names in this book follow the pinyin system of converting Chinese characters to the Roman alphabet. This system has been officially adopted by the People's Republic of China since 1979 and it closely resembles actual Mandarin pronunciation. Since this is a relatively new system you may find that it takes you a while to get used to seeing Beijing for Peking and Sichuan instead of Szechuan. I have used the new system throughout except for the spellings of very well known dishes, such as Peking Duck and dim sum, and for a few ingredients which are Cantonese. In the case of the better known places in China the pinyin spelling is followed by the other spelling, as, for example, Guangzhou (Canton).

This book accompanies the BBC Television series *Chinese Cookery*, first broadcast on BBC2 from October 1984.

Series producer and book editor: Jenny Stevens
Consultant: Margaret Leeming
Photographer: Bryce Attwell
Stylist: Roisin Nield
Illustrations: Ken Astrop and David Brown (map)

Published to accompany a series of programmes prepared in consultation with the BBC Continuing Education Advisory Council

© Ken Hom 1984
Hardback edition first published 1984
This edition published 1985
by Book Club Associates by arrangement with
BBC Publications
Reprinted 1988

Typeset in 11 on 12pt Melior
Typeset by Phoenix Photosetting, Chatham
Printed and bound in Great Britain by Mackays of Chatham Ltd, Kent
Colour and cover origination by Bridge Graphics, Hull
Colour and cover printed by Chorley and Pickersgill Ltd, Leeds

CONTENTS

CONVERSION TABLES

All these are *approximate* conversions, which have either been rounded up or down. In a few recipes it has been necessary to modify them very slightly. Never mix metric and imperial measures in one recipe. Stick to one system or the other.

Weights	
½ oz	10 g
1	25
1½	40
2	50
3	75
4	110
5	150
6	175
7	200
8	225
9	250
10	275
12	350
13	375
14	400
15	425
1 lb	450
1¼	550
1½	700
2	900
3	1·4 kg
4	1·8
5	2·3

Volume	
1 fl oz	25 ml
2	50
3	75
5 (¼ pint)	150
10 (½)	300
15 (¾)	400
1 pint	570
1¼	700
1½	900
1¾	1 litre
2	1·1
2¼	1·3
2½	1·4
2¾	1·6
3	1·7
3¼	1·8
3½	2
3¾	2·1
4	2·3
5	2·8
6	3·4
7	4·0
8 (1 gal)	4·5

Measurements	
¼ inch	0·5 cm
½	1
1	2·5
2	5
3	7·5
4	10
6	15
7	18
8	20·5
9	23
11	28
12	30·5

Oven temperatures		
Mk 1	275°F	140°C
2	300	150
3	325	170
4	350	180
5	375	190
6	400	200
7	425	220
8	450	230
9	475	240

INTRODUCTION

Good food has been an important part of my life since my earliest childhood. I well remember my family gathered around the dinner table endlessly discussing what we were to eat, how it would be prepared, what our favourite dishes were, the best methods for cooking various delicacies, and so forth. In fact this is a common experience for most Chinese – food is our favourite topic of conversation. For us food is more than a passion, it is an obsession, and good eating is believed to be essential to good living. We Chinese have an expression: 'Chi fan le mei you?', which literally means: 'Have you eaten yet?'. It is used universally as a greeting, just as one would ask in English, 'How are you?'. It is also a wish for one's health and happiness. It is an entirely appropriate phrase since food to the Chinese has always meant much more than mere sustenance, and the processes of cultivating, selecting, cooking and consuming it are completely embedded into Chinese culture.

Like all Chinese children I absorbed a great deal of knowledge about Chinese cuisine simply by listening to the dinner table conversations of my relations. My real culinary training, however, took place in my uncle's restaurant in Chicago where I started to work part-time at the age of 11. In those early days I had all the routine, unpleasant jobs. I remember peeling hundreds of pounds of prawns, a tedious and painful chore. I also have memories of cleaning what seemed like mountains of huge sea snails which were delivered to the kitchen in enormous burlap bags. All the time I was thus employed I was surrounded by the wonderful aromas of the mouth-watering dishes being prepared by the expert chefs. Slowly they taught me why a particular spice went with a certain meat, why this sauce suited that vegetable, in short, the essence of Chinese cooking technique.

Although my family were originally from Guangdong (Kwantung Province), my uncle employed chefs from many different parts of China. Many people think that all Chinese cooking is similar, which is understandable since all Chinese cooks share a common technique, and since so many restaurants in the West blur the distinctions between the various regional styles. But China is a vast country with great variations in climate, agricultural tradition and available foodstuffs. It is no wonder then, that there are actually many variations in culinary style within China. They can be separated into four key regional categories:-

The Southern School
This is the region of Guangdong (Cantonese) cuisine which is probably the best known in the West because in the nineteenth century many Chinese families emigrated from this area to Europe

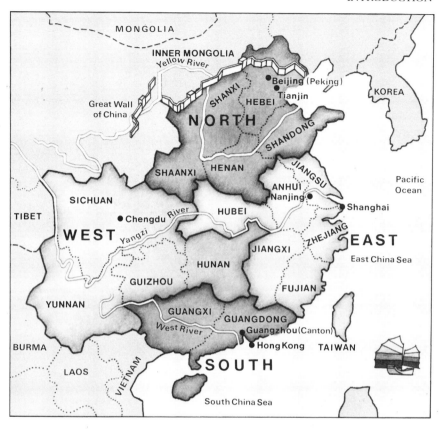

and America. Cantonese cooking is regarded by many as the *haute cuisine* of China. Some people attribute this to the influence of the brilliant chefs of the Imperial Court who fled to Guangzhou (Canton) when the Ming dynasty was overthrown in 1644. The Cantonese are especially interested in exotic delicacies such as dog, snake, frog's legs and turtle. The area is famous for its sweet and sour dishes, such as Sweet and Sour Pork, for its *dim sum* — a range of delicious snacks which are served as a light lunch or afternoon tea, and for its widespread use of soy, hoisin and oyster sauces.

The Cantonese prefer their food slightly undercooked so that the natural flavours and colours are preserved, and for this reason stir-frying and steaming are two of the most popular methods of cooking. They also avoid the heavy use of garlic, spices and oils, and concentrate instead on achieving a subtle, yet harmonious blend of colours, textures, aromas and flavours. Rice is the staple of the Cantonese diet and the area is known as one of the 'rice-bowls' of China.

9

The Northern School

This area stretches from the Yangzi (Yangtze) River to the Great
Wall of China and embraces the culinary styles of Shandong
(Shantung), Henan and Beijing (Peking). A distinguishing feature
of its cuisine is the use of grains, rather than rice, as the staple
food, particularly wheat, corn and millet, which the northerners
eat in the form of bread, noodles, dumplings and pancakes.
Because of the harshness of the climate, fresh vegetables are only
available at certain times of the year. To compensate for this,
northerners have learned how to preserve foods to see them
through their long winters. Vegetables like sweet potatoes, turnips,
onions and cabbages which store well are widely used, and the
region specialises in a range of preserved ingredients such as dried
mushrooms, dried and smoked meats, and pickled fruits and
vegetables. Unlike all the other regions of China, meat is in much
shorter supply, although beef, mutton and goat are available as well
as pork. This area contains many of China's four million Moslems
who shun pork, and their presence has greatly affected its cuisine.

The Imperial Court of China was based in Beijing (Peking) and
its influence on the culinary style of the area is still reflected in
some of its more complicated and spectacular dishes such as the
celebrated Peking Duck. Of all the elaborate banquet dishes in
Chinese cuisine, this is the most glorious. Its subtlety and
sophistication are a distinct contrast to other more strongly
flavoured dishes which characterise northern cooking, depending
heavily as it does on garlic, spring onions, leeks, sesame seeds and
oil, and sweet bean sauce.

The Eastern School

This region stretches from the eastern coast to central China. It
contains the cooking styles of Fujian (Fukien), Jiangxi, Zhejiang
and, most important of all, Shanghai, which is the biggest city in
China and its greatest port. The region contains some of the most
fertile land in all China which provides a rich variety of fresh fruit
and vegetables, and the area is noted for its vegetarian cuisine. The
countryside is dominated by the magnificent Yangzi (Yangtze)
River and the coastline is very long. Consequently fresh fish and
shellfish are also plentiful.

Eastern cooks prefer light and delicate seasonings to maximise
the natural flavours of their fresh ingredients. The preferred
cooking techniques are stir-frying, steaming, red-cooking (slow
simmering in a dark soy sauce) and blanching. Soy sauce from this
area is reputed to be the best in China. The region is also famous for
some special ingredients, notably black vinegar, which is used

10

both for cooking and as a dipping sauce; Zhejiang ham, which is rather like raw English smoked bacon; and rice wine. Sugar is widely used in the cooking of meat and vegetables, as is a great deal of oil, earning this area a reputation for rich food.

The Western School

This area is entirely inland and includes the provinces of Sichuan (Szechuan) and Hunan, the birthplace of Chairman Mao. This 'land of abundance', as it is sometimes called, is virtually surrounded by mountains and was almost cut off from the rest of China until this century. Nowadays Sichuan cuisine in particular is fast gaining popularity in the West. In this area summers are hot and sultry and the winters mild. Fruit and vegetables are plentiful as are pork, poultry and fish. The distinguishing aspect of the culinary style is its reliance on very strong flavourings and hot spices, particularly red chillis, Sichuan peppercorns, ginger, onions and garlic. Outsiders used to suggest that such ingredients were used to mask the taste of the food which had deteriorated in the area's muggy heat. However, regional chefs stand by their cuisine and their command of the art of seasoning. Dishes from this area are usually artful combinations of many flavours and can be hot, sour, sweet and salty all at once.

Chinese cooking outside China

The Revolution in China in 1949 and its aftermath had con-sequences for cooking as well as profound political and social effects. Within China, the great cookery tradition became for quite some time almost moribund. Revolutionaries deemed the art of cooking an elitist and reactionary enterprise, a reminder of Imperial days and therefore best repressed. Only recently has an effort been made to revive the tradition, to train young chefs and to allow small private restaurants to start up or re-open.

Countries outside China benefited from the demise in Chinese cuisine brought about by this revolutionary zeal. Relaxed immigration rules, particularly in North America, allowed the entry into Western countries of Chinese people from all parts of Mainland China. Cantonese restaurants which had been pre-dominant were now joined by Sichuan (Szechuan), Hunanese and Shanghai restaurants, to the great enrichment of Western palates! Increasing familiarity with and availability of Chinese ingredients, coupled with the rapid rise in the popularity of the wok, has encouraged many non-Chinese people to experiment with Chinese cooking.

The grand tradition of Chinese cookery has not only survived but has been developed to a high degree of excellence in Taiwan and Hong Kong. Many food critics and gourmets now consider Hong Kong to be the greatest centre of Chinese cookery in the world. The best and most traditional ingredients of Chinese cooking flow over the Chinese border into Hong Kong and China is Hong Kong's chief food supplier. In its eagerness to earn foreign currency, China has fostered a trade which has ensured the maintenance of traditional Chinese cooking in Hong Kong, and Hong Kong's economic prosperity has supported the preservation of the best of this cuisine. In this bustling, energetic place there are over 40,000 restaurants and food stalls, all competing for the custom of the inhabitants, many of whom eat most of their meals out. Perhaps no other people in the world are so food-conscious. Even the smallest food stall sells delicious dishes of excellent quality and the top restaurants are regarded as being among the best in the world.

This book contains recipes from all the cooking traditions of China as well as some from Hong Kong. It also has a chapter on techniques (page 37) which covers a range of the cooking methods used such as braising, deep-frying, steaming and stir-frying. If you are new to Chinese cooking, do not feel that you have to prepare a meal which consists entirely of dishes from one particular region. Instead, select dishes which will provide a variety of colours, textures and tastes. On pages 51 to 56 I have given advice on how to put together a Chinese meal, and have suggested menus of varying complexity. Start with some of the simple ones which will give you experience in the basic cooking methods. At first try just one or two Chinese dishes at a time, perhaps incorporating them into a European meal. Chinese snacks and soups, for example, make wonderful starters for any meal and there are many Chinese dishes which can be successfully combined with Western-style meats and salads.

When you prepare your first entirely Chinese meal, select just two or three dishes and serve them with some plain steamed rice. Never select dishes which are all stir-fried or you will have a traumatic time in the kitchen trying to get everything ready at the same time and will arrive at the table hot and flustered. Choose instead to do one braised dish, a cold dish, or something which can be prepared ahead of time then warmed through, and limit your stir-frying to just one dish. This way not only will you gain the confidence needed to try more ambitious recipes, but your meal will be all the more authentic for embracing a harmonious blend of cooking techniques.

The Chinese diet is a very healthy one since it depends upon cooking methods which preserve vitamins and use small quantities of meat and no dairy produce. Underlying all Chinese cooking is the ancient yin yang theory of food science which is closely related to Chinese beliefs about health. In China, all foods are divided into one of three groups: yin, for cooling foods; yang, for heating foods; and yin yang for neutral foods. To the foreigner there is little obvious logic in the way foodstuffs are assigned to these categories. Yin foods include items as diverse as beer, crab, duck and soda water. Yang foods include brandy, beef, coffee and smoked fish. Neutral foods include bread, steamed rice, carrots, pigeon and peaches. Not only are all foods sub-divided in this way, but people are too. A yin person is quiet and introverted, while a yang person is a more active, outgoing type. The effect of different foods on an individual will depend upon the way they conflict with or complement his personality type. The idea is to construct a meal and one's whole diet to achieve the right balance or harmony. Most Chinese have some knowledge of the yin yang food science as the idea is instilled into them from a very young age.

Apart from a sensible mixture of yin and yang foods, the art of Chinese cookery also lies in achieving a harmonious blend of colour, texture, aroma and flavour. A typical Chinese meal consists of two parts—the fan which is the staple grain, be it rice, noodles or dumplings, and the cai which covers the rest of the dishes: meat, poultry, fish and vegetables. The average meal comprises three to four cai dishes, one fan dish and a soup. The cai dishes should each have a different main ingredient; for example, one meat, one fish and one vegetable. A variety of techniques will be used to cook these dishes. A fish may be steamed, a meat braised, while the vegetables may be stir-fried. The meal will also be designed so that each dish varies and yet complements the others in terms of appearance, texture and flavour. One dish will be spicy and another mild; one may be chewy and another crisp. The total effect should appeal to all the senses. All these dishes will be placed in the centre of the table and shared between the diners who help themselves and each other to a little of this, and then a little of that. Eating for the Chinese is a communal experience, and a shared meal is regarded as the visible manifestation of the harmony which should exist between family and friends.

The subtle and distinctive taste of Chinese food depends in part on the use of some special Chinese ingredients. Of the recipes I have given here, some use ingredients which are more complicated than others. Where possible I have suggested suitable Western alternatives, but I'm afraid that if you want to cook authentic

Chinese food there is ultimately no alternative but to track down a reliable source of the key Chinese ingredients. Fortunately it is becoming easier to find some of these in supermarkets, and Chinese grocers are proliferating, many of whom offer a mail-order service (see page 262). The chapter on ingredients (pages 15 to 30) lists all the specialist ingredients which I have used in the recipes and it will help you to know what to look or ask for. You may find it useful to refer to this before embarking on a shopping trip to your nearest Chinese grocer.

Your Chinese grocer may also be a good place to buy a wok. Although it is perfectly possible to cook Chinese food successfully using ordinary Western kitchen utensils, you will probably want to invest in a wok eventually to use for stir-frying at least. The beauty of the wok is that its shape ensures that heat is evenly distributed all over the pan, making for fast cooking, and its depth allows you to stir and toss foods rapidly when they need to be fried quickly. Equally important, you need use far less oil for deep-frying than you would with a deep-fat fryer. Woks usually work better on gas, although it is possible to get a flat-bottomed variety which is more suitable for electric cookers. I have given some advice on choosing and seasoning a wok on pages 32 and 33.

There is an old Chinese proverb which says 'To the ruler, people are heaven; to the people, food is heaven'. Once you have embarked on the exciting road to discovering the mysteries and pleasures of Chinese cooking you will soon find how sublime Chinese food can be. I wish you happy cooking and happy eating.

INGREDIENTS

Chinese cooking would not be 'Chinese' without the use of a number of specialist ingredients which give Chinese foods their distinctive flavours. All the ingredients used in the recipes in this book can be obtained in this country, if not from your local supermarket then certainly from a Chinese grocer. There are now many Chinese grocers throughout the UK and a list has been given at the back of this book (page 262) of those who offer a mail-order service. It is well worth the effort to find your nearest Chinese grocer and to build up a stock of the most frequently used ingredients. Many, particularly soy sauce, vary enormously in quality, but most Chinese grocers stock good authentic brands at reasonable prices.

The following is a list of the special ingredients which I have used in this book. There are also some notes on vegetables in the introduction to the vegetable chapter on page 185 and information on rice, noodles and flour in the introduction to Rice, Noodles and Doughs on page 215. One ingredient commonly used in China which you will *not* find mentioned here is monosodium glutamate (also known as MSG, Ve Tsin, Accent, seasoning or taste powder). This is a white crystalline extract of grains and vegetables widely used to tenderise and enhance the natural flavour of certain foods, particularly meat, in Japan and China and in Western food processing. Some people have an adverse reaction to it, experiencing symptoms such as headaches, excessive thirst and palpitations. This allergic response is sometimes known as 'Chinese restaurant syndrome'. I believe that the freshest and finest ingredients need no enhancing and I therefore never use it.

Bamboo shoots

Bamboo shoots are the young edible shoots of some kinds of bamboo. Unfortunately in this country they are only available tinned. Pale yellow with a crunchy texture, they come peeled and either whole or thickly sliced. They can be bought in most supermarkets, delicatessens and in Chinese grocers. Rinse them thoroughly before use and transfer any remaining shoots to a jar, cover them with fresh water and keep in the refrigerator. If the water is changed daily they will keep for up to a week.

Beancurd

Beancurd is also known by its Chinese name *doufu* or by its Japanese name *tofu*. It has played an important part in Chinese cookery for over 1000 years since it is highly nutritious, being rich in protein. Beancurd has a distinctive texture but a bland taste. It is

16

made from yellow soyabeans, which are soaked, ground, mixed with water and then cooked briefly before being solidified. In this country it is usually sold in two forms: firm cakes, or as a thickish junket, but it is also available in several dried forms and fermented. The soft junket-like variety (sometimes called silken *tofu*) is used for soups, while the solid type is used for stir-frying, braising and poaching. Solid beancurd 'cakes' are white in colour and are sold in Chinese grocers and in many health food shops. They are packed in water in plastic containers and may be kept in this state in the refrigerator for up to five days, providing the water is changed daily. To use solid beancurd, cut the amount required into cubes or shreds using a sharp knife. Do this with care as it is delicate. It also needs to be cooked carefully as too much stirring can cause it to disintegrate.

Black beans

These small black soya beans, also known as salted black beans, are preserved by being fermented with salt and spices. They have a distinctive, slightly salty taste and a pleasantly rich smell, and are used as a seasoning, often in conjunction with garlic or fresh ginger. They are inexpensive and can be obtained from Chinese grocers, usually in tins, as 'Black Beans in Salted Sauce' but you may also see them packed in plastic bags. Rinse them before use; I prefer to chop them slightly too. Transfer any unused beans and liquid to a sealed jar and the beans will keep indefinitely if stored in the refrigerator.

Chillis

Chillis are used extensively in western China and somewhat less frequently in the south. They are the seed pods of the capsicum plant and can be obtained fresh, dried or ground.

Fresh chillis

Fresh chillis can be distinguished by their small size and elongated shape. They should look fresh and bright with no brown patches or black spots. There are several varieties. Red chillis are generally milder than green ones because they sweeten as they ripen.

To prepare fresh chillis, first rinse them in cold water. Then, using a small sharp knife, slit them lengthways. Remove and discard the seeds. Rinse the chillis well under cold running water, and then prepare them according to the instructions in the recipe. Wash your hands, knife and chopping board before preparing other foods, and be careful not to touch your eyes until you have washed your hands thoroughly with soap and water.

17

Dried red chillis

Dried red chillis are small, thin and about ½ inch (1 cm) long. They are used to season oil for stir-fried dishes, sauces and for braising. They are normally left whole or cut in half lengthways and the seeds left in. The Chinese like them to blacken and be left in the dish during cooking, but as they are extremely hot and spicy you may choose to remove them after using them to flavour the cooking oil. They can be found in most supermarkets and in Chinese and Asian grocers, and will keep indefinitely in a tightly covered jar.

Chilli powder

Chilli powder is made from dried red chillis and is also known as cayenne pepper. It is pungent, aromatic, and ranges from hot to very hot; it is thus widely used in many spicy dishes. You will be able to buy it in any supermarket.

Cinnamon sticks or bark

Cinnamon sticks are curled, paper-thin pieces of the bark of the cinnamon tree. Chinese cinnamon comes as thicker sticks of this bark. It is highly aromatic and more pungent than the more common cinnamon sticks, but the latter are an adequate substitute. They add a robust taste to braised dishes and are an important ingredient of five spice powder. Store cinnamon sticks or bark in a tightly sealed jar to preserve their aroma and flavour. Ground cinnamon is not a satisfactory substitute.

Citrus peel

Dried citrus peel made from tangerines or oranges is used extensively in Chinese cookery to flavour braised and smoked dishes. It also adds an intense aroma and taste to stir-fried dishes. Drying the peel concentrates the flavour but you can use fresh peel instead. Chinese dried citrus peel can be found in Chinese grocers, usually in cellophane or plastic packets. It is, however, simple to make your own dried peel.

To make dried citrus peel

Peel the skin off a tangerine or orange, scraping away as much of the white pith as possible. Lay the peel on kitchen paper and dry it in the sun, in an airing cupboard, or in a warm but switched-off oven until it is dry and very hard. Store in a cool dry place in a well sealed container.

To use dried citrus peel

Soak the required amount of peel in warm water until it softens, then chop or slice it according to the recipe.

18

Coriander (Chinese parsley)

Fresh coriander is one of the relatively few herbs used in Chinese cookery. It looks like flat parsley but its pungent, musky, citrus-like flavour gives it a distinctive character which is unmistakable. Its feathery leaves are often used as a garnish or it can be chopped and then mixed into sauces and stuffings. Parsley may be used as a substitute but for an authentic Chinese flavour it is well worth trying to obtain the real thing. Many Asian and Chinese grocers stock it, as do some greengrocers and supermarkets now. When buying fresh coriander, look for deep green, fresh-looking leaves. Yellow and limp leaves indicate age and should be avoided.

To store coriander, wash it in cold water, drain it thoroughly and wrap in kitchen paper. Store it in the vegetable compartment of your refrigerator; it should keep for several days.

Cornflour

In China there are many flours and types of starch, such as waterchestnut powder, taro starch and arrowroot, which are used to bind and thicken sauces and to make batter. These exotic starches and flours are difficult to obtain but I have found cornflour works just as well in my recipes. As part of a marinade it helps to coat the food properly and it gives dishes a velvety texture. It also protects food during deep-frying by helping to seal in the juices, and can be used as a binder for minced stuffings. Cornflour is invariably blended with cold water until it forms a smooth paste before it is used in sauces.

Five spice powder

Five spice powder is less commonly known as five-flavoured powder or five fragrance spice powder, and is available in many supermarkets (in the spice section) and in Chinese grocers. This brownish powder is a mixture of star anise, Sichuan peppercorns, fennel, cloves and cinnamon. A good blend is pungent, fragrant, spicy and slightly sweet at the same time. The exotic fragrance it gives to a dish makes the search for a good mixture well worth the effort. It keeps indefinitely in a well sealed jar.

Garlic

Garlic has been an essential seasoning in Chinese cookery for thousands of years. Chinese food would be inconceivable without the distinctive, highly aromatic smell and taste of garlic. The Chinese use it in numerous ways: whole, finely chopped, crushed

19

and pickled. It is used to flavour oils as well as spicy sauces, and is often paired with other equally pungent ingredients such as spring onions, black beans or fresh ginger.

Select fresh garlic which is firm and preferably pinkish in colour. It should be stored in a cool, dry place but not in the refrigerator where it can easily become mildewed or begin sprouting.

Ginger
Fresh root ginger is indispensable in Chinese cookery. Its pungent, spicy and fresh taste adds a subtle but distinctive flavour to soups, meats and vegetables. It is also an important seasoning for fish and seafood since it neutralises fishy smells. Root ginger looks rather like a gnarled Jerusalem artichoke and can range in size from 3 inches (7·5 cm) to 6 inches (15 cm) long. It has pale brown, dry skin which is usually peeled away before use. Select fresh ginger which is firm with no signs of shrivelling. It will keep in the refrigerator, well wrapped in clingfilm, for up to two weeks. Fresh ginger can now be bought at many greengrocers and supermarkets and in most Chinese and Asian grocers. Dried powdered ginger has a quite different flavour and cannot be substituted for fresh root ginger.

Ham
Chinese ham has a rich salty flavour and is used primarily as a garnish or seasoning to flavour soups, sauces, stir-fried dishes, noodles and rice. One of the most prized Chinese smoked hams comes from Zhejiang Province. Unfortunately Chinese hams are not available in this country but a good substitute is either Parma ham which can be found in delicatessens and good supermarkets, or lean English smoked bacon (with any rind or fat cut away).

Chinese mushrooms
Mushrooms are a popular ingredient in Chinese cookery. There are many varieties and they are used both fresh and dried. The most common are:

Chinese dried mushrooms
There are many varieties of these which add a particular flavour and aroma to Chinese dishes. They can be black or brown in colour. The very large ones with a lighter colour and a highly cracked surface are the best and so they are usually the most expensive. They can be bought in boxes or plastic bags from Chinese grocers, and are fairly pricey. Keep them stored in an air-tight jar.

To use Chinese dried mushrooms

Soak the required amount of dried mushrooms in hot water for about 25 minutes until they are soft. Squeeze out any excess liquid and remove the tough, inedible stem. The mushrooms are now ready for use.

Straw mushrooms

These are among the tastiest mushrooms found in China. When fresh they have deep brown caps which are moulded around the stem. In this country they are only available in tins, and can be bought in Chinese grocers and in some supermarkets and delicatessens. Drain them and rinse in cold water before use.

Oils

Oil is the most commonly used cooking medium in China. The favourite is groundnut (peanut) oil. Animals fats, usually lard and chicken fat, are also used in some areas, particularly in north China. I prefer always to use oil since I find animal fats too heavy.

Throughout this book I have indicated where oils can be re-used. Where this is possible simply cool the oil after use and filter it through cheesecloth or a fine strainer into a jar. Cover it tightly and keep in a cool, dry place. If you keep it in the refrigerator it will become cloudy but it will clarify again when the oil returns to room temperature. I find oils are best re-used just once, and this is healthier since constantly re-used oils increase in saturated fat content.

Groundnut oil

This is also known as peanut oil or arachide oil. I prefer to use this for Chinese cookery because it has a pleasant, mild taste which is unobtrusive. Although it has a higher saturated fat content than some oils, its ability to be heated to a high temperature makes it perfect for stir-frying and deep-frying. Many supermarkets stock it, but if you cannot find it, use corn oil instead.

Corn oil

Corn or maize oil is also quite suitable for Chinese cooking. It has a high heating point although I find it rather bland and it has a slightly disagreeable smell. It is high in polyunsaturates and is therefore one of the healthier oils.

Other vegetable oils

Some of the cheaper vegetable oils available include soyabean, safflower and sunflower oils. They are light in colour and taste, and can also be used in Chinese cooking.

21

Sesame oil

This is a thick, rich, golden brown oil made from sesame seeds, which has a distinctive, nutty flavour and aroma. It is widely used in Chinese cookery as a seasoning but is not normally used as a cooking oil because it heats rapidly and burns easily. It is often added at the last moment to finish a dish. Sold in bottles you can obtain it in many supermarkets and in Chinese grocers.

Peanuts

Raw peanuts are used in Chinese cooking to add flavour and a crunchy texture and are especially popular when marinaded or added to stir-fry dishes. They can be bought at health food shops, good supermarkets and Chinese grocers. The thin red skins need to be removed before you use the nuts. To do this simply immerse them in a pot of boiling water for about 2 minutes. Drain them and let them cool and the skins will come off easily.

Rice wine

This wine is used extensively for cooking and drinking throughout China, and the finest variety is believed to be that from Shaoxing in Zhejiang Province in eastern China. It is made from glutinous rice, yeast and spring water. Available from Chinese grocers, it should be kept at room temperature, tightly corked. A good quality, dry, pale sherry can be substituted but cannot equal the rich, mellow taste of Chinese rice wine.

Sauces and pastes

Chinese cookery involves a number of thick tasty sauces or pastes. They are essential to the authentic taste of Chinese cooking and it is well worth making the effort to obtain them. Most are sold in bottles or tins in Chinese grocers and some supermarkets. Tinned sauces, once opened, should be transferred to screw-top glass jars and kept in the refrigerator where they will last indefinitely.

Chilli bean sauce

This is a thick dark sauce or paste made from soyabeans, chillis and other seasonings, which is very hot and spicy. Widely used in cooking in western China, it is usually available here in jars in Chinese grocers. Be sure to seal the jar tightly after use and store in the larder or refrigerator. Do not confuse it with chilli sauce (see below) which is a hot, red, thinner sauce made without beans and used mainly as a dipping sauce for cooked dishes.

Chilli sauce

Chilli sauce is a bright red, hot sauce which is made from chillis, vinegar, sugar and salt. It is sometimes used for cooking, but it is mainly used as a dipping sauce. There are various brands available in many supermarkets and Chinese grocers and you should experiment with them until you find the one you like best. If you find it too strong, dilute it with hot water. Do not confuse this sauce with the chilli bean sauce mentioned above which is a much thicker, darker sauce used for cooking.

Hoisin sauce

This is a thick, dark, brownish red sauce which is made from soyabeans, vinegar, sugar, spices and other flavourings. It is sweet and spicy and is widely used in southern Chinese cookery. In the West it is often used as a sauce for Peking Duck instead of the traditional sweet bean sauce. Hoisin sauce is sold in tins and jars (it is sometimes also called barbecue sauce) and is available in Chinese grocers and some supermarkets. If refrigerated it should keep indefinitely.

Oyster sauce

This thick brown sauce is made from a concentrate of oysters cooked in soy sauce and brine. Despite its name, oyster sauce does not taste fishy. It has a rich flavour and is used not only in cooking but as a condiment, diluted with a little oil, for vegetables, poultry or meats. It is usually sold in bottles and can be bought in Chinese grocers and some supermarkets. I find it keeps best in the refrigerator.

Sesame paste

This rich, thick, creamy brown paste is made from sesame seeds. It is used in both hot and cold dishes, and is particularly popular in northern and western China. It is sold in jars at Chinese grocers. If you cannot obtain it, use peanut butter, which resembles it in taste and texture.

Soy sauces

Soy sauce is an essential ingredient of Chinese cooking. It is made from a mixture of soyabeans, flour and water, which is then naturally fermented and aged for some months. The liquid which is finally distilled is soy sauce. There are two main types:

Light soy sauce   As the name implies this is light in colour but it is full of flavour and is the best one to use for cooking. It is saltier than dark soy sauce. It is known in Chinese grocers as Superior Soy.

23

Dark soy sauce This sauce is aged for much longer than light soy sauce, hence its darker, almost black colour. It is slightly thicker and stronger than light soy sauce and is more suitable for stews. I prefer it to light soy as a dipping sauce. It is known in Chinese grocers as Soy Superior Sauce.

Most soy sauces sold in supermarkets are dark soy. Chinese grocers sell both types and the quality is superior. Be sure you buy the right one as the names are very similar.

Whole yellow bean sauce
This thick, spicy, aromatic sauce is made with yellow beans, flour and salt which are fermented together. It is quite salty but adds a distinctive flavour to Chinese sauces. There are two forms: whole beans in a thick sauce; and mashed or puréed beans (sold as crushed yellow bean sauce). I prefer the whole bean variety because it is slightly less salty and has a better texture.

Chinese sausages
Chinese sausages look exactly like thin salami and are about 6 inches (15 cm) long. They are made from duck or pork liver, or from pork meat and are cured. They are dark red in colour with white flecks of fat. Their tasty flavour varies according to type but they are sweet rather than spicy. They must be cooked before they can be eaten and are most commonly used to season chicken and rice dishes. They are obtainable from Chinese grocers.

Sherry
If you cannot get rice wine you can use a good quality, dry, pale sherry instead. Do not use sweet or cream sherries.

Sichuan peppercorns
Sichuan peppercorns are known throughout China as 'flower peppers' because they look like flower buds opening. They are reddish brown in colour with a strong pungent odour which distinguishes them from the hotter black peppercorns. They are actually not from peppers at all, but are the dried berries of a shrub which is a member of the citrus family. I find their smell reminds me of lavender while their taste is sharp and mildly spicy. They can be ground in a conventional peppermill and are very often roasted before they are ground to bring out their full flavour. They are sold wrapped in cellophane or plastic bags in Chinese grocers and are inexpensive. They will keep indefinitely if stored in a well sealed container.

To roast Sichuan peppercorns

Heat a wok or heavy frying-pan to a medium heat. Add the peppercorns (you can cook up to about 5oz (150g) at a time) and stir-fry them for about 5 minutes until they brown slightly and start to smoke. Remove the pan from the heat and let them cool. Grind the peppercorns in a peppermill, clean coffee grinder or with a mortar and pestle. Seal the mixture tightly in a screw-top jar until you need. Alternatively keep the whole roasted peppercorns in a well sealed container and grind them when required.

Sichuan preserved vegetable

There are many types of Chinese pickled vegetables. One of the most popular is Sichuan preserved vegetable, a speciality of Sichuan Province. This is the root of the mustard green which is pickled in salt and hot chillis. It is sold in tins in Chinese grocers, and gives a pleasantly crunchy texture and spicy taste to dishes. Before using it, rinse in cold water and then slice or chop as required. Any unused vegetable should be transferred to a tightly covered jar and stored in the refrigerator where it will keep indefinitely.

Spring roll skins

These are the paper-thin pastry wrappers which are filled with bean sprouts and other vegetables to make spring rolls. They are about 6 inches (15 cm) square, white in colour, and are made from a soft flour and water dough. They are very thin and probably too tricky to make at home, so I suggest you buy them frozen in packets of 20 from Chinese grocers. Keep them in the freezer well wrapped in clingfilm.

Star anise

The star anise is a hard, star-shaped spice and is the seed-pod of the anise bush. (It is also known as Chinese anise or whole anise.) It is similar in flavour and fragrance to common aniseed but is more robust and liquorice-like. Star anise is an essential ingredient of five spice powder and is widely used in braised dishes to which it imparts a rich taste and fragrance. It is sold in plastic packs by Chinese grocers, and should be stored in a tightly covered jar in a cool, dry place.

Sugar

Sugar has been used in the cooking of savoury dishes in China for a thousand years. Properly employed it helps balance the various flavours of sauces and other dishes. Chinese sugar comes in several forms: as rock or yellow lump sugar, as brown sugar slabs, and as maltose or malt sugar. I particularly like to use rock sugar which is rich and has a more subtle flavour than that of refined granulated sugar. It also gives a good lustre or glaze to braised dishes and sauces. You can buy it in Chinese grocers where it is usually sold in packets. You may need to break the lumps into smaller pieces with a wooden mallet or rolling pin. If you cannot find it use white sugar or coffee sugar crystals (the amber, chunky kind) instead.

Chinese black tea

Chinese black tea is a full-bodied, fragrant and smooth tea with a rich aroma and a superb bouquet. There are various kinds of which Keemun is one of the most well known. Tea is used in smoked dishes or for simmering, as in the Marbled Tea Eggs (page 253). You can purchase Chinese black teas in Chinese grocers, delicatessens and in many supermarkets. I prefer to store tea in tins since these keep the tea in the freshest possible condition.

Vinegar

Vinegars are widely used in Chinese cooking. Unlike Western vinegars they are usually made from rice and there are many varieties, ranging in flavour from the spicy and slightly tart to the sweet and pungent.

White rice vinegar

White rice vinegar is clear and mild in flavour. It has a faint taste of glutinous rice and is used for sweet and sour dishes.

Black rice vinegar

Black rice vinegar is very dark in colour and rich though mild in taste. It is used for braised dishes, sauces, and sometimes as a dipping sauce for crab.

Red rice vinegar

Red rice vinegar is sweet and spicy in taste and is usually used as a dipping sauce for seafood.

All these vinegars can be bought from Chinese grocers. They are sold in bottles and will keep indefinitely. If you cannot get Chinese vinegars I suggest you use cider vinegar instead. Malt vinegar can be used but its taste is stronger and more acidic.

Waterchestnuts

Waterchestnuts do not actually belong to the chestnut family at all, but are a sweet root vegetable or bulb about the size of a walnut. They are white and crunchy. In China they are eaten as a snack, having first been boiled in their skins, or peeled and simmered in rock sugar. They are also used in cooked dishes, especially in southern China.

Here, fresh waterchestnuts can sometimes be obtained from Chinese grocers or good supermarkets. They are tastier than tinned ones and will keep, unpeeled, in a paper bag in the refrigerator for up to 2 weeks. Peel them before use and if you have any left over, put them back in the refrigerator covered with cold water. Tinned waterchestnuts are sold in many supermarkets and Chinese grocers. They have a good texture but little taste. Rinse them well in cold water before you use them, and store any unused ones in a jar of cold water. They will keep for several weeks in the refrigerator if you change the water daily.

Wuntun skins

Wuntun skins are made from egg and flour and can be bought fresh or frozen from Chinese grocers. They are thin pastry-like wrappings which can be stuffed with minced meat and fried, steamed or used in soups. They are sold in little piles of 3¼ inch (8cm) yellowish squares, wrapped in plastic. The number of squares or skins in a packet varies from about 30 to 36, depending upon the supplier. Fresh wuntun skins will keep for about 5 days if stored in clingfilm or a plastic bag in the refrigerator. If you are using frozen wuntun skins, just peel off the number you require and thaw them thoroughly before you use them.

Dipping sauces and mixtures

Many Chinese dishes and snacks are dipped into a variety of dipping sauces before being eaten. The most popular of these are chilli sauce, which can be bought ready-made, and Chilli Oil, which can easily be made at home. Soy sauce and red and black Chinese rice vinegars are also widely used as dips. The recipes on the following pages are some of my favourite dipping sauces, most of which, once made, will keep for several months.

CHILLI OIL
Region: western

For those who like hot and spicy food, chilli oil is a must. It can be purchased ready-made from Chinese grocers, but it is also easy to make yourself. Chilli oil can be added as a final spicy touch to dishes during cooking or it can be used as a dipping sauce either on its own or combined with vinegar and soy sauce, as for the Potsticker Dumplings (page 239).

5 fl oz	150ml	oil, preferably groundnut
1 tablespoon		dried red chillis, chopped
2 teaspoons		unroasted Sichuan peppercorns (optional)

Heat a wok or frying-pan over a high heat and add the oil. Continue to heat until the oil begins to smoke. Remove the wok or pan from the heat and add the chillis and peppercorns. Allow the mixture to cool undisturbed and then pour it into a jar. Let the mixture sit for 2 days, and then strain the oil. It will keep indefinitely.

SWEET AND SOUR SAUCE
Region: southern

This is my version of a subtle and tasty sweet and sour sauce which can be used for any deep-fried foods such as the Fried Wuntun (page 248). It keeps well in a tightly sealed jar in the refrigerator.

2 tablespoons	ginger marmalade
2 tablespoons	orange marmalade
¼ teaspoon	salt
1 tablespoon	cider vinegar or Chinese white rice vinegar
1 tablespoon	hot water

Combine all the ingredients together in a small bowl. Be sure to mix them thoroughly. Transfer the mixture to a small dish if it is to be used at once or put it in a jar and refrigerate until needed.

GINGER AND SPRING ONION SAUCE

Region: southern

In this simple sauce the oil is heated and then poured over the seasonings to bring out their full taste and fragrance. It is a dipping sauce best used with poultry and meat dishes like Twice-cooked Chicken (page 136) and Braised Chicken with Leeks (page 128).

3 tablespoons	spring onions, finely chopped
2 teaspoons	fresh ginger, finely chopped
2 teaspoons	salt
1 teaspoon	light soy sauce
3 tablespoons	oil, preferably groundnut

Put all the ingredients except the oil in a small heatproof bowl and mix them well. Heat a wok or frying-pan and add the oil. Continue to heat until the oil is almost smoking. Remove the pan from the heat and pour the hot oil into the bowl with the other ingredients. The sauce should sizzle for a few seconds and is ready for use.

GINGER SHERRY OR RICE WINE

Region: all

This is simply sherry or rice wine flavoured with fresh ginger. The mixture works very well as a variation in recipes which call for sherry or rice wine. Putting fresh ginger in sherry or rice wine is also a good method of preserving it and it can then be eaten as a snack.

3 tablespoons		fresh ginger, finely chopped
3 fl oz	75 ml	dry sherry or rice wine

Combine the ginger and the sherry or rice wine and put the mixture into a jar in the refrigerator until you are ready to use it. It will keep for at least 2 months.

29

ROASTED SALT AND PEPPER

Region: all

This roasted salt and pepper mixture which is made with Sichuan peppercorns is used throughout China as a dip for deep-fried foods. The dry-roasting method releases all the flavours of the peppercorns.

2oz	50g	**Sichuan peppercorns**
3oz	75g	**coarse sea salt**

Heat a wok or heavy frying-pan to a medium heat. Add the peppercorns and the salt and stir-fry them until the mixture begins to smoke slightly and brown a little. Remove the pan from the heat and let the mixture cool. Then grind it using a grinder, clean coffee mill or mortar and pestle. Seal the mixture tightly in a jar until you are ready to use it.

FIVE SPICE SALT

Region: northern and western

This dipping mixture is similar to the Sichuan peppercorn and salt mixture but has the distinctive fragrance of five spice powder. It is best served with fried meat like chicken and pigeon, or fried fish.

3 tablespoons	salt
1 teaspoon	**five spice powder**

Heat a wok or frying-pan until it is hot. Then add the salt and stir-fry for a minute or so until it is quite hot. Remove the pan from the heat and stir in the five spice powder. Mix well and allow to cool, then put the mixture in a sealed jar until needed.

30

EQUIPMENT

Traditional Chinese cooking equipment is not essential for cooking Chinese food but there are a few items which will make it very much easier. Most items can be bought very cheaply, especially if you seek out authentic implements from a Chinese grocer rather than the more expensive versions sold in many department stores.

Wok

The most useful piece of equipment is the wok, which is easier to use than a large frying-pan because its depth makes it easier to toss foods quickly without spilling them. It also requires far less oil for deep-frying than a deep-fat fryer, although you may find the latter easier and safer to use. Another advantage is that the shape of the wok allows the heat to spread evenly over its surface, thus making for rapid cooking which is fundamental to stir-frying.

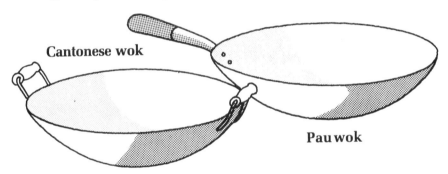

Cantonese wok

Pau wok

There are two types of wok: the Cantonese wok which has a short, rounded handle on either side, and the pau wok which has one long handle. The Cantonese wok is best for steaming and deep-frying since it can be set steadily onto a stand over the heat, and is easier to move when it is full of liquid. The pau wok is better for stir-frying since it is easier to shake it over the heat with one hand while your free hand wields a long-handled spoon or spatula. It also distances you from the heat and hot oil and makes for more comfortable, safer frying. Woks with rounded bases should only be used on gas hobs. It is now possible to buy woks with flattish bottoms which are specifically designed for electric hobs. Although these really defeat the purpose of the traditional design, which is to concentrate intense heat at the centre, they do have the advantage of having deeper sides than a frying-pan.

Choosing a wok

Choose a large wok—preferably about 14 inches (35·5 cm) in diameter, with good deep sides. Some woks on the market are too shallow and are no better than a large frying-pan. It is easier to cook a small quantity in a large wok than to try to accommodate a large quantity in a small one. Select one which is heavy and if possible made of carbon steel rather than a light stainless steel or aluminium. The latter types tend to scorch. I do not like non-stick woks; not only are they more expensive, but they cannot be seasoned like an ordinary wok, which detracts from the flavour of the food. I also dislike electric woks because I find they do not heat up to a sufficiently high temperature and tend to be too shallow.

Seasoning a wok

All woks (except non-stick ones) need to be seasoned. Many need to be scrubbed first as well to remove the machine oil which is applied to the surface by the manufacturer to protect it in transit. This is the *only* time you will ever scrub your wok—unless you let it rust up. Scrub it with a cream cleanser and water to remove as much of the machine oil as possible. Then dry it and put it on the hob on a low heat. Add 2 tablespoons of cooking oil and rub this over the inside of the wok using kitchen paper until the entire surface is lightly coated with oil. Heat the wok slowly for about 10–15 minutes and then wipe it thoroughly with more kitchen paper. The paper will become blackened. Repeat this process of coating, heating and wiping until the kitchen paper wipes clean. Your wok will darken and become well seasoned with use.

Cleaning a wok

Do not scrub a seasoned wok. Just wash it in plain water without detergent. Dry it thoroughly, preferably by putting it over a low heat for a few minutes before putting it away. This should prevent the wok from rusting, but if it does, scrub the rust off with cream cleanser and repeat the seasoning process.

Wok accessories
Wok stand

This is a metal ring or frame designed to keep a conventionally
shaped wok steady on the hob,
and is essential if you want to
use your wok for steaming,
deep-frying or braising. Stands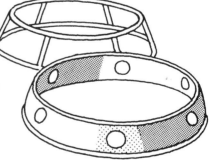
come in two designs. One is a solid metal ring punched with about six ventilation holes. The other is like a circular thin wire frame. If you have a gas cooker use *only the latter type* as the more solid design does not allow for sufficient ventilation and may lead to a build-up of gas which could put the flame out completely.

Wok lid

A wok lid is a dome-like cover, usually
made from aluminium, which is used for
steaming. It may come with the wok or it can be
purchased separately from a Chinese grocer, but
any large, domed pot lid which fits snugly over the
top of the wok can be used instead. Alternatively you
could use aluminium foil.

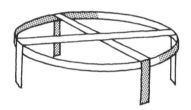

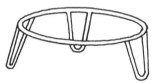

Spatula

A long-handled metal spatula shaped rather like a
small shovel is ideal for scooping and tossing food in a wok.
Any good long-handled spoon can be used instead.

Rack

If you use your wok or a large pot as a steamer you will need a
wooden or metal rack or trivet to stand above the water level and
support the plate of food to be steamed. Some woks are sold with a
metal stand, but most Chinese grocers, department stores and
hardware shops stock triangular wooden stands or round metal
stands which can be used for this purpose. You can improvise a
stand by using an empty, inverted tin can of suitable height.

Bamboo brush

This bundle of stiff, split bamboo
is used for cleaning a wok without
scrubbing off the seasoned surface.
It is an attractive, inexpensive implement but not essential. A soft
washing-up brush will do just as well.

Deep-fat fryers

These are very useful and you may find them safer and easier to use
for deep-frying than a wok. The quantities of oil given in the
recipes are based on the amount required for deep-frying in a wok.
If you are using a deep-fat fryer instead you will need about double
that amount, but never fill it more than half-full with oil.

Cleavers

No self-respecting Chinese cook would be seen with a knife instead of a cleaver. These heavy, lethal-looking choppers serve many purposes. They are used for all kinds of cutting ranging from fine shredding to chopping up bones. A Chinese  cook would usually have three types: a lightweight one with a narrow blade for cutting delicate foods including vegetables, a medium-weight one for general cutting, chopping and crushing purposes, and a heavy one for heavy-duty chopping. Of course you can prepare Chinese food using good sharp knives, but if you decide to invest in a cleaver you will be surprised at how easy it is to use. Choose a good quality stainless steel one and keep it sharp.

Chopping board

The Chinese traditionally use a soft wood block for chopping. Not only is this difficult to maintain but it accumulates bacteria. I prefer to use a hardwood or a white acrylic board. Both are strong, easy to clean and last indefinitely. There is so much chopping and slicing to be done when preparing food for Chinese cooking that it really is essential to have a large, steady cutting board. (For hygiene reasons never cut cooked meat on a board which you have also used for chopping raw meat or poultry. Keep a separate board for this purpose.)

Steamers

Bamboo steamers are among the most ancient of Chinese cooking utensils. These attractive round 'boxes' come in several sizes of which the 10inch (25·5cm) size is the most suitable for home use. Bamboo steamers are filled with food and placed on top of a 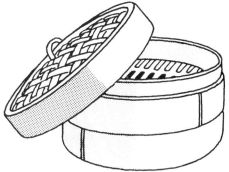 pot or over a wok of boiling water. Clean, damp cheesecloth is sometimes placed over the open slats under the food to prevent sticking. A tight-fitting bamboo lid is put on top to prevent the steam escaping. One of the advantages of the design is that several steamers can be stacked one on top of the other for multiple cooking. Bamboo steamers can be bought at Chinese grocers. (Alternatively, any

35

European kind of wide, metal steamer can be used.) Before using a bamboo steamer for the first time wash it and steam it empty for about 5 minutes.

Rice cookers

Electric rice cookers are increasing in popularity. They cook rice perfectly and keep it warm throughout a meal. A rice cooker also has the advantage of freeing a burner or element, making for a less cluttered hob. They are relatively expensive, however, so unless you eat rice frequently I do not think they are worth the expense.

Sand or clay pots

These attractive light-weight clay pots are also known as sand pots because their unglazed exteriors have a sandy texture. They come in a variety of shapes and sizes, equipped with matching lids and sometimes are encased in a wire frame. The pots are designed to be used on the hob (since most Chinese do not have ovens) and are used for braised dishes, soups and for cooking rice. Never put an empty sand pot onto the heat, or put a hot sand pot onto a cold surface. In both cases the pot will crack. Any good casserole or cast-iron pot can be used as a substitute.

Chopsticks

Chopsticks are not just used for eating. They are also used when cooking, for stirring, beating and whipping. Specially long chopsticks are available for these purposes, but it is perfectly all right to use Western cooking implements instead.

Table chopsticks come in wood, plastic and, most luxurious of all, ivory. They can be bought at many department stores, Chinese grocers and from many Chinese restaurants or takeaways. For instructions on how to eat with chopsticks see page 53.

TECHNIQUES

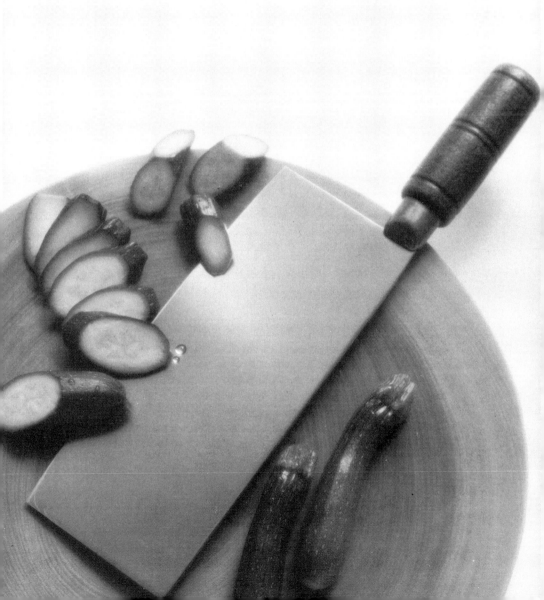

The preparation of food for cooking is probably more important and more time-consuming in Chinese cookery than in any other cuisine. Although many dishes are cooked rapidly, this presupposes that every ingredient has been properly prepared beforehand and has been chopped into smallish, well shaped pieces to ensure even and quick cooking. This means that food can be cooked for a minimum of time so that it retains its natural texture and taste. The other reason for careful cutting is to enhance the visual appeal of a dish. This is why most Chinese cooks are so specific about cutting techniques, particularly where vegetables are concerned. The Chinese always use a cleaver for these tasks, wielding it with skill and dexterity. Of course a sharp knife can be used instead.

Chinese cookery is a sophisticated cuisine which involves a number of cooking methods which are relatively uncommon in the West. Sometimes several different techniques are used in the preparation of a single dish. Most can be easily mastered with a little practice. When you are planning a meal, be sure to select dishes which use a range of techniques, and limit yourself to one stir-fried dish per meal until you have become used to this important method of cooking.

Cutting techniques
Slicing

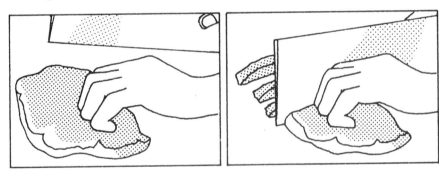

This is the conventional method of slicing food. Hold the food firmly on the chopping board with one hand and slice the food straight down into very thin slices. Meat is always sliced across the grain to break up the fibres and to make it more tender when it is cooked. If you use a cleaver rather than a knife for this, hold the cleaver with your index finger over the far side of the top of the cleaver and your thumb on the side nearest you to guide the cutting edge firmly. Hold the food with your other hand, turning your fingers under for safety. Your knuckles should act as a guide for the blade.

Horizontal or flat slicing

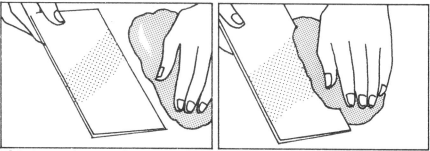

This is a technique for splitting food into two thinner pieces while retaining its overall shape. It is often used for cutting kidneys. The cleaver with its wide blade is particularly suitable for this. Hold the blade of the cleaver or knife parallel to the chopping board. Place your free hand on top of the piece of food to keep it steady. Using a gentle cutting motion slice sideways into the food. Depending on the recipe you may need to repeat this process, cutting the two halves into further thin flat pieces.

Diagonal slicing

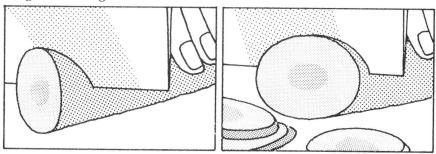

This technique is used for cutting vegetables such as asparagus, carrots or spring onions. The purpose is to expose more of the surface of the vegetable for quicker cooking. Angle the knife or cleaver at a slant and cut.

Roll cutting

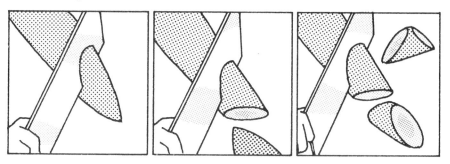

This is rather like diagonal slicing but is used for larger vegetables such as courgettes, large carrots, aubergines and Chinese white radish (mooli). As with diagonal slicing this technique allows more of the surface of the vegetable to be exposed to the heat, thereby speeding up the cooking time. Begin by making one diagonal slice at one end of the vegetable. Then turn it 180 degrees and make the next diagonal slice. Continue in this way until you have chopped the entire vegetable into evenly sized, diamond-shaped chunks.

Shredding

This is the process by which food is cut into thin, fine, matchstick-like shreds. First cut the food into slices and then pile several slices on top of each other and cut them *lengthways* into fine strips. Some foods, particularly meat and chicken breasts, are easier to shred if they are first stiffened slightly in the freezer for about 20 minutes.

Dicing

This is a simple technique of cutting food into small cubes or dice. The food should first be cut into slices. Stack the slices and cut them again *lengthways* into sticks just as you would for shredding (above). Stack the strips or sticks and cut *crossways* into evenly sized cubes or dice.

Mincing

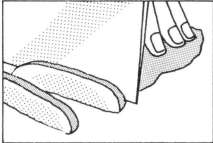

This is a fine-chopping technique. Chefs use two cleavers to mince, rapidly chopping with them in unison for fast results. One cleaver or knife is easier for the less expert although the process will of course take a little longer! First slice the food and then, using a sharp knife or cleaver, rapidly chop the food until it is rather spread out over the chopping board. Scrape it into a pile and chop again, and continue chopping until the food reaches the desired state. You may find it easier to hold the knife or cleaver by the top of the blade (rather than by the handle) with two hands, as though you were chopping parsley. A food processor may also be used for this but be careful not to over-mince the food or you will lose out on texture and taste.

Chopping

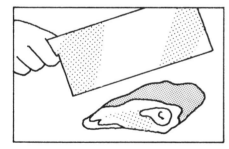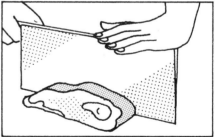

This is a term which is used for any technique which requires food to be completely cut through. Usually this applies to whole birds or to cooked food with bones which need to be cut into smaller pieces. The food to be chopped should be placed on a firm cutting surface. Use a straight, sharp, downward motion with the cleaver or knife. To chop through bones, hit down with the blade and then finish off the blow with the flat of your other hand on the top edge of the cleaver or knife. A heavy-duty cleaver or knife is best for these tasks.

41

Scoring

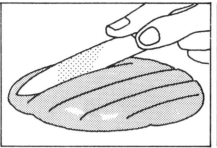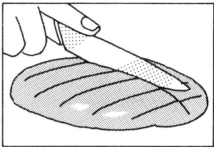

This is a technique used to pierce the surface of foods to help them cook faster and more evenly. It also gives them an attractive appearance. Use a cleaver or a sharp knife and make cuts into the food at a slight angle to a depth of about ⅛inch (33mm). Take care not to cut all the way through. Make cuts all over the surface of the food, cutting criss-cross to give a wide, diamond-shaped pattern.

Other preparation techniques

Marinading

This is a process in which raw meat or poultry is steeped for a time in a liquid such as soy sauce, rice wine or sherry and cornflour to improve its flavour and to tenderise it. Sometimes other spices or seasonings such as sugar, chillis, five spice powder or Sichuan peppercorns are added. The marinading time is usually at least 20 minutes in order to infuse the meat or poultry properly with the flavours of the marinade. Once marination is complete the food is usually lifted out of the marinade with a slotted spoon before it is cooked.

Thickening

Cornflour blended with an equal quantity of water is frequently used in Chinese cookery to thicken sauces and glaze dishes. Always make sure the mixture is smooth and well blended before adding it.

Velveting

Velveting is used to prevent delicate foods like chicken breasts from overcooking. The food is coated with a mixture of unbeaten egg white, cornflour and sometimes salt. It is then put into the refrigerator for about 20-30 minutes to ensure that the coating adheres to the food. This protects the flavour and texture of the food when it is put into oil or hot water.

42

Cooking techniques

Blanching

This involves putting food into hot water or into moderately hot oil for a few minutes to cook it briefly but not entirely. It is a sort of softening-up process to prepare the food for final cooking. Chicken is often blanched in oil or water after being velveted (see page 42). Meat is sometimes blanched to rid it of scum in order to ensure a clean taste and appearance. Blanching in water is common with harder vegetables such as broccoli or carrots. The vegetable is plunged into boiling water for several minutes. It is then drained and plunged into cold water to arrest the cooking process. In such cases blanching usually precedes stir-frying to finish the cooking.

Poaching

This is a method of simmering food until it is partially cooked. It is then put into soup or combined with a sauce and the cooking process continued.

Stir-frying

This is the most famous of all Chinese cooking techniques and it is possibly the most tricky since success with it depends upon having all the required ingredients prepared, measured out and immediately at hand, and on having a good source of fierce heat. Its advantage is that, properly executed, stir-fried foods can be cooked in minutes in very little oil so they retain their natural flavours and textures. It is very important that stir-fried foods are not overcooked or greasy. Once you have mastered this technique you will find that it becomes almost second nature. Using a wok is definitely an advantage when stir-frying as its shape not only conducts the heat well but its high sides enable you to toss and stir ingredients rapidly, keeping them constantly moving while cooking. Having prepared all the ingredients for stir-frying the steps are:

● Heat the wok or frying-pan until it is very hot *before* adding the oil. This prevents food sticking and will ensure an even heat. Add the oil and, using a metal spatula or long-handled spoon, distribute it evenly over the surface. It should be very hot indeed—almost smoking—before you add the next ingredient unless you are going on to flavour the oil (see next point).

● If you are flavouring the oil with garlic, spring onions, ginger, dried red chilli or salt, do not wait for the oil to get so hot that it is almost smoking. If you do, these ingredients will burn and become bitter. Toss them quickly in the oil for a few seconds. In some recipes these flavourings will then be removed and discarded before cooking proceeds.

43

● Now add the ingredients as described in the recipe and proceed to stir-fry by tossing them over the surface of the wok or pan with the metal spatula or long-handled spoon. If you are stir-frying meat let each side rest for just a few seconds before continuing to stir. Keep moving the food from the centre of the wok to the sides. Stir-frying is a noisy business and is usually accompanied by quite a lot of splattering because of the high temperature at which the food must be cooked.

● Some stir-fried dishes are thickened with a mixture of cornflour and cold water. To avoid getting a lumpy sauce be sure to remove the wok or pan from the heat before you add the cornflour mixture, which must be thoroughly blended before it is added. The sauce can then be returned to the heat and thickened.

Deep-frying

This is one of the most important techniques in Chinese cooking. The trick is to regulate the heat so that the surface of the food is sealed but does not brown so fast that the food is uncooked inside. Although deep-fried food must not be greasy the process does require a lot of oil. The Chinese use a wok for deep-frying which requires rather less oil than a deep-fat fryer, but I think you should avoid using the wok unless you are very sure of it. If you do, be certain that it is fully secure on its stand before adding the oil and on no account leave the wok unsupervised. Most people will find a deep-fat fryer easier and safer to use. Be careful not to fill this more than half-full with oil.

Some points to bear in mind when deep-frying are:

● Wait for the oil to get hot enough before adding the food to be fried. The oil should give off a haze and almost produce little wisps of smoke when it is the right temperature, but you can test it by dropping in a small piece of food. If it bubbles all over then the oil is sufficiently hot. Adjust the heat as necessary to prevent the oil from actually smoking or overheating.

● Be sure to dry food to be deep-fried thoroughly first with kitchen paper as this will prevent splattering. If the food is in a marinade, remove it with a slotted spoon and let it drain before putting it into the oil. If you are using batter make sure all the excess batter drips off before adding the food to the hot oil.

● Oil used for deep-frying can be re-used. Cool it and then strain it into a jar through several layers of cheesecloth or through a fine mesh to remove any particles of food which might otherwise burn if re-heated and give the oil a bitter taste. Label the jar according to

44

what food you have cooked in the oil and only re-use it for the same thing. Oil can be used up to three times before it begins to lose its effectiveness.

Shallow-frying
This technique is similar to sautéeing. It involves more oil than stir-frying but less than for deep-frying. Food is fried first on one side and then on the other. Sometimes the excess oil is then drained off and a sauce added to complete the dish. A frying-pan is ideal for shallow-frying.

Slow-simmering and steeping
These processes are very similar. In slow-simmering food is immersed in liquid which is brought almost to the boil and then the temperature is reduced so that it simmers, cooking the food to the desired degree. This is the technique used for making stock. In steeping, food is similarly immersed in liquid (usually stock) and simmered for a time. The heat is then turned off and the remaining heat of the liquid finishes off the cooking process.

Braising and red-braising
This technique is most often applied to tougher cuts of meat and certain vegetables. The food is usually browned and then put into stock which has been flavoured with seasonings and spices. The stock is brought to the boil, the heat reduced and the food simmered gently until it is cooked. Red-braising is simply the technique by which food is braised in a dark liquid such as soy sauce. This gives food a reddish brown colour, hence the name. This type of braising sauce can be saved and frozen for re-use. It can be re-used many times and becomes richer in flavour.

Steaming
Steaming has been used by the Chinese for thousands of years. Along with stir-frying and deep-frying it is the most widely used technique. Steamed foods are cooked by a gentle moist heat which must circulate freely in order to cook the food. It is an excellent method for bringing out subtle flavours and so is particularly wonderful for fish. Bamboo steamers are used by the Chinese but you could use any one of several utensils:

● *Using a bamboo steamer in a wok* For this you need a large bamboo steamer about 10 inches (25·5 cm) wide. Put about 2 inches (5 cm) of water in a wok. Bring it to a simmer. Put the bamboo steamer containing the food into the wok where it should rest safely perched on the sloping sides. Cover the steamer with its matching lid and steam the food until it is cooked. Replenish the water as required.

45

● *Using a wok as a steamer*   Put about 2 inches (5 cm) of water
into a wok. Then put a metal or wooden rack into the wok. Bring
the water to a simmer and put the food to be steamed onto a plate.
Lower the plate onto the rack and cover the wok tightly with a wok
lid. Check the water level from time to time and replenish it with
hot water when necessary.

● *Using a large roasting pan or pot as a steamer*   Put a metal or
wooden rack into the pan or pot and pour in about 2 inches (5 cm)
of water. Bring it to a simmer and put the food to be steamed onto a
plate. Lower the plate onto the rack and cover the pan or pot with a
lid or with aluminium foil. Replenish the water as necessary.

● *Using a European steamer*   If you have a metal steamer which
is wide enough to take a plate of food then this will give you very
satisfactory results. Keep an eye on the level of the water in the
base.

If you do not have a metal or wooden rack you could use a small
empty tin can to support the plate of food. Remember that the food
needs to remain above the water level and must not get wet. The
water level should always be at least 1 inch (2·5 cm) below the edge
of the food plate. (Be sure to use a heatproof plate.)

Roasting
In China roasting is only done in commercial establishments since
most homes do not have ovens. The Chinese roast food in large
metal, drum-shaped ovens which stand about 5 feet (1·5 m) high
and are fuelled by charcoal. The food is hung on hooks inside the
oven over intense heat. The idea is to expose all the surface of the
food to the heat to give it a crisp outer surface and a moist interior.
You can approximate the Chinese method by putting food on to a
rack in a roasting pan so that the hot air of the oven can circulate
round it.

Barbecuing
This is a variation on roasting and it is not very common.
Marinaded meat is placed over a charcoal fire and the meat
constantly basted to keep it moist. Today modern grills and
outdoor barbecues produce much the same result.

Twice-cooking
As the name implies this is a two-step process involving two quite
different techniques, such as simmering and stir-frying. It is used to
change the texture of food, to infuse it with flavour and to render
foods which are difficult to cook into a more manageable state. It is
especially useful for removing fat from meat before final cooking.

Re-heating foods

Steaming is one of the best methods of re-heating food since it warms it without cooking it further and without drying it out. To re-heat soups and braised dishes, bring the liquid slowly to a simmer but do not boil. Remove it from the heat as soon as it is hot to prevent overcooking.

Garnishes

The Chinese pay much attention to the presentation of their cuisine. This is why cutting techniques are so important since the size and shape of individual ingredients should harmonise with each other. We also like to decorate dishes with various kinds of garnish ranging from the simple spring onion brush to the elaborate tomato rose. Here are some instructions for making some simple, attractive garnishes.

Spring onion brushes

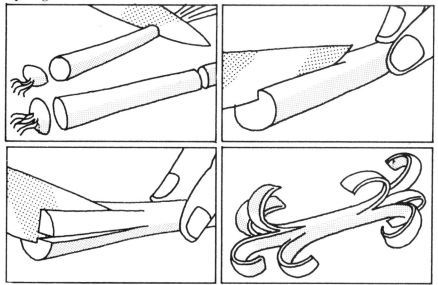

1   Cut off the green part of the spring onion and trim off the base of the bulb. You should have a 3 inch (7·5 cm) white segment left.

2   Make a lengthways cut about 1 inch (2·5 cm) long at one end of the spring onion. Roll the spring onion 90° and cut again. Repeat this process at the other end.

3   Soak the spring onions in iced water and they will curl into flower brushes. Spin or pat them dry before use.

Radish roses

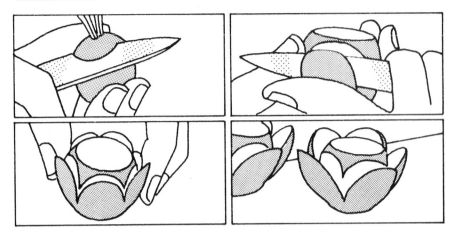

1 Remove any leaves, trim the top and the root end of the radish.

2 Make thin, rounded cuts to form petals.

3 Soak the radishes in iced water for about an hour.

Carrot flowers

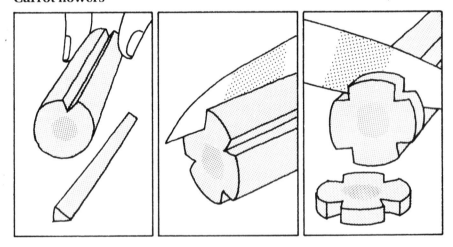

1 Peel the carrots and cut them into 3 inch (7·5 cm) chunks.

2 Cut a V-shaped slice down the length of each chunk. Repeat, making 3–4 more lengthways cuts around each.

3 Now slice the carrots crossways to form thin flower shapes. Soak them in cold water until required.

Fresh chilli flowers

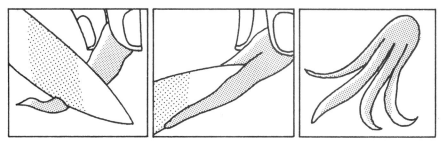

1   Trim the tip of the chilli but do not remove the stem.

2   Make 4 cuts lengthways from the stem of the chilli to the tip, to form 4 sections. Remove and discard any seeds.

3   Soak the chillis in cold water. They will 'flower' in the water.

Tomato roses

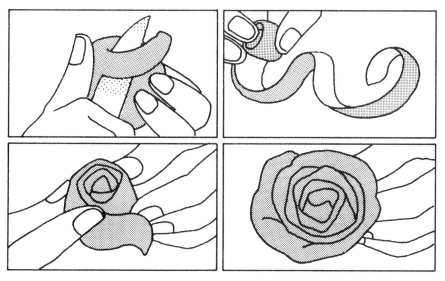

1   Select firm tomatoes and, using a very sharp knife, peel off the skin from the top in one piece as though you were peeling an apple. Do not break the strip.

2   Roll the strip of tomato skin into a tight coil.

3   Turn the coil over and you should have a tomato rose.

49

Cucumber fans

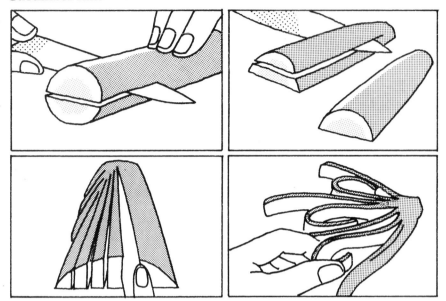

1   Using a sharp knife, cut off the rounded end of half a cucumber. Then cut it in half *lengthways*.

2   Turn each cucumber piece so that the skin side is uppermost. Make a horizontal slice to reduce the thickness of each cucumber piece, so that you end up with a slice which is mainly skin with just a little flesh.

3   Now make parallel cuts down the length of the slice, as shown in the diagram. The cuts will have to curve slightly so that you will be able to splay the slices out like a fan.

4   Starting with the second slice, bend every alternative slice in towards the base of the cucumber piece, tucking them in so that they stay securely in place.

5   Keep the cucumber fans in cold water until you are ready to use them.

MENUS
AND HOW TO EAT
CHINESE FOOD

Chinese meals always consist of a soup, a rice, noodle or bread dish, a vegetable dish and at least two other dishes which may be mainly meat, fish or chicken. The meal may be preceded and concluded with tea, but during the meal itself soup will be the only beverage. Soup is drunk not as a first course as it is in the West but throughout the meal. The exception to this is a banquet when soup, if it is served at all, comes at the end of the meal or as a palate-cleanser at several points during the dinner. On such occasions, wine, spirits, beer or even fruit juice will be drunk with the food. At banquets (which are really elaborate dinner parties) dishes are served one at a time so that the individual qualities of each dish can be properly savoured. There may be as many as eight to twelve courses. Rice will not be served except at the end of the meal when fried rice might be offered to anyone who has any appetite left.

At ordinary family meals all the dishes comprising the meal are served together, including the soup. The food is placed in the centre of the table. Each person has his own rice bowl into which he puts a generous amount of steamed rice. Then, using his chopsticks, he helps himself to a little of one dish, transferring this to his rice bowl. Once he has eaten this together with some rice he will have a chopstick-full of another dish. No Chinese would dream of heaping his rice bowl with what he regarded as his full share of any dish before proceeding to eat. Eating is a communal affair and each diner will take care to see that everyone else at the table is receiving a fair share of everything.

Of course you can eat Chinese food any way you like. I think it blends deliciously with many European dishes, and when you are new to Chinese cooking you may find it easier to familiarise yourself with the cuisine by trying out just one or two dishes at a time and incorporating them into a non-Chinese menu. Chinese soups, for example, make excellent starters and stir-fried vegetables are delicious with grills and roasts.

When you do devise an all-Chinese meal, try to see that you have a good mix of textures, flavours, colours and shapes. Apart from a staple dish, such as steamed rice, you should opt for a variety of meat, poultry and fish. It is better to serve one meat and one fish dish rather than two meat dishes, even if the meats are different. It will also be a better-balanced meal (and easier to prepare) if you use a variety of cooking methods. Serve a stir-fried dish with a braised, steamed or cold dish. It's important to try to select one or two things which can be prepared in advance. Avoid doing more than two stir-fried dishes which will make for frantic activity at the last minute.

Table-setting

You don't need any special crockery or cutlery for serving Chinese food, although I think it tastes infinitely better when it is eaten with chopsticks rather than a fork. Knives are definitely unnecessary since Chinese food is always cut into bite-sized pieces before it is served. Each person will need a rice bowl, a soup bowl, a teacup if you are serving tea, and a small plate for any bones or debris. A small dish or saucer each will also be needed if you are having any dipping sauces. Soup or cereal bowls will do for the rice and soup. Chopsticks are usually set to the right of the rice bowl where a knife would normally be put. A spoon, metal or china, will be needed for soup and as an adjunct to chopsticks for noodles.

The Chinese always help themselves (and others) to the food using their own chopsticks. Some people provide separate serving chopsticks but these are usually abandoned in the enthusiasm of eating.

Using chopsticks

Using chopsticks just takes a little practice and the hungrier you are the quicker you learn!

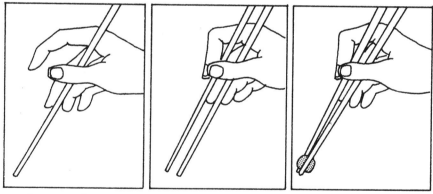

1   Put one chopstick into the crook of your hand between your thumb and first finger, holding the chopstick about two-thirds the way up from the thinner end. Let it rest on your third finger.

2   Put the second chopstick between your thumb and forefinger so that its tip is level with the first chopstick below.

3   Keep the lower chopstick steady and move the top one to pick up food.

When eating rice and other tricky morsels it is perfectly acceptable to lift your rice bowl under your chin and 'shovel' rice into your mouth with your chopsticks. The Chinese do this all the time.

What to drink

If you want to be authentic serve soup with your Chinese meals. If you prefer you could serve tea, preferably Chinese tea which is drunk without milk and sugar. There are three different types of Chinese tea. Green or unfermented tea is made from green leaves which, when infused, result in a pale yellowish tea with a refreshing astringent taste. Black tea is made from fermented black leaves and is red when infused. It has a hearty, robust flavour. Oolong tea is made from partially fermented leaves and is strong and dark. Of all these I think green jasmine tea is the nicest with food. (Do not confuse any of these teas with 'China tea' which is a tea blended for the British market.)

Chinese wines are usually made from fermented rice, the most famous being Shaoxing which is also used for cooking. It has a very different flavour from wine made from grapes and is rather an acquired taste. Many European wines go very well with Chinese food, particularly dry whites and light reds. In recent years whiskey and cognac have become very popular with the more affluent Hong Kong Chinese who drink these neat with their meals.

Menus and servings

Throughout this book I have given some suggestions about what accompanying dishes would go with a particular recipe. There is of course no need to stick rigidly to these ideas. Although most Chinese meals consist of at least three dishes, rice and soup, I recommend that you concentrate on achieving success with relatively few dishes until you become more familiar with Chinese cooking techniques and with the recipes themselves. Chefs apart, the Chinese themselves would not expect to be proficient in cooking the real delicacies of their cuisine. These they would order in a restaurant and would not attempt at home. (The Chinese who live in towns and cities eat out a great deal, although many restaurants are very humble, simple places.)

Chinese cooking can be very time-consuming. The recipes in this book are based on the expectation that you will cook two meat, chicken or fish dishes per meal. (This is in addition to a vegetable dish, rice or noodles and, probably, a soup.) This way the total meat, chicken and fish allowance per head will be about 6–8 oz (175–225 g). If you prefer to cook just one such dish then you will probably have to double the quantities given in the recipe. Doing this at least means you will have a chance to try the authentic taste of Chinese food without quite so much work. Once you gain confidence you will be able to cope with preparing more dishes and be able to serve a more authentic Chinese meal.

54

SUGGESTED MENUS

Here are some suggestions for a variety of menus:

Everyday family meals

● Tomato Eggflower Soup
  Steamed Fish with Garlic, Spring Onions and Ginger
  Stir-fried Beef with Orange
  Lettuce with Oyster Sauce
  Steamed Rice

● Kidney and Beancurd Soup
  Stir-fried Minced Pork
  Cold Marinaded Bean Sprouts
  Stir-fried Ginger Broccoli
  Steamed Rice

● Beef Noodle Soup
  Fried Wuntun
  Stir-fried Cucumbers with Hot Spices
  Peaches in Honey Syrup
  (This menu is for a light lunch or supper.)

● Curried Sweetcorn Soup with Chicken
  Five Spiced Spareribs
  Fried Fish with Ginger
  Cold Spicy Noodles
  Stir-fried Mange-tout with Waterchestnuts

Summer dinner parties

● Sesame Prawn Toast
  Chinese Chicken Salad
  Stir-fried Pork with Spring Onions
  Stir-fried Spinach with Garlic
  Steamed Rice
  Fruit Compote

Serves 4

● Cold Spicy Noodles
Chicken Pieces in Black Bean Sauce
Stir-fried Scallops with Pig's Kidneys
Cold Sweet and Sour Chinese Leaves
Fresh Fruit

Winter dinner parties

Serves 4

● Hot and Sour Soup
Sichuan Prawns in Chilli Sauce
Five Spice Red Braised Pigeons
Braised Cauliflower with Oyster Sauce
Steamed Rice

Serves 4–6

● Wuntun Soup
Curried Chicken with Peppers
Peking Braised Lamb
Braised Spicy Aubergines
Steamed Rice

● Prawn Crackers
Mongolian Hot Pot
Stir-fried Pork with Spring Onions (optional)

Special dinner or banquet
This menu should be attempted when you feel reasonably
competent at Chinese cooking. It takes quite a lot of preparation
and you will find it easier to manage the whole meal if you have
already experimented with the individual dishes. It is designed so
that each dish is served as a separate course.

Serves 6–8

● Caramel Walnuts
Sweetcorn Soup with Crabmeat
Rainbow Beef in Lettuce Leaves **or** Peking Duck with Chinese
    Pancakes
Stir-fried Mange-tout with Waterchestnuts
Braised Pork with Beancurd
Fresh Fruit

SOUPS

In China soups are rarely served as a separate course except at banquets. During some formal banquets light soups are served at various stages of dining. They signal the end of a course and are used to cleanse the palate in preparation for the next one. Most commonly a thin clear soup will be served at the end of the dinner but before the dessert. At family meals soup is served at the same time as all the other dishes. In this case it complements the various tastes and textures of the meal and also serves as a beverage.

There are two basic types of soup in Chinese cookery: light and heavy. Light soups are clear broths garnished with a little meat, fish, seafood or vegetable. Such soups are a liquid accompaniment to other dishes. (Drinks such as water, wine and tea are rarely served with a meal in China.) I remember family gatherings when a large tureen of clear soup would dominate the centre of the table, with all of the other dishes arranged round it. It was considered good form always to drink a good helping of it during the meal.

The heavy soups are more like separate courses or meals in their own right. They are substantial in texture, more like stews than soups, and are made from a rich stock with the addition of meat, fish or seafood, chopped vegetables and seasonings. These soups are generally thickened with a starch such as cornflour or waterchestnut flour. They are made in a heatproof casserole and simmered slowly until all the flavours marry. Shark's Fin is one of the most famous Chinese thick soups. It is a classic, gourmet soup. Its essential ingredient (shark's fin) is expensive to obtain, and it is time-consuming to make, so is not really suitable for the domestic kitchen and is best enjoyed in a restaurant.

The key to a good Chinese soup, as to any soup, is good stock. I learned about Chinese stock first by watching my mother making it with meticulous care in her kitchen. These lessons were reinforced for me in my uncle's restaurant where a large pot of stock was the heart of the kitchen. All the world's great cuisines emphasise the importance of stock. The French call it the *fonds de cuisine*, the basis or foundation of cooking. In China stock is essential in many recipes, and it is indispensable in soup. In Chinese cuisine stock is generally made from chicken, with pork bones sometimes being added to enrich the broth. Beef is rarely used because it is expensive and also because it is considered too strong for the Chinese palate.

All of the soups in the following chapter are easy to make, particularly if you have already made stock ahead of time. They can be served, Chinese-style, with other dishes, or as a separate course, or on their own as a light meal. You need not limit your enjoyment of these soups to an all-Chinese meal as Chinese soups blend deliciously with European food.

CHICKEN STOCK

Region: all

Chicken stock is an all-purpose base, not only for soups, but also for sauces and glazes. It is light and delicious, its chief ingredient is fairly cheap and it is easy to make. With such attributes it is small wonder that chicken stock is essential in Chinese cookery. Your first step on the path to success with Chinese cooking must be to prepare and maintain an ample supply of good chicken stock. I prefer to make large quantities of it at a time and freeze it. Once you have a supply of stock available you will be able to prepare any number of soups or sauces very quickly. Never ever use stock cubes for Chinese cooking. They contain too much salt and too little flavour and will never produce the sort of rich, thick stock on which so many Chinese dishes depend for their subtle taste. Here are several points to remember:

● Good stock requires meat to give it richness and flavour. It is therefore necessary to use at least some chicken meat, if not a whole bird.

● The stock should never boil. If it does it will be undesirably cloudy and the fat will be incorporated into the liquid.

● Simmer slowly and skim the stock regularly.

● Strain the finished stock well through several layers of cheesecloth or a fine mesh strainer.

● Let the stock cool thoroughly before freezing it.

The classic Chinese method to ensure a clear stock is to blanch the meat and bones before simmering. I find this is unnecessary. My method of careful skimming achieves the same result with far less work. Remember to save all your uncooked chicken bones and carcasses for stock. They can be frozen until you are ready to make it. (Be sure to wrap the bones well before freezing them.)

This recipe makes about 6 pints 3·4 litres		
		(If you find the portions too large for your needs cut the recipe in half)
4½lb	2kg	uncooked chicken bones (backs, feet, wings, etc.)
1½lb	700g	chicken pieces
6 pints	3·4ltr	cold water
2 slices		fresh ginger

2	spring onions
2	garlic cloves, unskinned
½ teaspoon	salt

Put the chicken bones and chicken pieces into a very large pot. (The bones can be put in either frozen or defrosted.) Cover them with the cold water and bring it to a simmer. Meanwhile cut the ginger into diagonal slices, 2 inches (5 cm) × ½ inch (1 cm). Remove the green tops of the spring onions. Lightly crush the garlic cloves leaving the skins on.

Using a large, flat spoon, skim off the scum as it rises from the bones. Watch the heat as the stock should never boil. Keep skimming until the stock looks clear. This can take from 20 to 40 minutes. Do not stir or disturb the stock.

Now turn the heat down to a low simmer. Add the ginger, white spring onions, garlic cloves and salt. Simmer the stock on a very low heat for between 2 and 4 hours, skimming any fat off the top at least twice during this time. The stock should be rich and full-bodied which is why it needs to be simmered for such a long time. This way the stock (and any soup you make with it) will have plenty of taste.

Strain the stock through several layers of dampened cheesecloth or through a very fine mesh strainer, and then let it cool thoroughly. Remove any fat which has risen to the top. It is now ready to be used or transferred to containers and frozen for future use.

PORK AND CHICKEN STOCK

Region: all

Pork is used extensively in Chinese cookery, and pork bones, when added to chicken stock, make for a richer, tastier and sweeter soup or broth. It was a favourite in our house not only as a beverage but as a 'rinse' for our rice bowls between courses. I also loved chewing on the cooked bones and looking for morsels of pork to dip in soy sauce.

60

This recipe makes about 4 pints 2·3 litres		
4 pints	2·3 ltr	Chicken Stock (page 59)
1½ lb	700g	uncooked pork bones
1 slice		fresh ginger
2		spring onions
½ teaspoon		salt

Cut the ginger into slices 2 inches (5 cm) × ½ inch (1 cm). Trim the green tops off the spring onions leaving the white part. Put the pork bones into a heavy pot or casserole together with the chicken stock. (Thaw the pork bones beforehand if they are frozen otherwise you will get a cloudy stock.) Bring the liquid to a simmer and skim off any scum that rises to the surface. Then add the ginger, spring onion whites and salt. Simmer on a very low heat for 1½ hours.

Strain the stock through dampened cheesecloth or through a fine mesh strainer, and then leave it to cool. When the stock is cold remove any fat which has risen to the surface. It is now ready to be used as soup or as a stock for other soups such as Ham and Marrow Soup (page 71). You can also freeze it for future use.

TOMATO EGGFLOWER SOUP

Region: southern

Tomatoes were introduced into China only 100 years ago. They were gradually adopted into southern Chinese cuisine and have become one of its most popular ingredients. Their intense, sweet flavour, brilliant colour and versatility lend them perfectly to Chinese cookery. Here they are used to enhance my adaptation of the traditional eggflower soup. The egg 'flowers' are simply strands of lightly beaten eggs which float on the surface of the soup like lilies on a pond. This effect is created by gently guiding the eggs over the soup in strands instead of dropping the mixture in all at once which would cause the egg to lump together. The egg mixture slightly thickens the soup, which nevertheless remains very light.

This is an impressive-looking soup but it is very easy to make. It is especially delightful in summer when fresh tomatoes are at their most plentiful. Although tinned tomatoes are acceptable, fresh ones are always preferable.

61

Serves 4 to 6	
2 pints 1·1ltr	**Chicken Stock (page 59)**
8oz 225g	**fresh or tinned tomatoes**
2	**small eggs**
½ teaspoon	**sesame oil**
1 teaspoon	**salt**
2 teaspoons	**light soy sauce**
1 tablespoon	**spring onions, white part only, finely chopped**
Optional garnish	
1 tablespoon	**green spring onion tops, finely chopped**

Put the chicken stock into a pot and bring it to a simmer. If you are using fresh tomatoes, peel, seed and cut them into 1 inch (2·5 cm) cubes. If you are using tinned tomatoes, chop them into small chunks. Lightly beat the eggs and then combine them with the sesame oil in a small bowl.

Add the light soy sauce and salt to the simmering stock, and stir to mix them in well. Then add the tomatoes and simmer for 5 minutes. Next stir in the spring onions and then add the egg mixture in a very slow, thin stream. Using a chopstick or fork, pull the egg slowly into strands. (I have found that stirring the egg in a figure of eight works quite well.) Garnish with the finely chopped spring onion tops.

CHICKEN AND SPINACH SOUP

Region: eastern

Spinach, with its distinctive taste and deep green colour, is a favourite of the Chinese. This soup is a thin one and is very attractive to look at. Its ingredients are blanched separately before they are combined with the stock. This way each ingredient retains its unique taste. This is an easy soup to make and many of the steps can be done in advance.

62

Serves 4 to 6		
6oz	175g	fresh spinach
6oz	175g	chicken breasts
2 pints	1·1ltr	Chicken Stock (page 59)
2 tablespoons		light soy sauce
2 teaspoons		sugar
2 tablespoons		spring onions, finely chopped

Remove the stems of the spinach and wash the leaves well. Blanch the leaves for a few seconds in a pot of boiling water until they are just wilted. Then freshen them in cold water to prevent further cooking.

Cut the chicken into thin slices about 2 inches (5 cm) long. In a separate pot of boiling water blanch the chicken slices for 2 minutes until they are slightly firm and white. Now drain both the spinach and the chicken slices. The soup can be prepared up to this point several hours ahead.

Just before you are ready to eat, bring the chicken stock to a simmer and season it with the soy sauce and sugar. Add the blanched spinach and chicken slices. Bring the soup back to simmering point and then add the spring onions. Serve at once.

WATERCRESS SOUP

Region: southern

Here is a soup from my childhood. My mother used to make it with pork pieces and its delightful fragrance emanating from the kitchen signified good things to come. I would remove the pork pieces from the soup and dip them in soy sauce before eating them. Then I would pour some of the soup into my rice bowl to flavour the rice. In our family restaurant, this soup was a favourite at staff meals because of its wonderfully delicate flavour and because it is so easy to make. Nowadays I prefer it plain, without any meat added. Use only the leaves of the watercress; the leftover stalks can be stir-fried and served as a vegetable. Spinach or Swiss chard can be used instead of watercress.

Serves 4 to 6	
2 pints 1·1ltr	Chicken Stock (page 59)
2 tablespoons	light soy sauce
1 teaspoon	sugar
8oz 225g	watercress leaves (about 3 bunches)
1 teaspoon	fresh ginger, finely chopped
1 tablespoon	spring onions, finely chopped

Bring the stock to a simmer in a large pot. Add the soy sauce and sugar and simmer for 3 minutes. Then add the watercress leaves, ginger and spring onions and continue to simmer the soup for another 4 minutes. Serve at once.

HAM AND BEAN SPROUT SOUP

Region: southern

This is a simple soup which typifies the fresh, light cooking of the south. Like many good soups, it takes a little effort to prepare, but it is worth it. It is best to use bean sprouts which are really fresh to give your soup a good crunchy texture. Chinese ham is traditionally used to produce the distinctive smoky flavour, but since it cannot be obtained here, lean English smoked bacon or Parma ham are satisfactory substitutes.

Serves 4 to 6	
2oz 50g	bean thread (transparent) noodles
3oz 75g	fresh bean sprouts
2 pints 1·1ltr	Chicken Stock (page 59)
1 tablespoon	light soy sauce
3oz 75g	Parma ham or lean English smoked bacon, shredded
2 tablespoons	fresh coriander, finely chopped
2 tablespoons	spring onions, finely chopped

Right: Rainbow Beef in Lettuce Leaves (page 98) and Hot and Sour Soup (page 75)

Soak the noodles in a bowl of warm water for about 20 minutes or until they are soft. Drain them thoroughly in a colander and cut them into 2 inch (5 cm) pieces. If you have the time, remove both ends of the bean sprouts. This will give the soup a cleaner look.

Bring the chicken stock to a simmer in a large pot. Add the drained noodles and soy sauce and simmer for 2 minutes. Then add the ham or bacon, coriander and spring onions, and simmer for 30 seconds. Finally, add the bean sprouts and simmer for another 30 seconds. Serve at once.

CHICKEN AND MUSHROOM SOUP

Region: southern

This soup combines two classic southern Chinese ingredients: chicken and dried mushrooms. Dark chicken meat from the legs and thighs is most often used for this soup to give it a rich, strong flavour and a good texture. Fresh button mushrooms can be used instead of dried ones, but you should try to use the dried Chinese mushrooms if you can get them as their smoky flavour enhances the total effect of the soup.

There are two techniques involved here. The chicken is first stir-fried to give it a rich flavour. Then all the other ingredients are simmered together with the fried chicken. The result is a good soup which would also go well with French bread and butter for a non-Chinese meal. It also re-heats nicely, tasting even better when made one day and eaten the next.

Serves 4 to 6		
4 oz	110 g	chicken thighs or legs, skinned
1 tablespoon		sherry or rice wine
1 tablespoon		light soy sauce
1 oz	25 g	Chinese dried mushrooms
2 pints	1·1 ltr	Chicken Stock (page 59)
1 tablespoon		spring onions, finely chopped

Left: Stir-fried Lamb with Garlic (page 105) and Tomato Eggflower Soup (page 61)

1 oz	25 g	Parma ham or lean English smoked bacon, shredded
1 tablespoon		light soy sauce
2 teaspoons		oil

Cut the chicken into ½ inch (1 cm) cubes, retaining any bones. Put them into a bowl together with the sherry or rice wine and 1 tablespoon of soy sauce and let the mixture stand for 10 minutes. Soak the mushrooms in warm water for 20 minutes. Then drain them and squeeze out the excess liquid. Remove and discard the stems and finely shred the caps into thin strips.

Bring the stock to a simmer in a large pot. Drain the marinade (but not the chicken cubes) into the stock. Add the mushrooms, spring onions, ham or bacon and soy sauce. Continue to simmer the soup and meanwhile heat the oil in a wok or large frying-pan. When it is hot, stir-fry the chicken cubes over a high heat until they are nicely brown. This should take about 5 minutes. Drain them on kitchen paper and then add them to the soup. Simmer together for 5 minutes, and the soup is ready to serve.

CURRIED SWEETCORN SOUP WITH CHICKEN
Region: southern

Curry is especially popular in southern China which has a long history of contact with India. The Chinese favour curry powder or paste which comes from Madras, but, unlike Indians, Chinese cooks use curry only as a light addition to the usual Chinese seasonings, a subtle touch rather than a dominant tone.

This is not a traditional Chinese soup but is my version of sweetcorn soup which has become popular in the West. It is easy to make and is delicious. If you use tinned creamed corn which is already quite thick, you could leave out the cornflour mixture. The rich golden sheen of the curried soup makes it a good, bright dish for a dinner which might include Stir-fried Pork with Spring Onions (page 81), a green vegetable such as spinach, and plain steamed rice.

Serves 4 to 6		
1 lb	450 g	fresh sweetcorn on a cob, or 10 oz 275 g tinned sweetcorn, plain or creamed
8 oz	225 g	boneless chicken breasts, skinned
1		egg white
1 teaspoon		cornflour
1 teaspoon		salt
1		egg
1 teaspoon		sesame oil
2 pints	1·1 ltr	Chicken Stock (page 59)
1 tablespoon		dry sherry or rice wine
1 tablespoon		curry powder or paste
1 teaspoon		salt
1 teaspoon		sugar
2 teaspoons		cornflour blended with 2 teaspoons water
Garnish		
2 tablespoons		spring onions, finely chopped

Clean the corn and remove the kernels with a sharp knife or cleaver. You should end up with about 10 oz (275 g). If you are using tinned corn, empty the contents into a bowl and set it aside. Using a cleaver or a sharp knife, thinly slice the chicken breasts into fine shreds about 3 inches long (7·5 cm). Mix the chicken shreds together with the egg white, 1 teaspoon cornflour and salt in a small bowl and set it aside. Beat the whole egg and sesame oil together in another small bowl and set it aside.

Bring a small pot of water to the boil. Quickly blanch the chicken shreds in it until they just turn white. (This should take about 20 seconds.) Remove them with a slotted spoon and drain them in a colander or sieve. Now bring the stock to a boil in a large pot and add the sweetcorn. Simmer for 10 minutes, uncovered, and then add the sherry or rice wine, curry powder, salt, sugar and, if you are using it, the cornflour mixture. Bring it back to the boil, then lower the heat and simmer for another 5 minutes. Now add the blanched chicken shreds, and then slowly pour in the egg and sesame oil mixture in a steady stream, stirring all the time. Transfer the soup to a tureen, garnish with spring onions and serve.

69

HAM AND PIGEON STEAMED IN SOUP

Region: eastern

This unusual technique for making soup is not difficult to master. It is called double-steaming, a process in which rich ingredients are steamed for hours in a covered casserole which is filled with soup. This extracts all the flavours from the ingredients, and is a technique often used for making the classic Shark's Fin and Bird's Nest Soups. The result is a distinctive soup, clear and rich but also light. Game birds other than pigeon, such as partridge, snipe, woodcock or quail, would work equally well. This soup is particularly suitable for a dinner party. For easy planning, I would make it in advance and freeze it, as it re-heats well.

Serves 4 to 6		
4		pigeons, each weighing about 8oz 225g
1oz	25g	Parma ham or lean English smoked bacon
4 slices		fresh ginger
2 pints	1·1ltr	Chicken and Pork Stock (page 60)
4		spring onions
2 tablespoons		dry sherry or rice wine
½ teaspoon		salt

Using a sharp, heavy knife or cleaver, cut the pigeons into quarters. Bring a pot of water to the boil, turn the heat down and add the pigeons. Simmer them in the water for 10 minutes. (This blanching rids the pigeons of some of their fat and impurities.) Remove them with a slotted spoon and discard the water. Cut the Parma ham or bacon into very fine shreds and cut the ginger into slices 2 inches (5cm) × ¼inch (0·5cm).

Set a rack into a wok or deep pan. Fill it with 2½inches (6cm) of water and bring it to the boil. Bring the stock to the boil in another large pot and then pour it into a heatproof glass or china casserole. Add the pigeon, ham, spring onions, ginger, sherry or rice wine and salt to the casserole, and cover it with a lid or foil. Put the casserole on the rack and cover the wok or deep pan tightly with a lid or foil. You now have a casserole within a steamer, hence the name 'double-steaming'. Turn the heat down and steam gently for 2–3 hours or until the pigeon is tender. Replenish the hot water

70

from time to time. An alternative method is simply to simmer the soup very slowly in a conventional pot, but the resulting taste will be quite different.

When the soup is cooked, remove all the ingredients with a slotted spoon and discard the spring onions, ginger and ham. Serve the soup together with the pigeon pieces. The soup can be served immediately or cooled and stored in the refrigerator or freezer to be re-heated when required.

HAM AND MARROW SOUP

Region: western

Although courgettes and marrows are not available in China, there are many similar members of the same family which are used in Chinese cookery. This is an adaptation of a traditional recipe which calls for 'hairy melon' or Chinese marrow, which is much more appetising than it sounds. The exterior of Chinese marrow is fuzzy and hairy, rather like a peach—hence its name. I think that marrow tastes very similar and makes an excellent alternative. This is basically a clear soup. It goes well with Sweet and Sour Pork (page 83) and Stir-fried Spinach with Garlic (page 211).

Serves 4 to 6		
8oz	225g	marrow or courgettes
2 pints	1·1 ltr	Chicken and Pork Stock (page 60)
2oz	50g	Parma ham or lean English smoked bacon, finely shredded
½ teaspoon		chilli bean sauce or chilli powder
1½ tablespoons		light soy sauce
½ teaspoon		salt
Garnish		
1 teaspoon		sesame oil

Trim the ends of the marrow or courgettes and, if you are using marrow, remove the seeds. Cut into ½inch (1cm) cubes. Bring the stock to a boil in a large pot. Add the ham or bacon, marrow or courgettes and all the other ingredients. Simmer the soup, uncovered, for 15 minutes. Add the sesame oil and give it a good stir. Serve the soup immediately in individual bowls or in a large soup tureen.

KIDNEY AND BEANCURD SOUP

Region: eastern

My mother often made kidney soup for our family dinner because it was tasty and inexpensive. Sometimes she added watercress or spinach to it. In this recipe the kidneys are cleaned in bicarbonate of soda and quickly blanched before being added to the stock. This prevents the kidney juices from clouding the soup. It is a light and nutritious soup which re-heats well. Serve it with Cashew Chicken (page 121) and Spicy Stir-fried Mushrooms (page 209).

Serves 4 to 6	
1lb 450g	pig's kidneys
1 teaspoon	bicarbonate of soda
2 teaspoons	cider vinegar or Chinese white rice vinegar
1 teaspoon	salt
14oz 400g	fresh beancurd
2 pints 1·1ltr	Pork and Chicken Stock (page 60)
1 teaspoon	fresh ginger, finely chopped
2 teaspoons	spring onions, finely chopped
2 tablespoons	light soy sauce
1 teaspoon	salt

Using a sharp knife, remove the thin outer membrane of the kidney. Then, with a sharp cleaver or knife, cut each kidney in half, cutting horizontally to keep the shape of the kidney. Now cut away the small knobs of fat and any tough membrane which surrounds them. Put the kidney halves flat on the cutting surface and score

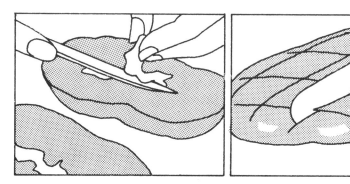

the top of each half, making light cuts in a crisscross pattern all over the surface. Then cut the halved kidneys into thin slices. Toss the kidney slices with the bicarbonate of soda and let them sit for about 20 minutes. Then rinse them thoroughly with cold water and toss them in the vinegar and salt. Put them into a colander and let them drain for at least 30 minutes or more.

Bring a pan of water to the boil. Blot the kidney slices dry with kitchen paper and blanch them in the water for about 2 minutes. Drain them in a colander or sieve and set aside. Cut the beancurd into ½ inch (1 cm) cubes.

In a separate pot, bring the stock to a simmer and add the rest of the ingredients. Simmer for about 5 minutes and then add the kidney slices to the soup. Give the soup several stirs and simmer another 2 minutes. Serve at once or allow to cool and re-heat gently when required.

WUNTUN SOUP
Region: southern

This is one of the most popular soups in southern China, and it is equally popular in Chinese restaurants in the West. Ideally, soup wuntun should be stuffed savoury dumplings poached in clear water and then served in a rich broth. Unfortunately in many restaurants the soup often arrives with wuntun skins but very little filling. This recipe will enable you to make a simple but authentic wuntun soup, perfect for any family meal. Wuntun skins can be obtained from Chinese grocers. They are yellowish in colour, square, and are packaged in small stacks. They can be bought fresh or frozen and can be found on the shop's cool shelf or in the freezer. (Be sure to thaw them thoroughly if they are frozen.) Wuntun can be filled and then frozen successfully, and thawed when required.

Serves 4 to 6	
1 packet	wuntun skins (about 30–35)
2 pints 1·1 ltr	Chicken Stock (page 59)
Filling	
12 oz 350g	minced pork
1 tablespoon	light soy sauce
2 teaspoons	dry sherry or rice wine
1½ tablespoons	spring onions, finely chopped
1 teaspoon	sesame oil
1	egg white
½ teaspoon	cornflour
1 teaspoon	sugar
½ teaspoon	salt
Garnish	
1 tablespoon	light soy sauce
1 tablespoon	spring onions, finely chopped
1 teaspoon	sesame oil

Combine the filling ingredients in a large bowl and mix them well. Using a small spoon, put a small amount of filling in the centre of each wuntun skin. Bring up the sides of the skin around the filling and pinch them together at the top so that the wuntun is well sealed. It should look like a small, filled bag.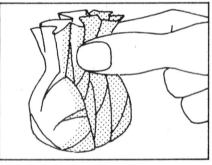

Bring a large pot of water to the boil and place the wuntun in the water for 1 minute until they float to the top. This poaching rids the wuntun of any excess flour and starch and will ensure that the soup itself is clear and has a clean texture. Remove the wuntun with a slotted spoon and put them on a plate.

Now bring the chicken stock to the boil in a large pot. Add the cooked wuntun and the garnish ingredients. Turn the heat low and simmer for 2 minutes. Although this soup can be re-heated, it is best eaten straightaway.

HOT AND SOUR SOUP
Region: northern and western

This Chinese soup has become quite popular in the Western world, perhaps because it is a heavy soup, suited to cold climates. It combines sour and spicy elements in a rich, tasty stock, and re-heats very well. The list of ingredients may be daunting but the recipe is, in fact, quite easy to make. I have suggested cider vinegar as a substitute for Chinese red vinegar which is harder to find.

Serves 4 to 6		
3 oz	75 g	boneless lean pork
1 oz	25 g	dried Chinese mushrooms
1 oz	25 g	bean thread (transparent) noodles
10 oz	275 g	fresh beancurd
2		small eggs
1 teaspoon		sesame oil
2 pints	1·1 ltr	Chicken Stock (page 59)
2 teaspoons		sugar
3 tablespoons		cider vinegar or Chinese red vinegar
½ teaspoon		white pepper
2 tablespoons		dark soy sauce
1 tablespoon		cornflour blended with 1 tablespoon water
2 tablespoons		spring onions, finely chopped
2 tablespoons		fresh coriander, finely chopped
1 teaspoon		sesame oil
1 teaspoon		Chilli Oil (page 28) (optional)

Cut the pork into thin shreds. Bring some water to the boil in a pot and blanch the pork in it for 2 minutes. Drain the meat and set it aside. Soak the mushrooms in warm water for 20 minutes, then drain them and squeeze out any excess liquid. Discard the stems and shred the caps finely. Soak the noodles for 5 minutes in warm water, and then drain them. Cut them into 5 inch (12·5 cm) lengths and set them aside. Drain the beancurd and shred it into thin strips. Beat the eggs and sesame oil together in a small bowl.

Bring the chicken stock to a simmer in a large pot. Add the prepared pork, mushrooms, noodles and beancurd together with the sugar, vinegar, white pepper and dark soy sauce. Simmer together for 3 minutes, and then thicken it with the cornflour mixture. Simmer for 2 minutes with the heat as low as possible.

75

Next pour the beaten egg mixture into the soup in a steady stream, and pull the egg into strands with a fork or chopsticks. Stir in the spring onions, fresh coriander, sesame oil and chilli oil. Pour the soup into a large tureen or individual bowls and serve at once.

SWEETCORN SOUP WITH CRABMEAT

Region: southern

My mother often made this soup using fresh sweetcorn. For convenience, tinned or frozen corn may be substituted but I think my mother's recipe is quite superior. It re-heats well and has a rich, thick texture, which goes well with Beef in Oyster Sauce (page 93) and Stir-fried Ginger Broccoli (page 195).

Serves 4 to 6	
1lb 450g	fresh sweetcorn on the cob, or 10oz 275g tinned or frozen sweetcorn
1	egg white
1 teaspoon	sesame oil
2 pints 1·1ltr	Chicken Stock (page 59)
1 tablespoon	dry sherry or rice wine
2 teaspoons	fresh ginger, finely chopped
1 teaspoon	salt
1 teaspoon	sugar
2 teaspoons	cornflour, blended with 2 teaspoons water
6oz 175g	fresh cooked, tinned or frozen crabmeat
Garnish	
2 tablespoons	spring onions, finely chopped

If you are using fresh corn, wash the cobs and, with a sharp knife or cleaver, remove the kernels. (You should end up with about 10oz (275g) of corn.) Mix the egg white and sesame oil together in a small bowl and set it aside.

Bring the stock to a boil in a large pot and add the corn. Simmer for 15 minutes, uncovered, and then add the sherry or rice wine, ginger, salt, sugar and cornflour mixture. Bring it back to the boil, then lower the heat to a simmer. Now add the crabmeat and then slowly pour in the egg white mixture in a steady stream, stirring all the time. Transfer the soup to a tureen and garnish.

MEAT

Whenever my family talked about meat we invariably referred to pork. On rare occasions we ate beef and even less frequently, lamb. This was probably because although I was brought up in the USA my family came from southern China where beef and lamb are less commonly eaten. Beef, mutton and goat are more popular in northern China, a reflection of the Moslem and Mongolian influence in this area. In the main, however, most Chinese think of meat as being pork, so, as you might expect, there are innumerable pork dishes in Chinese cuisine. It is an extremely versatile meat which can be prepared in many different ways and its subtle flavour lends itself to many complementary ingredients, seasonings and sauces. Pork fat is also highly prized and it is cooked in various ways which render it not only edible but delicious.

This chapter contains some recipes for beef and lamb although their flavour is less familiar to Chinese palates. If you like you can substitute beef for pork in some of the recipes. Stir-fried Pork with Spring Onions (page 81) and Stir-fried Minced Pork (page 82) will work just as well with beef.

Sheep and goat share the same Chinese character. Goat is more widely available in north China, but is also eaten in other areas. I prefer to use lamb instead. A Chinese poet once wrote 'There are seventy-two ways of cooking lamb; of these only eighteen or nineteen are palatable.' The recipes here are within the latter category!

The British cuts of meat which are most suitable for Chinese cooking are:

Pork
For stir-frying use loin chops with the bones and all the fat removed, or pork steaks or fillet. Pork belly is best for braising. The best minced pork comes from the blade which is a reasonably priced cut.

Beef
I prefer fillet steak for stir-frying since it is lean and tender and full of flavour. Although it is expensive a little goes a long way. Porterhouse, rump and T-bone steak are also suitable. My favourite cut for braising is brisket. Although it is fatty its taste and ability to absorb the flavours of a sauce are unbeatable. The Chinese love the texture of braised brisket. Shin and chuck steak are also suitable for slow-cooking.

Lamb

Loin chops with the bones and all the fat removed are perfect for stir-frying, as are lamb fillets (which come from the neck) and lamb steaks. The best cuts for braising are breast, scrag end of neck or shoulder.

Lack of refrigeration means that various meats which are preserved by drying or curing are also popular in Chinese cuisine. Dried beef is often eaten as a snack while cured ham is used in cooking. The regions of Zhejiang and Yunnan are famous for their hams which unfortunately are unobtainable here, though Parma ham or English smoked bacon are acceptable substitutes for Zhejiang ham which I frequently use. In Chinese cookery nothing is ever wasted. Every part of a beast is utilised. Offal is extremely popular and it is usually braised, except for liver which is commonly stir-fried.

I prefer to use meat which has not been frozen since it contains less water and I think it has a better flavour. This is particularly important when selecting meat for stir-frying which needs to be as dry as possible so that it will fry rather than steam in its own juices. Although the Chinese are very fond of meat they eat it in small quantities. This is one reason why Chinese food is so healthy.

PORK WITH BLACK BEAN SAUCE

Region: southern
Method: stir-frying

Pork goes particularly well with black beans, the salty and spicy flavour of which is so distinctively Chinese. This simple, homely, stir-fried dish is one which I often ate as a child. Sometimes my mother would vary the taste by adding an extra spicy touch of chilli powder. It is very quick to cook and goes well with plain rice and any stir-fried vegetable.

Serves 4	
12 oz 350 g	lean pork
2 teaspoons	dry sherry or rice wine
2 teaspoons	light soy sauce
½ teaspoon	cornflour
1 tablespoon	oil
1½ tablespoons	black beans, coarsely chopped
1½ teaspoons	garlic, finely chopped
1 tablespoon	spring onions, finely chopped
2 teaspoons	light soy sauce
1 teaspoon	sugar
2 teaspoons	chicken stock or water

Cut the pork into thin slices 2 inches (5 cm) long. Put the slices into a small bowl and mix them well with the dry sherry or rice wine, soy sauce and cornflour. Let them marinade for about 20 minutes.

Heat a wok or large frying-pan until it is hot. Add about ½ tablespoon of the oil and, when it is almost smoking, lift the pork out of the marinade with a slotted spoon and quickly stir-fry it for about 2–3 minutes. Then transfer it at once to a bowl.

Wipe the wok clean, re-heat it and add the rest of the oil. Then quickly add the black beans, garlic and spring onions. A few seconds later add the rest of the ingredients. Bring the mixture to a boil and then return the pork to the wok or pan. Stir-fry the entire mixture for another 5 minutes. Turn it onto a platter and serve.

STIR-FRIED PORK WITH SPRING ONIONS

Region: southern
Method: stir-frying

This is a simple stir-fried dish in the southern Chinese tradition. The key to success is not to overcook the pork.

Serves 3 to 4	
12 oz 350 g	boneless, lean pork
2 teaspoons	dry sherry or rice wine
2 teaspoons	light soy sauce
½ teaspoon	cornflour
4	spring onions
2 teaspoons	oil
½ teaspoon	salt
½ teaspoon	sugar

Cut the pork into thin slices 2 inches (5 cm) long. Put the sliced pork into a bowl and mix in the dry sherry or rice wine, soy sauce and cornflour. Let the mixture sit for 10–15 minutes so that the pork absorbs the flavours of the marinade. Cut the spring onions on the diagonal into 2 inch (5 cm) lengths.

Heat a wok or frying-pan to a very high heat. Add the oil. When it is almost beginning to smoke, add the pork slices and stir-fry them until they are brown. Add the spring onions, salt and sugar. Continue to stir-fry until the pork is cooked and slightly firm. This should take about 5 minutes. Remove and arrange the pork on a warm serving platter. Pour over any juices and serve at once.

STIR-FRIED MINCED PORK

Region: northern

Method: stir-frying

This is tasty, quick and inexpensive. The secret of its delicious flavour lies in the use of preserved vegetables which are typical of northern Chinese cuisine. Northern winters are long and cold and vegetables must be preserved by salting or pickling. You can use the Cold Sweet and Sour Chinese Leaves (page 200) instead of the Sichuan or Tianjin preserved vegetable, but it is worth the effort to get the latter from a Chinese grocer. I like to serve this as a stuffing for fresh lettuce leaves or Chinese pancakes (page 237). Plain steamed rice and a simple stir-fried vegetable dish such as Stir-fried Spinach with Garlic (page 211) would also go well with it.

Serves 4	
4oz 110g	**Cold Sweet and Sour Chinese Leaves (page 200), or 4oz 110g Sichuan or Tianjin preserved vegetable**
1½ tablespoons	oil, preferably groundnut
1lb 450g	minced pork
2 tablespoons	dark soy sauce
1 tablespoon	dry sherry or rice wine
2 teaspoons	sugar
Garnish	
3 tablespoons	spring onions, finely chopped

Rinse the Cold Sweet and Sour Chinese Leaves or preserved vegetable well in cold water. Drain them in a colander and then blot them dry with kitchen paper. Chop them finely and set them aside.

Heat a wok or large frying-pan over a high heat. Add the oil. When it is almost smoking add the pork and stir-fry it for 2 minutes. Stir constantly to break up any lumps. Then add the Chinese Leaves or preserved vegetable and the rest of the ingredients. Continue to stir-fry for another 5 minutes or until the pork is cooked. Turn it onto a warm serving platter.

If you are serving it with Chinese pancakes or lettuce leaves, each person piles a little of the meat mixture into a pancake or lettuce leaf, wraps it up well and eats it with his or her fingers.

SWEET AND SOUR PORK

Region: southern
Method: deep-frying and braising

Of all Chinese dishes, Sweet and Sour Pork is probably one of the best known in the West. Unfortunately for Westerners it is rarely properly made, often consisting of heavy, doughy balls containing a scrap of pork drenched in a hideously sweet, red sauce. Properly prepared, sweet and sour Chinese dishes are so delicately balanced that one is hard pressed to describe them as either strictly sweet or sour. In my version of this classic dish, you will find that balance. This dish is best served with plain steamed rice and a simple blanched vegetable such as cabbage or Chinese Leaves in Soy Sauce (page 200).

Serves 4		
12 oz	350 g	lean pork
1 tablespoon		dry sherry or rice wine
1 tablespoon		light soy sauce
½ teaspoon		salt
2 oz	50 g	green pepper (about ½)
2 oz	50 g	red pepper (about ½)
2 oz	50 g	carrots
2 oz	50 g	spring onions
1		egg, beaten
2 tablespoons		cornflour
15 fl oz	400 ml	oil, preferably groundnut (see Deep-fat fryers, page 34)
3 oz	75 g	tinned lychees, drained, or fresh orange segments
Sauce		
5 fl oz	150 ml	chicken stock
1 tablespoon		light soy sauce
½ teaspoon		salt
1½ tablespoons		cider vinegar or Chinese white rice vinegar
1 tablespoon		sugar
1 tablespoon		tomato paste
1 teaspoon		cornflour
1 teaspoon		water

Cut the pork into 1 inch (2·5 cm) cubes. Put the cubes into a bowl together with the sherry or rice wine, 1 tablespoon of light soy sauce and ½ teaspoon salt, and marinade for 20 minutes. Meanwhile, cut the green and red peppers into 1 inch (2·5 cm) squares. Peel and cut the carrots and spring onions into 1 inch (2·5 cm) cubes. (The uniform size of meat and vegetables adds to the visual appeal of the dish.) Bring a pot of water to the boil and blanch the carrots in it for 4 minutes; drain and set aside.

Mix the egg and cornflour in a bowl until they are well blended into a batter. Lift the pork cubes out of the marinade, put them into the batter and coat each piece well. Heat the oil in a deep-fat fryer or large wok until it is almost smoking. Remove the pork pieces from the batter with a slotted spoon, and deep-fry them. Drain the deep-fried pork cubes on kitchen paper.

Combine the chicken stock, soy sauce, salt, vinegar, sugar and tomato paste in a large saucepan. Bring it to the boil. Add all the vegetables, but not the lychees or oranges, and stir well. In a small bowl, blend together the cornflour and water. Stir this mixture into the sauce and bring it back to the boil. Turn the heat down to a simmer. Add the lychees or oranges and pork cubes. Mix well, and then turn the mixture onto a deep platter. Serve at once.

COLD PEKING PORK

Region: northern

Method: braising

Cold platters are commonly served at banquets in the north of China. This dish is a little like a European pâté and has a very good flavour. It should be prepared a day in advance and then served cold, making menu-planning easier. The pork is first blanched for a few minutes to rid it of any impurities, and is then slowly simmered in a rich liquid infused with Chinese spices. The cooked meat is removed and the braising liquid reduced. This is then poured over the pork which is left to marinade overnight. This dish is ideal for summertime and would make a tasty cold dish for a picnic.

	Serves 4 to 6	
1½lb	700g	pork leg, fillet end or shoulder, in one piece
	Braising liquid	
2 pints	1·1ltr	Chicken Stock (page 59)
3 slices		fresh ginger
3		spring onions, whole
2		star anise
2 tablespoons		dry sherry or rice wine
2 teaspoons		five spice powder
5 tablespoons		sugar or Chinese rock sugar
2 tablespoons		dark soy sauce
1 teaspoon		salt
2 teaspoons		whole Sichuan peppercorns, roasted (page 25) (optional)

Remove the rind from the pork but do not discard it. Bring a pan of water to the boil and blanch the rind and the pork in it for about 3–5 minutes. Remove them with a slotted spoon, discard the liquid and chop the rind into small pieces. Rinse the pot clean and return the pork to the pot. Add all the braising liquid ingredients and the pieces of rind. Bring the mixture to the boil, then turn the heat down to a very low simmer. Cover the pot and simmer for about 2 hours.

Remove the cooked pork from the pot with a slotted spoon and skim off as much fat as possible. Turn the heat back to high and reduce the liquid to about half. Put the pork into a bowl or deep dish. Strain the reduced liquid and pour it over the meat. Allow it to cool and put it into the refrigerator. Let it sit in the refrigerator for at least 8 hours before serving. Just before serving, remove the pork and slice it as thinly as possible. If the juice has jelled, cut it into cubes and arrange it as a garnish around the sliced pork, otherwise simply pour some of the cooled liquid over the pork slices and serve.

HONEY GLAZED PORK

Region: western

Method: braising

This is my adaptation of a famous Chinese dish called Honey Ham with Lotus Seed. Chinese ham is braised in sugar, rice wine and lotus seeds until the mixture is reduced to a syrup which glazes the ham like honey. This process usually takes about 4 hours but I have found that the method can be applied to thick pork chops, taking considerably less time, but with excellent results. Serve this with plain steamed rice and a simple green vegetable dish.

Serves 4 to 6		
1 lb	450g	boned pork chops, at least 1½ inches 3·5 cm thick
¼ teaspoon		salt
2		spring onions
2 slices		fresh ginger
1 tablespoon		oil
Braising sauce		
15 fl oz	400 ml	rice wine, or 5 fl oz 150 ml dry sherry mixed with 10 fl oz 300 ml chicken stock
4 oz	110g	sugar or Chinese rock sugar
1½ teaspoons		black peppercorns or roasted Sichuan peppercorns (page 25)

Lightly salt the meat and set it aside. Cut the spring onions into 3 inch (7·5 cm) lengths, and cut the ginger into slices 3 inches (7·5 cm) × ¼ inch (0·5 cm).

Heat the oil in a wok or large frying-pan. Reduce the heat and then add the spring onions and ginger. After a few seconds add the meat and cook it until it browns. Bring the braising sauce ingredients to the boil in a heavy pot or casserole, and then turn the heat down to a simmer. Add the browned pork, spring onions and ginger mixture. Turn the heat as low as possible, cover, and simmer for about 40 minutes or until the pork is tender.

When the chops are cooked, remove them from the liquid and let them cool slightly before you slice them, cutting them diagonally. Remove any surface fat from the braising liquid, and spoon some of it over the pork slices. Serve immediately. The rest of the braising liquid can be cooled and frozen for future use. (Remove any surface fat before transferring it to the freezer.)

BRAISED PORK WITH BEANCURD

Region: western
Method: braising

This is one of the most famous family dishes in China. It is sometimes known as 'Ma Po's' beancurd which means Mother Po's method of braising. My mother used to make a wonderful version of this simple peasant dish using a range of spices to transform fresh, but rather bland beancurd into truly delicious fare. This recipe is typical of the Chinese flair for stretching scarce meat, and it makes an economical, tasty and very nutritious dish. You can buy fresh beancurd from good health food shops and Chinese grocers.

Serves 6		
8oz	225g	fresh beancurd
2 teaspoons		oil
2 teaspoons		garlic, finely chopped
2 teaspoons		fresh ginger, finely chopped
8oz	225g	minced pork
1½ tablespoons		spring onions, finely chopped
½ teaspoon		chilli bean sauce or chilli powder
½ teaspoon		sugar
2 teaspoons		dry sherry or rice wine
1 tablespoon		dark soy sauce
1 tablespoon		whole yellow bean sauce
½ teaspoon		roasted Sichuan peppercorns, freshly ground (page 25) (optional)
2½floz	70ml	chicken stock
Optional garnish		
1 tablespoon		fresh coriander, finely chopped

Cut the beancurd into ½ inch (1cm) cubes and put them into a sieve to drain.

Heat a wok or large frying-pan. Add the oil, and then add the garlic and ginger. A few seconds later add the minced pork and stir-fry it for 2 minutes. Then add all the other ingredients except the beancurd. Bring the mixture to the boil and then turn the heat down to low. Add the beancurd and mix it in well but gently,

87

taking care not to break up the chunks. Let the mixture simmer slowly, uncovered, for about 15 minutes. If necessary add a little more chicken stock during this time. Garnish with the chopped, fresh coriander. (This dish may be cooked ahead of time and then gently re-heated.)

BRAISED PORK BELLY

Region: eastern

Method: braising

Pork belly is an inexpensive cut of pork which is very popular in Chinese cuisine and it has always been a favourite of mine. At first glance it might look rather fatty and unappetising but its gelatinous texture is highly prized by the Chinese and when it is properly cooked the taste is unbeatable. In this recipe the long simmering process renders down most of the fat, leaving a juicy, delicious dish which goes very well with some plain steamed rice.

		Serves 6
1½lb	700g	belly pork, including the bones
1 tablespoon		salt
1 tablespoon		oil, preferably groundnut
		Braising liquid
3 slices		fresh ginger
17floz	500ml	Chicken Stock (page 59)
10floz	300ml	rice wine or dry sherry
5floz	150ml	light soy sauce
3oz	75g	plain sugar or Chinese lump sugar
1 teaspoon		five spice powder
3		spring onions, whole

This joint can be cooked with its bones left in. If you get your butcher to remove them be sure to add them to the pot with the braising liquid for greater flavour. Rub the fresh pork belly with the salt and let it stand for 1 hour. Then carefully rinse the salt off. This helps to clean the pork and to firm it up by drawing out some of the moisture from the meat. Dry the meat with kitchen paper.

Heat a wok or large frying-pan. Add the oil, and in it brown the pork belly, rind side only, until it is crisp and brown. Add more oil if necessary. Cut the fresh ginger into slices 3 inches (7·5 cm) × ¼ inch (0·5 cm). Put the ginger together with the rest of the braising liquid ingredients into a large pot or casserole. Bring the liquid to a simmer and then add the browned pork belly. Cover the pot and simmer it slowly for 1½–2 hours or until the pork is tender.

When the pork is cooked, remove it from the pot and let it cool slightly. (The braising sauce liquid can now be cooled and frozen for re-use. Remove any surface fat before transferring it to the freezer.) Then slice the meat thinly. The Chinese would serve the pork rind and fat as well as the meat, but do remove it if you prefer. If you like, some of the braising liquid may be thickened with a little cornflour and served as a sauce over the sliced pork. If you do this be sure to remove all traces of fat from the sauce before thickening it.

STEAMED PORK WITH SPICY VEGETABLES

Region: western

Method: steaming

Preserved vegetables are often used to flavour meats in China. This dish can be made with Cold Sweet and Sour Chinese Leaves (page 200) or with Sichuan preserved vegetable which can be bought tinned from Chinese grocers and which has a pleasant crunchy texture. This recipe employs the technique of steaming which keeps the dish moist and hot without any risk of overcooking the pork. It is a tasty and homely dish and it re-heats well. It goes well with Stir-fried Rice Noodles with Vegetables (page 231).

Serves 3 to 4	
5oz	150g	Cold Sweet and Sour Chinese Leaves (page 200), or 2½oz 70g Sichuan preserved vegetable
12oz	350g	minced pork
1 tablespoon		dry sherry or rice wine
1 teaspoon		chilli bean sauce or chilli powder
1 teaspoon		dark soy sauce
½ teaspoon		light soy sauce
1 tablespoon		spring onions, finely chopped
½ tablespoon		fresh ginger, finely chopped

Rinse the preserved vegetable or Cold Sweet and Sour Chinese Leaves thoroughly under running water and drain them in a sieve or colander. Then chop them finely and put them into a bowl. Add the pork and all the other ingredients and mix everything together very well. Put the mixture onto a deep plate, and make a well in the centre where the juices can collect during cooking.

Set up a steamer or fill a wok or deep casserole with at least 2½inches (6cm) of water. Put a rack into the wok or casserole and bring the water to the boil. Now lower the plate of meat into the steamer or onto the rack and cover the pot tightly. Gently steam on a low heat for 50 minutes or until the pork is done. Serve this dish on the plate in which it is steamed.

CHILLI PORK SPARERIBS
Region: western
Method: deep-frying and braising

Here is a spicy and delicious way of preparing pork spareribs. Although the recipe involves a series of techniques, much of the work can be done ahead of time and the dish can be quickly completed at the last moment. The combination of spices and sauces are the hallmark of dishes from western China. It is worthwhile getting the chilli bean sauce for an authentic taste, although chilli powder is a reasonably acceptable substitute. The spareribs can be finished in the oven, under a grill or on a barbecue.

		Serves 2 to 4
1 pint	570ml	oil, preferably groundnut (see Deep-fat fryers, page 34)
1½lb	700g	pork spareribs, separated into individual ribs
		Braising sauce
1½pts	900ml	Chicken Stock (page 59)
1 tablespoon		chilli bean sauce, or 2 teaspoons chilli powder
2 teaspoons		sugar
2½floz	70ml	dry sherry or rice wine
1 tablespoon		dark soy sauce
1 tablespoon		light soy sauce
2 teaspoons		garlic, finely chopped
1 tablespoon		spring onions, finely chopped
1 tablespoon		whole yellow bean sauce
1½ tablespoons		hoisin sauce

Heat the oil in a deep-fat fryer or large wok, and deep-fry the spareribs until they are brown and crisp. Do this in several batches, draining each cooked batch well on kitchen paper.

Combine all the sauce ingredients in a large pot and bring it to the boil. Add the deep-fried spareribs and simmer them, covered, for about 40 minutes or until they are tender. Drain off the sauce and remove any remaining fat. This sauce can now be frozen and re-used the next time you want to make this dish. The dish may be prepared up to this point the day before.

Pre-heat the oven to gas mark 4, 350°F (180°C). Put the spareribs onto a rack in a roasting tin and bake them in the oven for 15–20 minutes until they are nice and brown. Baste them from time to time with the braising sauce if you like. You can also cook the spareribs under a grill or on a barbecue, until they are brown. Using a cleaver or a sharp, heavy knife, chop the spareribs into pieces 2½inches (6cm) long and serve.

FIVE SPICE SPARERIBS

Region: northern
Method: deep-frying and braising

This is a delightful meat dish which engages the senses with many contrasting tastes. The spareribs are first marinaded, next deep-fried in oil, and then slowly braised in an unusual, piquant sauce. It can be easily re-heated and the taste improves if it is cooked the day before it is eaten.

Serves 2 to 4	
1½lb 700g	pork spareribs
1 pint 570ml	oil, preferably groundnut (see Deep-fat fryers, page 34)
Marinade	
1 tablespoon	dry sherry or rice wine
1 tablespoon	light soy sauce
1 tablespoon	cider vinegar or Chinese white rice vinegar
½ teaspoon	sesame oil
Sauce	
1 tablespoon	garlic, finely chopped
1 tablespoon	five spice powder
1½ tablespoons	spring onions, finely chopped
1 tablespoon	sugar
1 tablespoon	light soy sauce
2 teaspoons	fresh orange peel, finely chopped
2½floz 70ml	cider vinegar or Chinese black rice vinegar

Have your butcher cut the spareribs into individual ribs, and then into chunks which are approximately 3 inches (7·5 cm) long.

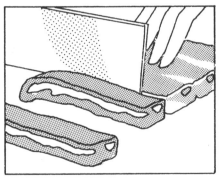
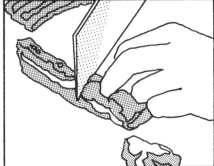

Alternatively do this yourself using a heavy sharp cleaver which can cut through the bones. Mix the marinade ingredients together in a bowl and steep the spareribs in the marinade for about 25 minutes at room temperature.

Heat the oil in a deep-fat fryer or large wok. Slowly brown the marinaded spareribs in several batches until they are brown. Drain each cooked batch on kitchen paper. (Leave the cooking oil to cool. Strain it through a filter once it has cooled if you want to keep it for re-use when cooking pork.)

Put the sauce ingredients into a clean wok or frying-pan. Bring the sauce to the boil and then reduce the heat. Add the spareribs and simmer them slowly, uncovered, for about 40 minutes, stirring occasionally. Add a little water to the sauce if necessary to prevent it from drying up. Skim off any surface fat and serve.

BEEF IN OYSTER SAUCE

Region: southern

Method: stir-frying

This was one of the most popular dishes in our family's restaurant. A good brand of oyster sauce does not taste at all fishy. Rather, it has a meaty flavour and goes very well with beef or pork. This dish is easy to make and is delicious served with plain steamed rice and Chinese Leaves in Soy Sauce (page 200).

Serves 4	
12oz 350g	lean beef steak
2 teaspoons	light soy sauce
2 teaspoons	dry sherry or rice wine
1 teaspoon	cornflour
1½ tablespoons	oil
2½floz 70ml	chicken stock
1½ tablespoons	oyster sauce
1 teaspoon	cornflour, blended with 1 teaspoon water
Garnish	
1½ tablespoons	spring onions, finely chopped

Cut the beef into thin slices 2 inches (5 cm) long and put them into a bowl. Add the soy sauce, sherry or rice wine and cornflour. Let the mixture marinade for 20 minutes.

Heat the oil in a wok or large frying-pan until it is very hot and almost smoking, and then stir-fry the beef slices. Remove them and drain them. Wipe the wok or pan clean and re-heat it over a high heat. Add the chicken stock and oyster sauce. Bring the liquid to the boil, and then add the cornflour mixture and simmer for 2 minutes. Return the drained beef to the pan and coat all the slices thoroughly with the sauce. Turn the mixture onto a serving platter and garnish it with the spring onions. Serve at once.

STIR-FRIED BEEF WITH ORANGE

Region: northern
Method: stir-frying

This is a northern Chinese beef speciality. I have adapted it by substituting fresh orange peel for the dried tangerine peel which is sometimes hard to get. The Chinese always use peel which has been dried. The older the skin, the more prized the flavour. It's quite easy to make your own dried peel (see page 18), but I find the tartness of the fresh orange peel works just as nicely to balance the robust taste of the beef. This is an easy dish to make and is a pleasant change of flavour from the usual stir-fried beef recipes. Serve it with rice and Sweetcorn Soup with Crabmeat (page 76).

Serves 4	
12 oz 350 g	lean beef steak
2 teaspoons	dark soy sauce
2 teaspoons	dry sherry or rice wine
1 teaspoon	fresh ginger, finely chopped
1 teaspoon	cornflour
1 teaspoon	sesame oil
2½ fl oz 70 ml	oil, preferably groundnut

2	dried red chillis, cut in half lengthways
1 tablespoon	fresh orange peel, coarsely chopped, or 2 teaspoons dried citrus peel, soaked and coarsely chopped (page 18)
½ teaspoon	roasted Sichuan peppercorns, finely ground (page 25) (optional)
2 teaspoons	dark soy sauce
¼ teaspoon	salt
1 teaspoon	sugar
½ teaspoon	sesame oil

Cut the beef into thin slices 2 inches (5 cm) long, cutting against the grain. Put the beef into a bowl together with the soy sauce, sherry or rice wine, fresh ginger, cornflour and 1 teaspoon of sesame oil. Mix well, and then let the mixture marinade for about 20 minutes.

Heat the oil in a wok or large frying-pan until it is very hot. Remove the beef from the marinade with a slotted spoon. Add it to the pan and stir-fry it for 2 minutes until it browns. Remove it and leave to drain in a colander or sieve. Pour off most of the oil, leaving about 1 teaspoon. Re-heat the pan over a high heat and then add the dried chillis. Stir-fry them for 10 seconds, and then return the beef to the pan. Add the rest of the ingredients and stir-fry for 4 minutes, mixing well. Serve the dish at once.

95

STIR-FRIED BEEF WITH GINGER

Region: southern

Method: stir-frying

This typically Cantonese dish is one of the quickest and tastiest ways to cook beef. The ginger adds a subtle and fragrant spiciness. Serve it with Ham and Bean Sprout Soup (page 64) and Lettuce with Oyster Sauce (page 207).

Serves 4	
12 oz 350 g	lean beef steak
¼ teaspoon	salt
2 teaspoons	light soy sauce
2 teaspoons	dry sherry or rice wine
½ teaspoon	sesame oil
1 teaspoon	cornflour
1 slice	fresh ginger
1 tablespoon	oil
1 tablespoon	chicken stock or water
½ teaspoon	sugar

Put the beef in the freezing compartment of the refrigerator for 20 minutes. This will allow the meat to harden slightly for easier cutting. Then cut it into thin slices 1½ inches (3·5 cm) long. Put the beef slices into a bowl and add the salt, soy sauce, sherry or rice wine, sesame oil and cornflour. Mix well, and let the slices steep in the marinade for about 15 minutes. Meanwhile, finely shred the ginger slice and set it aside.

Heat a wok or large frying-pan and add the oil. When it is very hot, remove the beef from the marinade with a slotted spoon and stir-fry it for about 2 minutes. When all the beef is cooked, remove it, wipe the wok or pan clean and re-heat it. Add a little oil and stir-fry the ginger for a few seconds. Then add the stock or water and sugar. Quickly return the meat to the pan and stir well. Turn the mixture onto a platter and serve at once.

STIR-FRIED PEPPER BEEF WITH MANGE-TOUT

Region: southern
Method: stir-frying

This is my adaptation of a stir-fried beef dish which is popular in Chinese restaurants in the USA. What makes this recipe so adaptable is that any fresh vegetable can be substituted for the mange-tout. It is extremely simple to make and is perfect for a quick but delicious, wholesome family meal. Try it with plain steamed rice and Steamed Fish with Garlic, Spring Onions and Ginger (page 163).

Serves 4		
12 oz	350 g	lean beef steak
2 teaspoons		light soy sauce
2 teaspoons		dry sherry or rice wine
1 teaspoon		cornflour
4 oz	110 g	red or green pepper (about 1)
1½ tablespoons		oil, preferably groundnut
2 oz	50 g	mange-tout, trimmed
2½ floz	70 ml	chicken stock or water
1 tablespoon		dark soy sauce

Cut the beef into thin slices 2 inches (5 cm) long. Put the slices into a bowl and add the light soy sauce, sherry or rice wine and cornflour. Mix well with the beef and allow the mixture to marinade for 15 minutes. Cut the pepper into 2 inch (5 cm) strips.

Heat a wok or large frying-pan until it is very hot. Add 1 tablespoon of the oil and when it is almost smoking, stir-fry the beef for 3 minutes. Remove the beef slices and drain them in a colander or sieve. Clean the wok or pan, add the remaining ½ tablespoon of oil and re-heat. When it is hot, stir-fry the pepper and mange-tout for 2 minutes. Then add the chicken stock and dark soy sauce. Bring the mixture to the boil. Return the cooked beef to the pan and give the mixture a few quick stirs to mix it well. Serve immediately.

97

RAINBOW BEEF IN LETTUCE LEAVES

Region: southern
Method: stir-frying

Some have speculated that this dish is not traditionally Chinese but an invention of some Hong Kong restaurant. Whatever the truth, it doesn't hide the fact that it is a truly delightful dish to eat. Various colourful vegetables constitute the 'rainbow', and they are stir-fried with beef and garnished with crispy bean thread (transparent) noodles and hoisin sauce to create a delicious combination of tastes and textures.

This dish makes a good starter for a dinner party or festive occasion. The rainbow beef mixture, crispy noodles and lettuce leaves are served on individual platters, and the hoisin sauce in a small bowl. Each guest puts a helping of each ingredient into a hollow lettuce leaf (rather like stuffing a pancake) and eats the filled leaf with his or her fingers.

Serves 4 to 6		
12 oz	350 g	lean beef steak
2 teaspoons		dry sherry or rice wine
2 teaspoons		light soy sauce
3 oz	75 g	carrots
2 oz	50 g	tinned bamboo shoots
2 oz	50 g	courgettes
2 oz	50 g	red or green pepper (about ½)
½ oz	10 g	Chinese dried mushrooms (optional)
8 oz	225 g	iceberg lettuce
1 oz	25 g	bean thread (transparent) noodles
10 fl oz	300 ml	oil (see Deep-fat fryers, page 34)
1 tablespoon		oil
1 teaspoon		light or dark soy sauce
2 teaspoons		dry sherry or rice wine
2–3 tablespoons		hoisin sauce

Right: Stir-fried Pepper Beef (page 97) and Beancurd with Vegetables (page 193)

Put the beef in the freezer for 20 minutes if possible as this will allow the meat to harden slightly for easier cutting. Then cut it into thin slices 2 inches (5 cm) long. Put the beef slices into a small bowl together with the dry sherry or rice wine and light soy sauce and let them marinade for about 20 minutes.

Meanwhile peel and cut the carrots into 2 inch (5 cm) long, fine shreds. Cut the bamboo shoots, courgettes and pepper into 2 inch (5 cm) fine shreds also. If you are using the dried mushrooms, soak them in warm water for 20 minutes, drain them and squeeze out any excess liquid. Trim off the stems and shred the caps into 2 inch (5 cm) long strips. Separate and wash the lettuce leaves, wiping off any excess water and set them aside.

In a deep-fat fryer or large wok, heat 10 fl oz (300 ml) of oil until it is almost smoking. Deep-fry the noodles until they are crisp and puffed up. Drain them on kitchen paper. (Leave the oil to cool; it can be saved for future use.)

Put one tablespoon of the oil in which you have fried the noodles into a wok or frying-pan and heat it. Then stir-fry the beef for about 1 minute. Remove the beef and put it into a bowl. Wipe the wok or pan clean. Re-heat the pan and when it is hot, add 1 tablespoon of fresh oil. When it is smoking slightly, stir-fry the carrots for 1 minute, and then add the rest of the vegetables (except the lettuce), together with the soy sauce and sherry or rice wine. Stir-fry the mixture for 3 minutes and then return the beef to the pan. Mix well and continue to stir-fry for 1 more minute. Turn the mixture on to a platter. Arrange the lettuce and noodles each on separate platters, put the hoisin sauce into a small bowl, and serve at once.

Left: Cold Peking Pork (page 84), Cold Sesame Broccoli (page 197), Caramel Walnuts (page 252) and Pickled Vegetables (page 213)

STEWED BEEF NORTHERN-STYLE

Region: northern
Method: braising

Beef in China is often tough and braising is therefore the preferred method of cooking it. Chinese cooks long ago learned to make a virtue of this necessity by using spices and seasonings during the long braising process to imbue the meat with subtle and complex flavours. This recipe is really a Chinese version of a beef stew and uses many of the favourite seasonings of northern China. Be sure to use an inexpensive cut of beef such as brisket or shin. One of the ingredients is Chinese white radish, sometimes called mooli. It can be bought in many greengrocers and in Chinese and Asian grocers. If you cannot find it you could use turnips or carrots instead. Plain steamed rice is a perfect accompaniment.

Serves 4 to 6		
12oz	350g	stewing beef, such as brisket or shin
1		spring onion
2 teaspoons		oil, preferably groundnut
1 slice		ginger
1 clove		garlic, lightly crushed
1		dried red chilli (optional)
4oz	110g	Chinese white radish (mooli)
Braising sauce		
10floz	300ml	Chicken Stock (page 59)
2 teaspoons		sugar
1½ teaspoons		light soy sauce
1 tablespoon		dark soy sauce
2 teaspoons		dry sherry or rice wine
2 teaspoons		five spice powder
2 tablespoons		hoisin sauce
2 teaspoons		whole yellow bean sauce

Cut the meat into 1 inch (2·5cm) cubes. Slice the spring onion at a slight diagonal into 2 inch (5cm) segments. Heat the oil in a wok or large frying-pan, and when it is hot add the beef. Stir-fry until it is brown. (This should take about 10 minutes.) Then pour off any excess fat, leaving 1 tablespoon of oil in the pan. Add the spring onion, ginger, garlic and chilli and stir-fry with the beef for about 5 minutes.

Transfer this mixture to a large casserole or pot. Add the braising sauce ingredients. Bring the liquid to the boil, skim off any fat from the surface and turn the heat as low as possible. Cover and braise for 1½ hours. Peel the Chinese white radish and cut it at a slight diagonal into 2 inch (5 cm) chunks. Add these to the meat and continue to cook for another 30 minutes or until the beef is quite tender. Then turn the heat up to high and rapidly reduce the liquid for about 15 minutes. The sauce should thicken slightly. It can be served immediately or cooled and re-heated later.

STEAMED BEEF MEATBALLS

Region: southern

Method: steaming

Since my days as an apprentice in our family restaurant I have always enjoyed these steamed meatballs. The secret of making them light and fluffy lies in the egg white and cornflour. We used to mince the beef by hand with two cleavers, one in each hand, adding egg white and cornflour as we chopped until it was all fully incorporated into the meat. Then we added the seasonings and continued to chop until the meat was almost a light paste. Such chopping requires concentration! But when that stage was over we all sat about chatting as we rolled the meat into balls. Today with a blender or food processor, this long process takes only a few minutes. The texture will be smoother, of course, but it does mean a lot less work. The meatballs re-heat well by steaming and are perfect for dinners, for parties or with drinks.

Serves 4		
12 oz	350g	**minced beef**
1		**egg white**
1 tablespoon		**very cold water**
½ teaspoon		**salt**
1 tablespoon		**light soy sauce**
1 teaspoon		**freshly ground black pepper**
2 teaspoons		**sesame oil**
1 tablespoon		**coriander, finely chopped**
1½ tablespoons		**spring onions, finely chopped**
1 teaspoon		**cornflour**
1 teaspoon		**sugar**

Mix the beef in a blender or food processor for a few seconds. Slowly add the egg white and cold water and mix them for a few more seconds until they are fully incorporated into the meat. Then add the rest of the ingredients and mix for about a minute until the meat mixture has become a light paste.

Using your hands, form the mixture into 1½ inch (3·5cm) balls—about the size of a golf ball. (This recipe makes about 10 balls.) Put the meatballs on a plate and set it into a steamer. (Alternatively put a rack into a wok or deep pan filled with simmering hot water.) Cover, and steam the meat balls gently for about 20 minutes. Pour off any liquid which has accumulated on the plate. Put the steamed meatballs on a clean platter and serve.

STIR-FRIED LAMB WITH GARLIC

Region: northern
Method: stir-frying

Lamb is especially delicious when it is stir-fried. This way of preparing it with lots of garlic and spring onions to balance its strong taste is a popular one. The tenderest parts of the lamb, such as steaks or chops are best for this dish. Serve it with rice and Braised Spicy Aubergines (page 190).

Serves 3 to 4		
12 oz	350g	lean lamb steaks or fillet, or boned, loin chop meat
2 teaspoons		dry sherry or rice wine
2 teaspoons		dark soy sauce
2 teaspoons		light soy sauce
½ teaspoon		sesame oil
2 teaspoons		oil
1½ teaspoons		spring onions, finely chopped
3		garlic cloves, peeled and thinly sliced
½ teaspoon		fresh ginger, finely chopped

Cut the lamb into thin slices and put it into a bowl. Mix in the sherry or rice wine, soy sauces and sesame oil and let the meat marinade for 20 minutes. Then drain off the marinade liquid.

Heat a wok or large frying-pan. When it is very hot, add the oil. Then add the marinaded lamb pieces with just a little of the marinade. Stir-fry for 2 minutes. Now add the spring onions, garlic and ginger, and continue to stir-fry for another 4 minutes. Serve immediately.

105

PEKING BRAISED LAMB

Region: northern

Method: braising

The Chinese usually cook mutton and goat rather than lamb, which is scarce, and have many exciting ways of braising both these meats with spices which help to mask their strong taste. This tasty and filling family dish is perfect for the winter. It goes well with plain steamed rice and Chinese Leaves in Soy Sauce (page 200).

Serves 4		
1 lb	450 g	boned shoulder of lamb
2		spring onions
2 slices		ginger
1 tablespoon		oil
½		small onion, finely chopped
Braising sauce		
15 fl oz	400 ml	Chicken Stock (page 59)
2		whole star anise (optional)
2 oz	50 g	sugar
1½ tablespoons		dark soy sauce
1 tablespoon		dry sherry or rice wine
½		cinnamon stick or Chinese cinnamon bark
2 teaspoons		sesame paste or peanut butter
1 tablespoon		hoisin sauce

Cut the meat into 2 inch (5 cm) cubes. Next, blanch the lamb by plunging it into boiling water for 5 minutes. Then remove the meat and discard the water. Slice the spring onions at a slight diagonal into 3 inch (7·5 cm) pieces. Slice the ginger diagonally into pieces 3 inches (7·5 cm) × ¼ inch (0·5 cm).

Heat the oil in a wok or large frying-pan and when it is hot, add the pieces of lamb. Stir-fry them until they are brown, then remove any excess fat, leaving just 1 tablespoon. Now add the spring onions, ginger and onion to the pan and continue to stir-fry for 5 minutes. Transfer this mixture to a large casserole or pot and add the braising sauce ingredients. Bring the liquid to the boil, skim off any fat from the surface, and turn the heat down as low as possible. Cover and braise for 1½ hours or until the lamb is quite tender. (The remaining liquid can be frozen and re-used another time to braise lamb.) Arrange the cooked meat on a platter and serve.

MONGOLIAN HOT POT

Region: northern
Method: simmering

This northern dish is similar in style to a European fondue. It was introduced into China after the Mongolian conquest in the thirteenth century, and soon could be found throughout China with regional touches added. Beef was sometimes substituted for the traditional lamb and the Cantonese developed their 'Chrysanthemum Fire Pot' which includes edible flower petals. In this recipe, which follows the traditional method, thin slices of lamb and vegetables are simmered in a broth. Each diner cooks his own food at the table in the pot of stock. The cooked food is then dipped into various sauces before being eaten. Towards the end of the meal, bean thread (transparent) noodles are cooked in the remaining broth which is then drunk as a soup. The Chinese use a special charcoal-burning 'fire pot' for this dish, but you could use either a large fondue pot or a small portable electric element and heatproof pot instead. (If you have an authentic Chinese fire pot only use it in a well ventilated room with the windows open, or use it out of doors. Otherwise the carbon monoxide fumes arising from the charcoal can be dangerous.)

Serves 4 to 6		
2–3lb	900g–1·4kg	lean lamb
4oz	110g	bean thread (transparent) noodles
8oz	225g	spinach
8oz	225g	Chinese leaves
2 pints	1·1 ltr	Chicken Stock (page 59)
1 teaspoon		fresh ginger, finely chopped
2 tablespoons		spring onions, finely chopped
1 teaspoon		garlic
1 tablespoon		fresh coriander, finely chopped
Dipping sauce		
2 tablespoons		sesame paste or peanut butter
1 tablespoon		light soy sauce
1 tablespoon		dry sherry or rice wine
2 teaspoons		chilli bean sauce
1 tablespoon		sugar
1 tablespoon		hot water

107

Using a cleaver or sharp knife, slice the lamb into very thin slices. Soak the bean thread (transparent) noodles in warm water for 5 minutes, then drain them and cut them into 5 inch (12·5 cm) lengths. Separate the spinach leaves from the stalks and wash them well. Discard the stalks. Cut the Chinese leaves into 3 inch (7·5 cm) pieces. Combine all the ingredients for the dipping sauce in a small bowl and mix them well.

Everyone should have his own small portion of dipping sauce. Serve each guest a plate containing his share of lamb, spinach and Chinese leaves. When you are ready to begin, bring the stock to the boil and light the fondue. Ladle the stock into the fondue and put the ginger, spring onions, garlic and coriander into the stock.

Each person selects a piece of food and cooks it quickly in the pot. When all the meat and vegetables have been eaten, add the noodles to the pot, let them heat through, then ladle the soup into soup bowls.

This dish also works successfully with other foods such as steak, fish balls, oysters, prawns, squid, mushrooms and lettuce, although it will no longer be a *Mongolian* hot pot, but more like the Cantonese Chrysanthemum Pot.

STIR-FRIED LIVER IN SPICY SAUCE

Region: southern

Method: stir-frying

Pig's liver is another Chinese speciality which is delicious when it is properly prepared. My uncle used to make a delectable pig's liver dish with vegetables. His secret was to cut the liver into thin slices, to stir-fry them quickly and then to drain them to get rid of any bitter juices.

This recipe has a robust and tasty sauce containing spices which help to balance the rich flavour of the liver. Cooked this way, the liver tastes a little like beef. (You could also use beef or veal liver for this recipe.) I like to serve this dish with plain steamed rice and some green vegetables.

108

Serves 4		
8oz	225g	fresh liver, preferably pig's
3		spring onions
2½floz	70ml	oil, preferably groundnut
Marinade		
1		egg white
1 tablespoon		dry sherry or rice wine
2 teaspoons		salt
2 teaspoons		fresh ginger, finely chopped
2 teaspoons		cornflour
Sauce		
2 teaspoons		light soy sauce
2 teaspoons		dry sherry or rice wine
1 teaspoon		sugar
1½ tablespoons		whole yellow bean sauce
½ teaspoon		chilli bean sauce or chilli powder

Cut the pig's liver into thin slices 3 inches (7·5 cm) long. Mix the marinade ingredients together in a bowl, add the liver slices and coat them thoroughly with marinade. Cover the bowl tightly with clingfilm and let it sit in the refrigerator for at least 20 minutes. Meanwhile cut the spring onions into 2 inch (5 cm) diagonal segments. In a separate bowl mix together the sauce ingredients.

Heat the oil in a wok or large frying-pan until it is almost smoking. Lift the liver out of the marinade with a slotted spoon and stir-fry it in the oil for 2 minutes. Drain the cooked liver in a colander or sieve, leaving about 2 teaspoons of the oil in the pan. (Discard the rest of the oil.)

Re-heat the wok or pan and add the spring onions. Stir-fry them for 1 minute and then add the sauce ingredients. When the sauce comes to the boil, return the liver to the wok or pan and toss it well, coating it with the sauce. Stir-fry for 30 seconds and then serve.

109

STIR-FRIED LAMB'S KIDNEYS

Region: western

Method: stir-frying

Lamb's kidneys are delicious when they are simply stir-fried. As a young cook I was taught a wonderful technique for cleaning kidneys which I use to this day. First the kidneys should be scored and tossed in baking soda; this helps to tenderise them and to neutralise their acidity. Then the bicarbonate of soda is rinsed off and they are tossed in a mixture of vinegar and salt to remove any remaining bitterness. The result is a clean and fresh-tasting kidney. This dish can also be made with pig's kidneys. Serve it with Sweetcorn Soup with Crabmeat (page 76) and plain steamed rice.

Serves 4	
8oz 225g	lamb's or pig's kidneys
½ teaspoon	bicarbonate of soda
1 teaspoon	cider vinegar or Chinese white rice vinegar
½ teaspoon	salt
1 tablespoon	oil, preferably groundnut
1	dried red chilli
1 tablespoon	garlic, finely chopped
1 tablespoon	dark soy sauce
2 teaspoons	dry sherry or rice wine
½ teaspoon	roasted Sichuan peppercorns, finely ground (page 25) (optional)
½ teaspoon	sugar
¼ teaspoon	salt
1 teaspoon	sesame oil
Garnish	
2 teaspoons	spring onions, finely chopped

Using a sharp knife remove the thin outer kidney membrane. Then, with a sharp cleaver or knife, split the kidneys in half by cutting horizontally. Now cut away the small knobs of fat and any tough membrane surrounding them. Next, score the kidneys in a crisscross pattern (see diagram page 73) and cut them into thin slices. Toss the kidney slices with the bicarbonate of soda and let

110

them sit for about 20 minutes. Then rinse them thoroughly with cold water and toss them with the vinegar and salt. Put them into a colander and let them drain for at least 30 minutes, preferably longer.

Blot the kidney slices dry with kitchen paper. Heat a wok or large frying-pan over a high heat until it is very hot. Add the oil and the dried chilli. Stir-fry to flavour the oil for about 20 seconds. Then add the kidney slices and stir-fry, coating the kidneys with the oil, for about 1 minute. Now add the rest of the ingredients and toss them together well with the kidneys. Continue to stir-fry the mixture for about 2 minutes or until the kidney edges begin to curl. Turn the mixture on to a warm serving platter, garnish with the spring onions, and serve at once.

HOT AND SOUR KIDNEYS

Region: western
Method: stir-frying

Pig's kidneys are tender and tasty when stir-fried in this hot and sour sauce. The contrasting flavours of the sauce perfectly complement the robust taste of the kidneys. As in the kidney recipe on page 72, I suggest you marinade the kidneys in bicarbonate of soda and then toss them in vinegar and salt. This dish is inexpensive to make and goes well with plain steamed rice and any stir-fried vegetable.

Serves 4	
8oz 225g	pig's kidneys
½ teaspoon	bicarbonate of soda
1 teaspoon	cider vinegar or white rice vinegar
½ teaspoon	salt
1 tablespoon	oil, preferably groundnut
1 slice	fresh ginger

111

Sauce	
1 teaspoon	garlic, finely chopped
1 teaspoon	fresh ginger, finely chopped
1 teaspoon	chilli powder
1 teaspoon	cider vinegar or Chinese white rice vinegar
½ teaspoon	sugar
2 teaspoons	dark soy sauce
¼ teaspoon	roasted Sichuan peppercorns, ground (page 25) (optional)
1½ tablespoons	chicken stock or water

Using a sharp knife, remove the thin, outer kidney membrane. Then, with a sharp cleaver or knife, split the kidneys in half horizontally (see page 73). Now cut away the small knobs of fat and any tough membrane surrounding them. Score the kidneys in a crisscross pattern and cut into 1 inch (2·5cm) slices. Toss the kidney slices with the bicarbonate of soda and let them sit for about 20 minutes. Then rinse them thoroughly with cold water and toss them with the vinegar and salt. Put them in a colander and let them drain for at least 30 minutes, preferably longer.

Blot the kidney slices dry with kitchen paper. Heat a wok or large frying-pan over a high heat. Add the oil and the ginger. Stir-fry to flavour the oil for about 20 seconds. Then add the kidney slices and stir-fry them for about 1 minute. Now add the sauce ingredients and toss them together well with the kidneys. Continue to stir-fry the mixture for about 2 minutes or until the kidney edges begin to curl. Turn the mixture onto a warm serving platter and serve at once.

CHICKEN,
DUCK AND GAME

Chicken is the most highly regarded of all poultry in China. To impress a guest a Chinese hostess might announce that she has killed a chicken in his honour. It is frequently served on special occasions, on birthdays, and at festivals and banquets. At our family gatherings chicken was always the centrepiece. Early every Sunday morning my mother would bring home a live chicken from the market in Chinatown in Chicago where we lived. Its noisy clucking would usually wake me up. The chicken would be quickly despatched and then prepared in one of many ways. One of my favourites was when it had been slowly poached and then served with a soy sauce and spring onion dipping sauce.

In China most homes do not have ovens and poultry is usually roasted by professional cooks. Home-cooked chicken is braised, stir-fried, deep-fried, steamed or simmered. One of the virtues of chicken is that its distinctive but mild flavour blends very well with other seasonings, spices and sauces. It is a very versatile bird and is almost as popular in China as pork.

The Chinese prefer to buy their chickens live to ensure that they are at their freshest when cooked. Obviously this is almost impossible in the West! In Europe and North America there are plentiful supplies of relatively inexpensive chicken but because of modern farming methods, commercially produced chickens tend to lack taste. Frozen chicken is especially bland. Try to buy a fresh chicken for Chinese cooking. It should have a healthy pinkish colour, a fresh smell, and be firm in texture. If possible buy free-range chickens. Not only have they been raised by more humane methods but their taste is far superior. Whole cooked chickens are never carried to the table to be carved, but are always chopped into bite-sized pieces before being arranged on a platter. However, many of the recipes in this chapter can be made with chicken pieces rather than with a whole chicken. All parts of the chicken are used in China. The dark meat from the thighs and drumsticks is especially prized for its superior flavour. Roasting chickens are the most suitable for frying, steaming and braising. If possible use boiling fowl for stock to give you a rich liquid with a good flavour. Poussins are also suitable for stir-fried dishes.

Fresh chicken should be cooked as soon as possible. Keep it cold until you are ready to use it. If you wish to store the chicken, first remove any wrapping and the giblets. Rinse it carefully in cold water and blot it completely dry with kitchen paper. Wrap it loosely in clingfilm and put it in the refrigerator where it will keep for two days. If you are using frozen chicken be sure to thaw it thoroughly before proceeding with the recipe.

Duck is also popular in Chinese cookery with Peking Duck being one of the most famous of all Chinese dishes. Like chicken, it is never roasted at home. In domestic kitchens duck is cut up and then braised or stir-fried. It is also steamed and then deep-fried, a process which results in a very tender fat-free duck. Fresh duck is always preferable to frozen and should be stored in the same way as chicken. If you use frozen duck, be sure to defrost it thoroughly first.

Game birds are widely used in Chinese cookery, but because their flavour tends to be strong they are frequently stewed or put into soups together with medicinal herbs and seasonings. Pigeon and quail are two birds which are readily available here and which are ideal for Chinese cooking.

CHICKEN PIECES IN BLACK BEAN SAUCE

Region: southern
Method: stir-frying and braising

This recipe is a favourite one for me because it evokes childhood memories of the fragrance of black bean sauce mixed with garlic which often used to greet me at the door when I came home from school. My mother used to make this dish with chicken wings, the tender and juicy flesh of which is among the tastiest parts of the chicken. Wings are ideal for stir-frying because they cook quickly, but other parts of the chicken work just as well. Serve this dish with plain rice and Stir-fried Spinach with Garlic (page 211).

Serves 4	
1 lb 450g	chicken wings or chicken pieces, unskinned
1 tablespoon	light soy sauce
1 tablespoon	dry sherry or rice wine
2 teaspoons	oil, preferably groundnut
1 tablespoon	fresh ginger, finely chopped
1 tablespoon	garlic, finely chopped
1½ tablespoons	spring onions, finely chopped
1½ tablespoons	black beans, coarsely chopped
5 fl oz 150ml	chicken stock

115

If you are using chicken wings, cut them in half at the joint. If you are using chicken pieces, cut them into 2 inch (5 cm) chunks. Mix the soy sauce and sherry or rice wine together and pour it over the chicken pieces. Let the chicken marinade for about 1 hour, then drain the chicken and discard the marinade.

Heat a wok or large frying-pan. Add the oil, and when it is hot add the ginger. Stir-fry it for a few seconds and then add the garlic, spring onions and black beans. A few seconds later add the chicken wings or pieces and stir-fry them for 2–5 minutes at a high heat until they are brown. Then add the stock. Bring the mixture to the boil and then reduce the heat. Simmer for 15 minutes or until the chicken is cooked. (If you are using chicken breasts cook for just 5 minutes.) This dish can be cooked ahead of time and re-heated, and it is also delicious served cold.

SPICY CHICKEN WITH PEANUTS

Region: western

Method: stir-frying

This is a classic western Chinese dish which is better known in China as Gongbao chicken. According to one expert, the dish was named after a Chinese official, Ding Baozhen, who was Governor of Sichuan province in the nineteenth century. There are many versions of this recipe; this one is close to the original and is also quick and easy to make. Rice and Stir-fried Chinese Greens (page 204) would go well with it.

	Serves 4	
8 oz	225 g	boneless chicken breasts
1		dried red chilli
1½ tablespoons		oil
3 oz	75 g	raw peanuts, shelled (page 22)

Sauce	
1 tablespoon	chicken stock or water
1 tablespoon	dry sherry or rice wine
2 teaspoons	dark soy sauce
1 teaspoon	sugar
1 teaspoon	garlic, finely chopped
2 teaspoons	spring onions, finely chopped
½ teaspoon	fresh ginger, finely chopped
1 teaspoon	cider vinegar or Chinese white rice vinegar
½ teaspoon	salt
1 teaspoon	sesame oil

Cut the chicken into 1 inch (2·5 cm) cubes. Split the dried chilli in half lengthways. Heat the oil in a wok or large frying-pan, and add the chilli. (You may remove it when it turns black or leave it in.) Next add the chicken cubes and peanuts and stir-fry them for 1 minute. Remove the chicken, peanuts and chilli from the pan.

Put all the sauce ingredients, except the sesame oil, into the pan. Bring the sauce to the boil, and then turn the heat down. Return the chicken and peanuts to the pan and cook for about 2 minutes in the sauce. Add the sesame oil, and then serve immediately.

GARLIC CHICKEN WITH CUCUMBER

Region: western
Method: stir-frying

Cucumbers are never served raw in China and they are delicious cooked. In this recipe they are stir-fried with delicate chicken breasts and flavoured with garlic and chilli. This is an uncomplicated dish which goes well with Honey Glazed Pork (page 86) or Tomato Eggflower Soup (page 61).

Serves 4	
12 oz 350 g	boneless chicken breasts, skinned
½	cucumber
¼ teaspoon	salt
2 teaspoons	oil, preferably groundnut
2 teaspoons	garlic, finely chopped
1 tablespoon	spring onions, finely chopped
2 teaspoons	light soy sauce
2 teaspoons	dry sherry or rice wine
¼ teaspoon	chilli bean sauce or chilli powder

Cut the chicken into 1 inch (2·5 cm) cubes and set aside. Peel the cucumber, halve it and remove the seeds with a teaspoon. Then cut it into 1 inch (2·5 cm) cubes, sprinkle with the salt and put the cubes into a colander to drain for 20 minutes. (This removes the excess moisture from the cucumber.) Next rinse the cucumber cubes in cold running water and blot them dry with kitchen paper.

Heat the oil in a wok or large frying-pan. When it is hot, add the chicken cubes and stir-fry them for a few seconds. Add all the other ingredients except the cucumber and continue to stir-fry for another 2 minutes. Now add the cucumber cubes and keep stir-frying the entire mixture for another 3 minutes. Serve at once.

CURRIED CHICKEN WITH PEPPERS

Region: southern
Method: stir-frying

Curry blends well with chicken especially when used in the style of southern Chinese cuisine, namely as a light and subtle sauce which does not overpower the delicate chicken meat. Peppers provide the dish with a crunchy texture but carrots, if blanched first, can be used instead. Serve this with Tomato Eggflower Soup (page 61) and plain steamed rice.

Serves 3 to 4		
8oz	225g	boneless chicken breasts, skinned
1		egg white
1 teaspoon		salt
1 teaspoon		cornflour
8oz	225g	red or green peppers
5floz	150ml	oil, preferably groundnut
2½floz	70ml	chicken stock
2 teaspoons		good curry powder or paste
1 teaspoon		sugar
2 teaspoons		dry sherry or rice wine
1 tablespoon		light soy sauce
1 teaspoon		cornflour, blended with 1 teaspoon water

Cut the chicken breasts into 1 inch (2·5 cm) cubes. Combine them with the egg white, salt and 1 teaspoon of cornflour in a small bowl, and put the mixture into the refrigerator for about 20 minutes. Wash and de-seed the peppers and cut them into 1 inch (2·5 cm) cubes.

Heat the oil in a wok or large frying-pan until it is moderately hot. Add the chicken mixture and stir-fry it quickly in the oil to keep it from sticking. Cook it until it turns white, which should take about 2 minutes. Put the breasts immediately into a colander or sieve and drain off the remaining oil. (This oil, once cooled, may be saved for future stir-fried dishes using chicken.)

Clean the wok or pan and add about 1 tablespoon of the drained oil. Re-heat it until it is very hot. Add the peppers and stir-fry them for 2 minutes. Then add the rest of the ingredients and cook the mixture for another 2 minutes. Return the chicken to the pan and stir-fry for another 2 minutes, coating the chicken pieces thoroughly with the sauce. Serve at once.

119

LEMON CHICKEN

Region: southern
Method: stir-frying

The Hong Kong Chinese have made a speciality of chicken cooked with lemon. The tart lemon sauce goes very well indeed with the delicate flavour of chicken. Unlike many versions which employ a cloyingly sweet sauce, this recipe balances tartness with sweetness. Sometimes the lemon chicken is steamed, but I think it is equally good stir-fried. Serve it with plain steamed rice and Cold Sesame Broccoli (page 197).

Serves 3 to 4	
8oz 225g	boneless chicken breasts, skinned
1	egg white
2 teaspoons	cornflour
2½floz 70ml	oil, preferably groundnut
Sauce	
2½floz 70ml	chicken stock or water
1½ tablespoons	fresh lemon juice
2 teaspoons	sugar
2 teaspoons	light soy sauce
2 teaspoons	dry sherry or rice wine
½ teaspoon	garlic, finely chopped
1	dried red chilli, or ¼ teaspoon chilli powder
1 teaspoon	cornflour, blended with 1 teaspoon water

Cut the chicken breasts into strips 3 inches (7·5cm) long. Combine the chicken strips with the egg white and cornflour in a bowl, and put it into the refrigerator for about 20 minutes.

Heat the oil in a wok or deep frying-pan until it is moderately hot. Add the chicken strips and stir them quickly in the oil to keep them from sticking. Cook the strips until they turn white. (This takes about a minute.) Drain the breasts immediately in a colander or sieve. (The oil may be saved for future stir-fried chicken dishes.)

Wipe the wok or pan clean and re-heat it. Add all the sauce ingredients except for the cornflour mixture. Bring it to the boil over a high heat and then add the cornflour mixture. Simmer for 1 minute. Return the chicken strips to the sauce and stir-fry them long enough to coat them all well with the sauce. Turn onto a platter and serve at once.

120

CASHEW CHICKEN

Region: southern
Method: stir-frying

This dish exemplifies the Chinese penchant for contrasting
textures. Here, tender succulent pieces of chicken are used with
sweet crunchy cashew nuts. The original Chinese version would
have been made with peanuts because cashew nuts do not feature
in Chinese cookery. Nevertheless this dish uses the best Chinese
cooking principles: stir-frying to seal in the juices of the chicken,
and then stir-frying again with spices to flavour it.

Serves 3 to 4		
8oz	225g	boneless chicken breasts, skinned
1		egg white
1 teaspoon		salt
1 teaspoon		cornflour
5 floz	150ml	oil, preferably groundnut
2oz	50g	cashew nuts
2 teaspoons		dry sherry or rice wine
1 tablespoon		light soy sauce
Garnish		
1 tablespoon		spring onions, finely chopped

Cut the chicken breasts into ½ inch (1 cm) cubes. Combine them
with the egg white, salt and cornflour in a small bowl, and put it in
the refrigerator for about 20 minutes.

Heat the oil in a wok or deep frying-pan until it is moderately
hot. Add the chicken mixture and stir-fry it quickly in the oil to
keep it from sticking. Cook it until it turns white which should take
about 2 minutes. Drain the chicken cubes in a colander or sieve and
drain off the oil. (The oil, once cooled, may be saved for future
stir-fried dishes using chicken.) Put about 1 tablespoon of the oil in
which you have cooked the chicken into a clean wok or pan.

Re-heat it until it is very hot. Add the cashew nuts and stir-fry
them for 1 minute. Then add the rest of the ingredients. Return the
chicken to the pan and stir-fry the mixture for another 2 minutes.
Garnish the dish with the spring onions and serve at once.

121

COUNTRY-STYLE CHICKEN

Region: western
Method: stir-frying

Not all western Chinese cooking is hot and spicy. Many simple homely recipes like this one use relatively little chilli. Rather, the accent is on seasonal vegetables. It is equally tasty without the fresh chilli if you prefer. Steamed rice is a perfect accompaniment to this dish.

Serves 3 to 4		
8oz	225g	boneless chicken breasts, skinned
2		small fresh green or red chillis
8oz	225g	tinned bamboo shoots
8oz	225g	courgettes
4oz	110g	red or green pepper (about 1)
2 tablespoons		oil, preferably groundnut
2 tablespoons		chicken stock
2 tablespoons		dry sherry or rice wine
1½–2 teaspoons		chilli bean sauce
2 teaspoons		sugar
2 tablespoons		dark soy sauce
1 tablespoon		cider vinegar or Chinese black rice vinegar
1 tablespoon		tomato paste

Cut the chicken breasts into shreds about 3 inches (7·5 cm) long. Cut the fresh chillis in half, carefully remove the seeds and shred the chillis. (Do not touch your eyes while doing this as it will make them sting.) Then prepare all the vegetables. Rinse the bamboo shoots in clean water and shred them. Trim the courgettes and shred them. Wash the pepper, remove the seeds and shred this too.

Heat 1 tablespoon of the oil in a wok or large frying-pan. When it is almost smoking quickly stir-fry the chicken shreds for 1 minute or until the chicken is slightly firm. Remove the cooked chicken and drain it.

Wipe the wok or pan clean. Re-heat it and add the rest of the oil. When it is hot, add the shredded chillis, bamboo shoots, courgettes and pepper. Stir-fry for about 2 minutes, and then add the rest of the ingredients. Mix them well and stir-fry for another minute. Return the chicken shreds and give the mixture a few quick stirs to finish cooking the chicken. Turn onto a serving platter and serve at once.

122

WALNUT CHICKEN

Region: eastern
Method: stir-frying

This recipe pairs the crunchy texture of walnuts with the delicate flavour of chicken in a classic stir-fry dish. For a variation try this recipe with other nuts such as cashews, pine nuts or almonds but be sure the nuts you use are very fresh. Stale nuts will ruin the flavour. I like to serve it with Fried Stuffed Cucumbers (page 206) and Sweetcorn Soup with Crabmeat (page 76).

Serves 3 to 4		
8oz	225g	boneless chicken breasts, skinned
1		egg white
1 teaspoon		salt
2 teaspoons		cornflour
3oz	75g	walnuts, shelled halves or pieces
5floz	150ml	oil, preferably groundnut
1 teaspoon		garlic, finely chopped
½ teaspoon		fresh ginger, finely chopped
1 tablespoon		spring onions, finely chopped
1 tablespoon		dry sherry or rice wine
1 tablespoon		light soy sauce

Cut the chicken breasts into ½inch (1cm) cubes. Combine the cubes with the egg white, salt and cornflour in a small bowl, and put it in the refrigerator for about 20 minutes. Blanch the walnuts in a small pot of boiling water for 5 minutes; then drain them.

Heat the oil in a wok or deep frying-pan until it is moderately hot. Add the chicken mixture and stir-fry it quickly in the oil to keep it from sticking, until it turns white. This will take about 2 minutes. Drain the cooked chicken in a colander or sieve. (The oil, once cooled, may be saved for future stir-fried dishes with chicken.)

Put about 1 tablespoon of the oil in which you have cooked the chicken into a clean wok or pan. Re-heat it until it is very hot. Add the walnuts and stir-fry them for 1 minute. Remove and set aside. Add the garlic, ginger and spring onions to the pan and stir-fry for a few seconds. Return the walnuts to the pan and then add the rest of the ingredients. Return the chicken to the pan and stir-fry the mixture for another 2 minutes. Serve at once.

123

SHREDDED CHICKEN WITH SESAME SEEDS

Region: western
Method: stir-frying

This is my version of a fragrant Sichuan dish popularly known as 'Strange Taste Chicken' because it incorporates so many flavours, being hot, spicy, sour, sweet and salty all at the same time. It is delicious as a hot dish but I find it an excellent cold dish as well. I simply let it cool and serve it at room temperature. The sesame seeds add a crunchy texture which contrasts nicely with the tender chicken meat. Serve this dish with Ham and Marrow Soup (page 71) and Stir-fried Broccoli with Hoisin Sauce (page 196.)

Serves 3 to 4		
8oz	225g	boneless chicken breasts, skinned
1		egg white
½ teaspoon		salt
2 teaspoons		cornflour
5floz	150ml	oil, preferably groundnut
1 tablespoon		white sesame seeds
Sauce		
1 teaspoon		dark soy sauce
1 teaspoon		cider vinegar or Chinese black rice vinegar
½ teaspoon		chilli bean sauce
½ teaspoon		sesame oil
1 teaspoon		sugar
2 teaspoons		dry sherry or rice wine
½ teaspoon		roasted Sichuan peppercorns (page 25) (optional)
2 teaspoons		spring onions, finely chopped

Cut the chicken breasts into fine shreds 3 inches (7·5cm) long. Combine them with the egg white, salt and cornflour in a small bowl, and place in the refrigerator for about 20 minutes.

Heat the oil in a wok or large frying-pan until it is moderately hot. Add the chicken mixture and stir-fry it quickly in the oil to keep it from sticking. Cook until it turns white, which should take about 1 minute. Drain the chicken immediately in a colander or sieve and drain off the oil. (The oil, once cooled, may be saved for future stir-fried dishes using chicken.)

Clean the wok or pan and add about 1 tablespoon of the drained oil. Re-heat it until it is hot. Add the sesame seeds and stir-fry them for 1 minute or until they are slightly brown. Then add the sauce ingredients and bring to the boil. Return the cooked chicken to the pan and stir-fry the mixture for another 2 minutes, coating the pieces thoroughly with the sauce and sesame seeds. Serve at once or let it cool and serve at room temperature.

STIR-FRIED CHICKEN SHREDS

Region: eastern

Method: stir-frying

This is a simple recipe which is quick and easy to make and is very suitable for family meals. The secret of cooking the chicken shreds without drying them out is to stir-fry them quickly in oil until they turn opaque and then remove them at once. You can substitute other vegetables such as asparagus, carrots or green peas for the ones I have used if you prefer. This dish goes nicely with rice and Ham and Marrow Soup (page 71).

Serves 3 to 4		
8oz	225g	boneless chicken breasts, skinned
1		egg white
½ teaspoon		salt
½ teaspoon		cornflour
6oz	175g	fresh bean sprouts
4oz	110g	mange-tout, trimmed
4oz	110g	waterchestnuts, tinned (drained weight) or fresh
5floz	150ml	oil, preferably groundnut
1 teaspoon		salt

Cut the chicken into very thin shreds and combine these with the egg white, salt and cornflour in a bowl. Mix well and place in the refrigerator for about 20 minutes. Meanwhile, trim the bean sprouts, finely shred the mange-tout lengthways, and shred or slice the waterchestnuts.

Heat the oil in a wok or large frying-pan and when it is almost smoking add the chicken. Stir-fry quickly for 1 minute. Drain the chicken in a colander or sieve immediately. Pour off the oil, leaving 1 tablespoon in the wok or pan. (The rest of the oil may be saved when it is cooled and used for future cooking with chicken.)

Re-heat the pan and stir-fry the vegetables for 2 minutes. Return the drained chicken to the pan, stir to mix well, and add the salt. Give the mixture a few more stirs and then turn it onto a warm serving platter.

SPICED DEEP-FRIED CHICKEN

Region: western

Method: deep-frying

This is a fragrant crispy chicken dish which has always brought me compliments. It is simple to make and should be served as soon as it is cooked. I like to serve this with Watercress Soup (page 63) and Rainbow Rice (page 220).

		Serves 4
12oz	350g	boneless chicken pieces
1 pint	570ml	oil (see Deep-fat fryers, page 34)
3oz	75g	plain flour
		Marinade
1 teaspoon		chilli bean sauce or chilli powder
2 teaspoons		dry sherry or rice wine
1 teaspoon		light soy sauce
1 teaspoon		dark soy sauce
2 teaspoons		fresh ginger, finely chopped
1 tablespoon		spring onions, finely chopped
1 teaspoon		sugar

Cut the chicken into strips 2 inches (5 cm) × ½ inch (1 cm) and put them into a large bowl. Blend the marinade ingredients together and pour the mixture over the chicken. Mix well to ensure an even distribution. Allow the chicken to marinade for 30 to 40 minutes at room temperature.

Heat the oil in a deep-fat fryer or large wok until it is quite hot. Lightly sprinkle the chicken strips with the flour and deep-fry them for 8 minutes. Remove them and drain on kitchen paper. Serve at once.

HOT SPICED CHICKEN

Region: western
Method: shallow-frying and braising

This hot and spicy chicken dish can easily be made ahead of time and re-heated. It is a good example of the combination of contrasting flavours which characterise the spicy cuisine of western China. The finished dish smells wonderfully fragrant and it has an equally delightful taste.

Serves 4		
12 oz–1 lb	350–450 g	chicken pieces
½ teaspoon		salt
2		spring onions
5 fl oz	150 ml	oil, preferably groundnut
1 teaspoon		oil
1		dried red chilli, halved lengthways
½ teaspoon		fresh ginger, finely chopped
1 teaspoon		chilli bean sauce, or ½ teaspoon chilli powder
10 fl oz	300 ml	Chicken Stock (page 59)
½ teaspoon		Sichuan peppercorns, roasted and ground (page 25) (optional)
½ teaspoon		sugar
2 teaspoons		dark soy sauce

Rub the chicken pieces with the salt and let them sit for about 30 minutes. Cut the spring onions into 2 inch (5 cm) pieces. Heat the oil in a wok or large frying-pan, and then add the dried chilli to flavour the oil. When it turns black, turn the heat down. (At this point you may remove the chilli or leave it in as the Chinese do.) Slowly brown the chicken pieces, a few at a time, skin-side down. Then turn them over and brown the other side. Drain the cooked pieces on kitchen paper.

Heat a clean wok or pan and add 1 teaspoon oil. Fry in it the spring onions, ginger and chilli bean sauce (or chilli powder) taking care not to have the heat too high or the sauce will burn. A few seconds later add the chicken stock, Sichuan peppercorns, sugar and dark soy sauce. Then turn the heat down low, and add the chicken pieces. Cover, and finish cooking the chicken in this sauce, turning the pieces from time to time. This should take about 20–30 minutes. Serve the chicken with the sauce, first removing any surface fat.

BRAISED CHICKEN WITH LEEKS

Region: northern
Method: stir-frying and braising

Leeks are popular in northern Chinese cooking. They have a flavour which is less pronounced than that of garlic or onions and which blends well with the mild taste of chicken. Leeks need to be thoroughly washed and I find it easier to do this after they have been chopped. This warm rich dish is perfect for cold winter days. I like to cook it in a Chinese clay pot but any heavy casserole will do. Serve with plain steamed rice or plain boiled noodles and Ginger and Spring Onion Dipping Sauce (page 29).

128

		Serves 4
12oz– 1lb	350– 450g	chicken pieces
2 teaspoons		dry sherry or rice wine
2 teaspoons		light soy sauce
4oz	110g	leeks
1		spring onion
1 slice		fresh ginger
1 tablespoon		oil, preferably groundnut
7½floz	210ml	chicken stock
2 teaspoons		dry sherry or rice wine
2 teaspoons		light soy sauce

Pat the chicken pieces dry with kitchen paper. Using a heavy cleaver or knife, cut them into smaller pieces about 2 inches (5cm) × 1 inch (2·5cm) and put them into a bowl. Add 2 teaspoons of dry sherry or rice wine and 2 teaspoons of light soy sauce. Mix well and set the chicken to one side.

Trim the leeks and discard any yellow parts. Cut the leeks at the point where they begin to turn green and discard the green parts. Then split the white parts in half and cut them at a slight diagonal into 2½ inch (6cm) segments. Now wash them well in cold water. (You may have to do this several times until there is no trace of dirt.) Cut the spring onion and ginger at a slight diagonal into 2½ inch (6cm) pieces.

Heat a wok or large frying-pan until it is hot. Add the oil and, when it is almost smoking, add the spring onion and ginger. Quickly lift the chicken pieces out of the marinade, using a slotted spoon, and add them to the pan together with the leeks. Stir-fry for about 5 minutes until they are thoroughly browned and then remove them from the pan with a slotted spoon and discard the oil.

Bring the stock to the boil in a medium-sized pot and add the sherry or rice wine and soy sauce. Then add the browned chicken and vegetables. Skim off any scum and then reduce the heat to a simmer. Cover the pot tightly and braise for about 25 minutes. Before serving, skim off any fat. Serve at once or let it cool and then refrigerate. (It re-heats beautifully.)

CHICKEN WITH GARLIC VINEGAR SAUCE

Region: northern

Method: steaming and deep-frying

I remember the first time I had this dish in a northern Chinese restaurant. I liked it so much that I immediately set out to re-create it. The secret was in steaming the chicken to keep it moist and then deep-frying it without batter. The result is a juicy chicken with a crisp, parchment-like skin. The chicken is served with a piquant sauce, and goes well with plain steamed rice and Stir-fried Ginger Broccoli (page 195).

Serves 6	
4 slices	fresh ginger
4	spring onions
1 whole 2½lb 1·1kg	chicken
2 teaspoons	salt
2 pints 1·1ltr	oil (see Deep-fat fryers, page 34)
Sauce	
1 tablespoon	garlic, finely chopped
2 tablespoons	cider vinegar or Chinese white rice vinegar
2 tablespoons	light soy sauce
2½ tablespoons	spring onions, finely chopped

Cut the ginger diagonally into slices 3 inches (7·5cm) × ¼inch (0·5cm). Cut the spring onions into 3 inch (7·5cm) pieces. Rub the whole chicken with the salt and stuff the cavity with the ginger and spring onions. Let the chicken sit at room temperature for 30 minutes.

Next set up a steamer or put a rack into a wok or deep pan and fill it with 2 inches (5cm) of water. Bring the water to the boil over a high heat. Put the chicken onto a plate and then carefully lower it into the steamer or onto the rack. Turn the heat to low and cover the pan tightly. Steam gently for 1 hour or until the chicken is cooked through to the bone. Remember to replenish the water from time to time.

Remove the cooked chicken and let it cool and dry. This takes at least 3 hours. Wipe the chicken completely dry and cut it in half, lengthways. Mix the sauce ingredients together and set aside.

130

Heat the oil in a deep-fat fryer or large wok. Deep-fry one chicken half until it is golden and crisp. Remove and then deep-fry the other half. Drain the cooked halves on kitchen paper. Cut the meat into bite-sized pieces, arrange them on a warm platter, and pour the sauce over the top. Serve at once.

DRUNKEN CHICKEN

Region: northern
Method: steeping and marinading

This dish isn't called Drunken Chicken without reason! You do need quite a lot of alcohol to cover the fowl during the steeping process, but it can be re-used. I think this traditional dish tastes best when it is made with Chinese rice wine rather than sherry. Because it can be prepared at least two days ahead, it makes an ideal dish for a party or a large gathering or special occasion.

Serves 4		
1 slice		fresh ginger
15 floz– 1 pint	400– 570 ml	water
½ teaspoon		salt
1		spring onion
12 oz	350 g	chicken pieces
5 floz	150 ml	rice wine, or 2½ floz 70 ml dry sherry mixed with 2½ floz 70 ml chicken stock

131

Cut the ginger into slices 2 inches (5 cm) × ¼ inch (0·5 cm). Fill a large casserole with the water. Bring it to the boil, and add the ginger, salt, whole spring onion and the chicken pieces. If they are not covered by the water add some more. Bring the liquid back to boiling point, and then turn the heat down. Simmer for 30–40 minutes, skimming any fat or scum off the surface all the time. Then turn the heat off, cover the casserole tightly and let the chicken sit in the liquid for 20–30 minutes.

Remove the cooked chicken to a large plate and let it cool. (The cooking liquid can be saved and used for stock.) If the chicken is not already in bite-sized pieces, cut it up and put it into a large bowl. Cover with the rice wine or sherry and stock mixture, and leave it for 2 days in the refrigerator, turning it over from time to time.

After 2 days remove the chicken and arrange it on a serving platter. Pour some of the wine over the chicken to moisten it. The remaining wine can be kept in the refrigerator and used for cooking other dishes which call for sherry or rice wine.

SOY SAUCE CHICKEN

Region: eastern and southern

Method: simmering and steeping

My friends are often surprised at their first taste of Soy Sauce Chicken. Instead of the saltiness they expect, given the name of the dish, they taste tender, succulent chicken bathed in a rich and subtle sauce. The technique of steeping used here ensures that the chicken is moist and tender, and allows the rich flavours of the sauce to gently permeate the meat. The chicken may be served hot but I think it is best cooled and served at room temperature, or refrigerated and served cold. It also makes a delicious picnic dish. The steeping liquid may be used as a sauce, and the rest may be frozen and re-used for making more Soy Sauce Chicken.

Right: Chicken Pieces in Black Bean Sauce (page 115) and Stir-fried Ginger Broccoli (page 195)

		Serves 6
4 slices		fresh ginger
1 whole		
2½lb	1·1kg	chicken
4		spring onions, whole
		Sauce
1¼pts	700ml	Chicken Stock (page 59) or water
1 pint	570ml	dark soy sauce
5floz	150ml	light soy sauce
10floz	300ml	rice wine, or 5floz 150ml dry sherry mixed with 5floz 150ml chicken stock
4oz	110g	sugar
3		whole star anise (optional)
3		cinnamon sticks
		Optional garnish
		fresh coriander sprigs

First make the sauce by combining all the sauce ingredients in a very large pot and bringing the liquid to a simmer. Meanwhile, cut the ginger into slices 2 inches (5 cm) × ¼ inch (0·5 cm). Stuff the cavity of the chicken with the whole spring onions and ginger slices. Put the chicken into the pot with the sauce mixture. If the liquid does not cover the chicken add a little more stock. Bring it back to a simmer and simmer for about 50–60 minutes uncovered, skimming all the while. Turn the chicken over so the breast is touching the bottom of the pot. Turn off the heat, cover the pot tightly and leave for about 20–30 minutes.

After this time remove the chicken from the liquid with a slotted spoon and put it on a plate to cool. It can now be put into the refrigerator or cut up into pieces and served. Remove any surface fat from the sauce and serve a little of it spooned over the chicken pieces. If you like, garnish with fresh coriander sprigs.

Left: Peking Duck (page 143), Chinese Pancakes (page 237), Hoisin Sauce (page 23) and Spring Onion Brushes (page 47)

TWICE-COOKED CHICKEN

Region: eastern

Method: steaming and deep-frying

This eastern Chinese recipe involves a two-step cooking process. First the chicken is marinaded and steamed. This cooks the flesh but retains the moisture and flavour of the bird. The chicken pieces are then dried and deep-fried to a golden, crispy brown.

Serves 4 to 6		
1½ lb	700g	chicken pieces, with the skin on
1 pint	570ml	oil, preferably groundnut (see Deep-fat fryers, page 34)
Marinade		
1 tablespoon		dry sherry or rice wine
1 tablespoon		light soy sauce
1 tablespoon		spring onions, finely chopped
1 teaspoon		fresh ginger, finely chopped
1 teaspoon		roasted Sichuan peppercorns, ground (page 25), or 1 teaspoon black peppercorns, freshly ground
2 teaspoons		sugar
½ teaspoon		salt

Combine the marinade ingredients together in a bowl. Next, rub the marinade mixture all over the chicken pieces and let them sit in a cool place for an hour or more.

Set up a steamer or put a rack into a wok or large deep pan and fill it with 2 inches (5 cm) of water. Bring the water to the boil. Arrange the chicken pieces on a deep plate with the breast pieces on the bottom and the joints on the top, and then gently lower the plate into the steamer or onto the rack. Cover the pan tightly and lower the heat. Gently steam the chicken for at least 1 hour. Top up the water level from time to time.

Remove the cooked chicken and let it cool and dry completely. The skin should become taut. This may take up to 1 hour or more. (The dish can be made a day ahead up to this point.)

Heat the oil in a deep-fat fryer or large wok until it is hot. Deep-fry the pieces of dried, steamed chicken, a few pieces at a time, until the skin is golden brown and heated right through. Drain the pieces on kitchen paper. Serve the chicken hot with one of the dipping sauces on pages 27 to 30.

CHINESE CHICKEN SALAD

Region: western
Method: steaming

I have often enjoyed serving this salad either as a first course or as a main course for dinner on a warm summer night. It has been a success at picnics too. It is easy to prepare and is served with a tasty dressing.

		Serves 6
8 oz	225 g	fresh bean sprouts
10 oz	275 g	cucumber
4 oz	110 g	carrots
1 whole		
2½ lb	1·1 kg	chicken, uncooked, or 1 plain roasted chicken
		Dressing
3 tablespoons		sesame paste or peanut butter
2 tablespoons		spring onions, finely chopped
2 teaspoons		sesame oil
2 tablespoons		cider vinegar or Chinese white rice vinegar
3 tablespoons		light soy sauce
1½ tablespoons		garlic, finely chopped
1 teaspoon		salt
2 teaspoons		sugar
5 floz	150 ml	chicken stock
1 tablespoon		dry sherry or rice wine

If you are using uncooked chicken, cut it into about 8 pieces, put it onto a large plate and set it inside a steamer. Alternatively set a rack into a wok or large pot and pour in about 2 inches (5 cm) water. Bring the water to a simmer and then lower the plate of chicken onto the rack, cover the pan and let it steam for about 1½ hours. Test it with a skewer to see if the juices run clear. If they are still pink continue to steam until the juices are clear and the chicken is just cooked.

Next prepare the vegetables. Trim the bean sprouts at both ends. Peel the cucumber, split it in half lengthways and remove the seeds with a teaspoon. Finely shred the cucumber into 3 inch (7·5 cm) lengths. Peel and finely shred the carrots into 3 inch (7·5 cm) lengths. Set the vegetables aside.

137

Take all the meat off the cooked chicken and shred it into fine strips using a sharp knife or cleaver. Arrange the chicken strips on a platter and surround them with the bean sprouts, cucumbers and carrots. Combine all the ingredients for the dressing and mix them thoroughly. (I find an electric blender is quite useful for this but you could use a screw-top jar and shake everything in it well.) Pour the dressing all over the chicken and vegetables and mix well. Serve at once.

CRISPY CHICKEN

Region: southern
Method: simmering and deep-frying

This is one of my favourite chicken dishes. I remember eating it at family gatherings on special occasions. Although it is usually served in restaurants it can easily be made at home. Some of the ingredients may be difficult to obtain, but it is worth the effort to achieve the authentic taste of the dish. It also requires a bit of patience to make, but much of the work can be done the day before.

Serves 6		
1 whole		
2½lb	1·1kg	chicken, cut in half lengthways
2 pints	1·1ltr	oil (see Deep-fat fryers, page 34)
Simmering sauce		
2 pints	1·1ltr	water
1		cinnamon stick or Chinese cinnamon bark
7½floz	210ml	dark soy sauce
1		whole star anise (optional)
1½ teaspoons		whole Sichuan peppercorns, roasted (page 25) (optional)
1 tablespoon		fresh orange peel, finely chopped or dried citrus peel, soaked and finely chopped (page 18)
2 slices		fresh ginger
2		spring onions
½oz	10g	sugar

	Glaze	
2½ tablespoons	honey	
10 floz 300 ml	water	
2 tablespoons	cider vinegar or Chinese white rice vinegar	
	Garnish	
1	lemon, cut in wedges	
	Roasted Salt and Pepper (page 30)	

Combine all the ingredients for the simmering sauce in a large casserole or pot and bring the mixture to the boil. Then turn the heat down to a simmer. Lower in the chicken halves and simmer them, uncovered, for 30–40 minutes. Remove the chicken halves and let them cool on a rack for at least three hours. The skin of the chicken should be completely dried.

In a pan or wok, heat the glaze ingredients to boiling point. Next, baste the skins of the dried chicken halves with this glaze. Let the chicken dry again for another 2 hours, keeping it in a very cool and airy place but not in the refrigerator. The dish can be prepared up to this point the day before you want to serve it.

Heat the oil in a deep-fat fryer or large wok, and lower in one of the chicken halves, skin-side down. Deep-fry it until it is a rich, dark brown colour and very crisp. Remove it and deep-fry the other half. Cut the meat into bite-sized pieces, arrange on a warm platter and garnish. Serve with Roasted Salt and Pepper (page 30).

FRIED CHICKEN LIVERS IN GINGER

Region: eastern
Method: shallow-frying and stir-frying

Chicken livers are extremely tasty when they are cooked properly and not overdone. In this recipe, the livers are marinaded briefly, coated with flour and shallow-fried before being finally stir-fried in a delicious sauce. Although this process is a little elaborate, the delectable taste and velvety texture of the dish make it all worthwhile. It is surprisingly good when served cold and is perfect for picnics.

Serves 4		
8oz	225g	fresh chicken livers
1oz	25g	plain flour, for dusting
5fl oz	150ml	oil, preferably groundnut
Marinade		
¼ teaspoon		salt
2 teaspoons		garlic, finely chopped
1 teaspoon		fresh ginger, finely chopped
1 tablespoon		spring onions, finely chopped
½ teaspoon		sugar
½ teaspoon		sesame oil
Sauce		
1½ teaspoons		fresh ginger, finely chopped
1½ teaspoons		light soy sauce
1 teaspoon		dry sherry or rice wine
1 teaspoon		cider vinegar or Chinese white rice vinegar
½ teaspoon		sugar
1 teaspoon		sesame oil

Clean the livers and discard any connecting membranes. Dry them well on kitchen paper. Combine the marinade ingredients with the chicken livers and let the livers marinade for about 30 minutes or more.

Drain the livers in a colander and discard the marinade. Dry them with kitchen paper and lightly dust with the plain flour. Heat the oil in a deep frying-pan or large wok until it is hot. Fry small batches of the livers at a time until they are crisp and brown. (Each batch should take about 2–3 minutes to reach this point.) Drain the cooked livers on kitchen paper.

Transfer about 1 tablespoon of the oil in which you have cooked the livers to a clean wok or frying-pan. Fry the ginger for a few seconds and then add the other sauce ingredients and bring the sauce to a simmer. Return the livers to the pan and quickly stir-fry them in this sauce for about 4 minutes until they are thoroughly coated and are firm to the touch. Serve immediately or, if you prefer, let them cool and put them in the refrigerator. They are delicious cold and make a wonderful addition to a cold meat platter.

CRISPY CHICKEN DUMPLINGS

Region: northern
Method: steaming and shallow-frying

These doughless dumplings are similar to French chicken quenelles and are usually eaten as part of a meal and not as a snack. Instead of poaching, the chicken paste mixture is steamed to cook it and to keep it moist at the same time. Then it is cut into dumplings which are shallow-fried to give them a crisp exterior. A spicy, cold garlic and vinegar sauce is then poured over the chicken. Although two techniques are involved here, the first step (the steaming) can be done up to a day in advance.

Serves 3 to 4		
8oz	225g	boneless chicken breasts, skinned
2		egg whites
2 teaspoons		cornflour
2 teaspoons		dry sherry or rice wine
1 teaspoon		fresh ginger, finely chopped
2 teaspoons		spring onions, finely chopped
1 teaspoon		salt
7½floz	210ml	oil, preferably groundnut
1oz	25g	cornflour, for dusting
Sauce		
1 tablespoon		cider vinegar or Chinese white rice vinegar
2 teaspoons		garlic, finely chopped
1 tablespoon		dark soy sauce
1 teaspoon		Chilli Oil (page 28) (optional)

Chop and then blend the chicken with the egg whites, cornflour, sherry or rice wine, ginger, spring onions and salt in a liquidiser or food processor until you have a fine paste. Alternatively, you could chop the chicken with a sharp knife or cleaver until it is very fine and then incorporate it with the other ingredients in a bowl.

Rub 1 tablespoon of the oil on a deep plate (this is to keep the mixture from sticking) and put the chicken mixture on it. Set up a steamer or put a rack into a wok or deep pan and pour in 2 inches (5 cm) of water. Bring the water to the boil and then set the plate of chicken mixture into the steamer or onto the rack. Cover it with a

141

lid and steam gently for about 15 minutes or until the chicken is firm and cooked. Remove the chicken and let it cool.

Divide the chicken mixture into bite-sized pieces and dust them lightly with the cornflour. Mix the sauce ingredients together and set them aside.

Heat the oil in a pot, wok or deep frying-pan until it is hot, and then fry the chicken pieces for 2 minutes or until they are golden brown. Drain them on kitchen paper. (You may have to do this in two batches.) Arrange the chicken pieces on a warm serving platter, pour the sauce over the top and serve.

CRISPY SICHUAN DUCK

Region: western
Method: steaming and deep-frying

In my family, duck was a treat reserved for special occasions and family banquets. I always remembered such feasts long afterwards. This duck recipe is one of my favourites. Don't be intimidated by the long preparation process. Most of the steps are quite simple and can be done up to a day ahead, and the results are well worth the labour. The technique of steaming renders out most of the fat, leaving the duck meat moist and succulent. The final deep-frying gives the duck skin a crispy texture. This is a dish for a special dinner party and should be served with Steamed Buns (page 234) and Roasted Salt and Pepper (page 30).

Serves 4 to 6	
1 whole 1·6kg–3½–4lb 1·8kg	**duck**
2 tablespoons	five spice powder
2 tablespoons	salt
4 slices	fresh ginger
4	spring onions
2 pints 1·1ltr	oil, preferably groundnut (see Deep-fat fryers, page 34)

If the duck is frozen, thaw it thoroughly. Blot it with kitchen paper until it is thoroughly dry, then rub it inside and out with the five spice powder and salt. Make sure these are rubbed on evenly. Wrap well in clingfilm and place in the refrigerator for at least 3 hours, preferably longer.

After this time, cut the ginger into slices 3 inches (7·5 cm) × ¼ inch (0·5 cm). Slice the spring onions into 3 inch (7·5 cm) lengths. Stuff the ginger and spring onions into the cavity of the duck, and put on a heatproof china or glass plate.

Set up a steamer or put a rack into a wok or deep pan. Pour about 2 inches (5 cm) of water into the pan and bring to the boil. Put the duck (and plate) into the steamer or onto the rack, cover it with a lid and steam gently for about 2 hours. Replenish the water from time to time to keep the steam constant. Remove the duck and pour off all the fat and liquid which may have accumulated. Discard the ginger and spring onions. Keep the duck on a platter in a cool dry place for about 2 hours until it has thoroughly dried and cooled. At this point the duck can be refrigerated.

Just before you are ready to serve it, cut the duck into quarters. Heat the oil in a deep-fat fryer or wok. When the oil is almost smoking deep-fry the duck quarters in 2 batches until each is crisp and warmed right through. Drain the quarters on kitchen paper and then chop them into smaller serving pieces.

To eat Crispy Sichuan Duck, dip a piece of duck meat in the Roasted Salt and Pepper mixture and then put the meat into a split, steamed bun and eat it rather like a sandwich.

PEKING DUCK

Region: northern
Method: blanching and roasting

The Chinese have a special reverence for duck, regarding it as a symbol of wholesomeness and fidelity. Of course its 'delectability' is its chief virtue. With Peking Duck Chinese cooks mastered the art of making the most of the duck's rich, succulent flesh while minimising its major flaw—its relatively large proportion of bone and fat. There is little doubt that this spectacular dish was first concocted in the Imperial kitchens. Its popularity spread as restaurants, staffed by former Imperial chefs, made it a speciality to be served at banquets. The dish can now be found in all parts of China.

The preparation and cooking of Peking Duck in China is an art form. Specially raised ducklings are fed a rich diet of maize, sorghum, barley and soyabeans for 1½ months before they are ready for the kitchen. After being killed and cleaned, air is pumped through the windpipe to separate the skin from the meat. (This allows the skin to roast separately and remain crisp while the fat melts, keeping the meat moist.) Hot water is then poured over the duck to close the skin pores and it is hung up to dry. During the drying process a solution of malt sugar is liberally brushed over the duck, which is then roasted in wood-burning ovens. The result is a shiny, crisp and aromatic duck with beautiful brown skin, moist flesh and no fat.

Preparing Peking Duck is a time-consuming task, but I have devised a simpler method which closely approximates the real thing. Just give yourself plenty of time and the results will be good enough for an emperor. Traditionally Peking Duck is served with Chinese Pancakes, spring onions cut into brush shapes and sweet bean sauce. In Hong Kong and in the West hoisin sauce is used instead. It is very similar to sweet bean sauce but contains vinegar. Each guest spoons some sauce onto a pancake. Then a helping of crisp skin and meat is placed on top with a spring onion brush and the entire mixture is rolled up like a stuffed pancake. It can be eaten using chopsticks or one's fingers. This makes an unforgettable dish for a very special dinner party.

Serves 4 to 6		
1 whole 3½–4lb	1·6kg–1·8kg	duck, fresh or frozen
Honey syrup mixture		
1		lemon
2 pints	1·1ltr	water
3 tablespoons		honey
3 tablespoons		dark soy sauce
5floz	150ml	dry sherry or rice wine
To serve		
8–12		Chinese Pancakes (page 237)
4–6 tablespoons		hoisin sauce
16–24		spring onion brushes (page 47)

If the duck is frozen, thaw it thoroughly. Rinse the duck well and blot it completely dry with kitchen paper. Insert a meat hook near the neck.

Using a sharp knife, cut the lemon into ¼ inch (0·5 cm) slices, leaving the rind on. Combine the lemon slices with the rest of the honey syrup ingredients in a large pot and bring the mixture to the boil. Turn the heat to low and simmer for about 20 minutes. Using a large ladle or spoon pour this mixture over the duck several times, as if to bathe it, until all the skin of the duck is completely coated with the mixture. Hang the duck in a cool, well ventilated place to dry, or alternatively hang it in front of a cold fan for about 4–5 hours, longer if possible. (Be sure to put a tray or roasting pan underneath to catch any drips.) Once the duck has dried, the surface of the skin will feel like parchment.

Pre-heat the oven to gas mark 9, 475°F (240°C). Meanwhile, place the duck on a roasting rack in a roasting pan, breast side up. Put 5 floz (150ml) of water into the roasting pan. (This will prevent the fat from splattering.) Now put the duck into the oven and roast it for 15 minutes. Then turn the heat down to gas mark 4, 350°F (180°C) and continue to roast for 1 hour and 10 minutes.

Remove the duck from the oven and let it sit for at least 10 minutes before you carve it. Using a cleaver or a sharp knife, cut the skin and meat into pieces and arrange them on a warm platter. Serve at once with Chinese Pancakes, spring onion brushes and a bowl of hoisin sauce.

BRAISED DUCK
Region: southern
Method: shallow-frying and braising

The braising sauce used for this duck recipe is the same as for the Soy Sauce Chicken (page 132). The sauce can be frozen and re-used. Unlike chicken, duck needs long braising to cook it thoroughly and to render out the fat in the skin. You can see this braised duck in food shops in Hong Kong (and in the USA and the UK) hanging picturesquely from hooks. It is easy to make at home and re-heats well, although I think it is best served at room temperature. It would go well with Hot Bean Thread Noodles (page 232) and Lettuce with Oyster Sauce (page 207).

		Serves 4 to 6
1 × 4 lb	1·8 kg	duck
10 floz	300 ml	oil, preferably groundnut
		Sauce
2 pints	1·1 ltr	Chicken Stock (page 59) or water
2 pints	1·1 ltr	dark soy sauce
10 floz	300 ml	light soy sauce
15 floz	400 ml	rice wine, or 7½floz 210ml dry sherry mixed with 7½floz 210ml chicken stock
4 oz	110 g	sugar
3		whole pieces of star anise (optional)
3		cinnamon sticks or Chinese cinnamon bark
		Garnish
		fresh coriander sprigs (optional)

Cut the duck into quarters. Dry these thoroughly with kitchen paper. Heat the oil in a wok or large frying-pan until it is almost smoking, and then shallow-fry 2 pieces of the duck, skin-side down. Turn the heat down and continue to fry slowly until the skin is browned. This should take about 15–20 minutes. Do not turn the pieces over but baste the duck as it fries. Drain the cooked duck on kitchen paper. Shallow-fry the rest of the duck in the same way.

Combine all the sauce ingredients together in a large pot and bring the mixture to a boil. Add the duck pieces and turn the heat down to a simmer. Cover the pot and slowly braise the duck for 1 hour or until it is tender.

Skim off the large amount of surface fat which will be left when the duck is cooked. This procedure will prevent the duck from becoming greasy. Now remove the duck pieces with a slotted spoon. Let them cool and then chop them into smaller pieces. Arrange on a warm platter, garnish with the fresh coriander and serve at once. Alternatively you can let the duck cool thoroughly and serve it at room temperature. Once the sauce has cooled, remove any lingering surface fat. Now the sauce can be frozen and re-used to braise duck or chicken.

FIVE SPICE RED BRAISED PIGEONS

Region: eastern
Method: blanching and braising

In this recipe, the five spice powder gives the pigeons a delicious flavour, while the soy braising sauce endows them with a rich brown colour. Chinese cooks often blanch pigeons before braising them to rid them of any impurities. Braising is a good technique to use as it keeps the pigeons moist. If you prefer you can substitute quails or other small game birds. This dish is excellent served cold and is perfect for an exotic picnic.

Serves 2 to 4		
4		pigeons, each weighing about 8 oz (225 g)
Sauce		
15 fl oz	400 ml	dark soy sauce
5 fl oz	150 ml	light soy sauce
2 tablespoons		five spice powder
5 fl oz	150 ml	dry sherry or rice wine
2 oz	50 g	sugar
Garnish		
2 tablespoons		spring onions, finely chopped
1 tablespoon		fresh ginger, finely chopped

Blanch the pigeons by immersing them in a large pot of boiling water for about 5 minutes. Remove them with a slotted spoon and discard the water.

Combine the sauce ingredients in a medium-sized pot and bring to the boil. Turn the heat down to a simmer and then add the pigeons. Cover the pot and braise the birds over a low heat for about 1½ hours or until they are tender. Then remove the pigeons with a slotted spoon and let them cool. (The braising sauce may be saved and frozen for the next time you cook this dish.) Chop the pigeons into bite-sized pieces and arrange them on a warm serving platter. Sprinkle the garnish ingredients on top and serve at once. If you want to serve the dish cold, let the pieces cool and then sprinkle them with the garnish ingredients. Refrigerate them well wrapped in clingfilm until you are ready to serve them.

147

DEEP-FRIED PIGEONS

Region: southern
Method: braising and deep-frying

On Sundays in Hong Kong one of the most popular outings is to Shatin, a town in the New Territories, to play the famous Chinese game Mahjong and to eat pigeon. Pigeons have a rich, gamy taste. The southern Chinese like to braise them quickly, let them dry and then deep-fry them just before serving. The result is a moist, highly flavoured pigeon with crisp skin. The secret to this dish lies in the braising liquid, which is used over and over again. In some restaurants it is used for years, like a vintage stock.

This dish takes time and patience but it is not difficult to make and much of the work can be done several hours in advance. It is an impressive dish for any special dinner party. Serve it with rice, Braised Spicy Aubergines (page 190) and Roasted Salt and Pepper (page 30).

	Serves 2 to 4
2	pigeons, each weighing about 8–12oz 225–350g
2 slices	fresh ginger
1½ pints 900ml	oil, preferably groundnut (see Deep-fat fryers, page 34)
	Braising sauce
2 pints 1·1ltr	Chicken Stock (page 59)
2 tablespoons	dark soy sauce
2 tablespoons	light soy sauce
5 floz 150ml	dry sherry or rice wine
2 tablespoons	honey
1 teaspoon	salt
2 pieces	fresh orange peel, finely chopped or dried citrus peel, soaked and finely chopped (page 18)
1	cinnamon stick or Chinese cinnamon bark
1	star anise (optional)
½ teaspoon	white pepper
1 teaspoon	sesame oil

Bring a large pot of water to the boil. Blanch the pigeons in the boiling water for about 2 minutes. This method helps to rid them of impurities and tightens the skin. Remove the pigeons from the

148

pot and discard the water. Cut the ginger into 3 inch (7·5 cm) slices.

Combine all the braising sauce ingredients together in a large pot and bring it to the boil. Add the pigeons and the ginger. Lower the heat to a simmer and cover the pot tightly. Let it simmer for about 1–1½ hours until the pigeons are just tender. Remove them with a slotted spoon and let them dry on a plate, or hang them up in a cool, dry, airy place for at least 2 hours. The braising liquid, once cooled, can be stored in a plastic container and frozen for future use.

After two hours the skin of the pigeons should feel like parchment paper. Just before you are ready to serve them, heat the oil in a deep-fat fryer or large wok. When it is hot, lower in the pigeons and deep-fry them until they are crisp and deep brown in colour. Turn them over frequently with a slotted spoon so that all sides are thoroughly cooked and browned. This should take about 10 minutes. Drain the cooked pigeons on kitchen paper and let them cool for a few minutes. Using a heavy cleaver or knife, chop them into 4–6 pieces and arrange on a warm serving platter. Serve at once.

BARBECUED QUAILS

Region: southern

Method: roasting

I enjoy being in southern China or Hong Kong in autumn because this is the season for rice birds. These very small birds are caught with nets in the rice fields and then simply barbecued on skewers with a zesty sauce. Unable to find rice birds in Europe or America, I discovered an excellent alternative—quails. They are easy and quick to prepare, and as they are also delicious cold they make a wonderful dish for a picnic. If you are serving them hot, Braised Spicy Aubergine (page 190) is an excellent accompaniment.

Serves 4	
6	quails, each weighing about 4 oz 110g
1 tablespoon	salt
Sauce	
3 tablespoons	hoisin sauce
1 tablespoon	dry sherry or rice wine
1 tablespoon	light soy sauce

Pre-heat the oven to gas mark 9, 475°F (240°C).

If the quails are frozen, make sure you thaw them thoroughly. Dry them well with kitchen paper and then rub each one inside and out with a little salt.

Mix the sauce ingredients in a small bowl. Rub each of the quails inside and out with this sauce. Put the quails in a small roasting pan and put them into the oven for 5 minutes. Then turn the heat down to gas mark 4, 350°F (180°C) and continue to roast the birds for another 20 minutes. Turn off the oven and leave them there for another 5 minutes. Take them out of the oven and let them rest for another 10 minutes before serving.

Serve the quails whole or, if you wish to serve them Chinese-style, use a cleaver or heavy knife and chop each of them into 4–6 pieces. Arrange on a warm platter and serve.

STIR-FRIED QUAILS

Region: southern
Method: stir-frying

Quails are popular in southern China because of their excellent flavour and their suitability for stir-frying. This technique seals in the taste and juices of the game-birds and precludes overcooking. The bamboo shoots and waterchestnuts provide a crunchy texture which complements the tenderness of the quail meat.

This recipe is an adaptation of a banquet dish from the Lee Gardens Rainbow Room Restaurant in Hong Kong. There, just the breasts of quails are served, an extravagance possible in a high-class restaurant staffed by expert chefs. I have found that this dish works equally well without the tedious job of boning these small birds. The robust flavours and rich colours of the dish make it a perfect main course for a dinner party. Serve it with the Sweetcorn Soup with Crabmeat (page 76) and rice.

Serves 4 to 6		
6		quails, each weighing about 4oz 110g
8oz	225g	waterchestnuts, tinned (drained weight) or fresh
8oz	225g	tinned bamboo shoots
6		spring onions
5floz	150ml	oil, preferably groundnut
10floz	300ml	Chicken Stock (page 59)
2 tablespoons		oyster sauce
2 teaspoons		sugar
2 teaspoons		cornflour mixed with 2 teaspoons water
Marinade		
2 tablespoons		dry sherry or rice wine
2 tablespoons		light soy sauce
1 tablespoon		cornflour
2 teaspoons		sesame oil

If the quails are frozen, thaw them thoroughly. Dry them inside and out with kitchen paper. Then, using a cleaver or heavy sharp knife, cut each quail into about 6 pieces. Put the pieces into a bowl with the marinade ingredients, mix them well and let them steep for about 20 minutes.

151

Next prepare the vegetables. If you are using fresh waterchestnuts, peel and slice them. If you are using tinned waterchestnuts, rinse them thoroughly in cold water before slicing them. Rinse the bamboo shoots in cold water and slice these too. Cut the spring onions at a slight diagonal into 3 inch (7·5 cm) segments.

Heat a wok or large frying-pan over a high heat. Remove half the quail pieces from the marinade using a slotted spoon. Add half the groundnut oil to the wok or pan and, when it is smoking slightly, stir-fry the quail pieces for about 5 minutes or until they are brown. Transfer them to a colander or sieve to drain and discard the cooking oil. Re-heat the wok or pan and stir-fry the rest of the pieces in the same manner using the other half of the groundnut oil. Again, drain the quail in a colander or sieve, but leave about 1 tablespoon of oil in the pan.

Re-heat the pan over a high heat. Add the spring onions, fresh waterchestnuts if you are using them and bamboo shoots, and stir-fry them for about 2 minutes. Then add the rest of the ingredients and bring the mixture to a boil. Return the quails to the pan and cook for about 3 minutes. Make sure you coat all the quail pieces thoroughly with the sauce. If you are using tinned waterchestnuts add these now and cook for 2 more minutes. Serve at once.

FISH
AND SHELLFISH

Of the many remarkable and fortunate food experiences I had growing up as a young Chinese I count the extensive consumption of fresh fish and seafood as among the most pleasurable. In my family, fish and seafood were regarded with special affection whether as part of a simple family dinner or a large banquet. The first question always asked about fish, however, was: 'How fresh is it?'. From this early childhood experience I learned, as do all Chinese, to value good fresh fish and seafood.

Fish and seafood are a major feature of Chinese cookery. China's long coastline gives it access to numerous saltwater varieties and its many rivers, lakes, streams and canals teem with freshwater fish and seafood all year round. It is estimated that there are several hundred species of fish and seafood which are used in Chinese cookery. Most are caught wild but a few species, such as carp, are raised on special fish farms. We Chinese prefer that no more than a few hours elapse between the catching and cooking of fish. Indeed, in many markets in Hong Kong fish is sold live. You can select the fish of your choice while it swims around in special glass tanks, and then take it straight home or to a restaurant to be cooked. The accent is always on freshness.

There are many cooking techniques which the Chinese use to ensure that the flesh of the fish or shellfish retains its natural juices and flavour. Steaming is a favourite method. Many Chinese chefs consider this to be the ideal way of cooking fish. It allows the fragrance and natural flavours of the fish to develop, while at the same time preserving the delicate texture, moistness and shape of the fish. Quick-braising is another popular method, and deep-frying and shallow-frying are also often used.

The Chinese prefer to cook fish whole although fish fillets and steaks can be satisfactorily used instead. We believe that the flesh remains moist and the flavour is best when the whole fish is used, head and tail included. To serve a fish whole is also a symbol of prosperity. The head of the fish should always point in the direction of the guest of honour, a courtesy that assures him or her good fortune.

Seafood is especially important in Chinese cuisine. Prawns, oysters, scallops, crab, lobster, squid and abalone are just some of the most popular varieties. Because seafood is so delicate it requires a minimum amount of handling and the simplest preparation. The most common techniques used are stir-frying, steaming, deep-frying and braising. Recipes for seafood are usually interchangeable; what works for prawns will work just as well for crab, lobster or scallops.

When fresh seafood is not available, Chinese cooks make imaginative use of dried seafood as the main ingredient or as a flavouring in soups, stir-fried dishes, braised dishes and stuffings. Drying concentrates the flavours of the seafood as well as preserving it.

The Chinese try to complement the delicate flavour, texture and colour of fish and seafood with contrasting flavourings and textures. For example, in the dish Sweet and Sour Prawns, the subtle taste and crisp texture of the prawns contrast nicely with the tasty spiciness of the sauce. Most Chinese recipes call for fresh, uncooked prawns. This will prove difficult for British cooks, since most prawns are sold cooked and are often frozen as well. If you are forced to use cooked prawns, look for the best and largest variety you can find, and just heat them through instead of cooking them for the full length of time called for in the recipe. Crabs can sometimes still be bought live, or at least freshly cooked. Instructions for dealing with live crab and crab cooked in the shell are given on page 181.

Fortunately the fish situation is much brighter. Cod and haddock are available everywhere and are perfect for deep-frying, stir-frying or braising. Plaice, Dover sole, lemon sole and flounder are perfect for steaming. Oily fish such as red mullet, carp and eel are best braised, and trout should be shallow-fried. Get to know your fishmonger and be assertive in asking for the freshest fish and seafood. Fresh fish should be firm, have clear eyes, bright gills and a shiny sheen to the skin. Seafood should be firm and not smell fishy. Learn to be as finicky about selecting fish and seafood as the Chinese are. It will open up a whole new world of flavour for you.

FRIED FISH WITH GINGER

Region: eastern

Method: shallow-frying

Ginger goes very well with fish. It is used rather as lemon is in European fish cookery. In this easy dish it imparts a subtle fragrance to the fish. This goes well with Braised Spicy Aubergines (page 190) and Garlic Chicken with Cucumber (page 117).

Serves 4	.	
8oz	225g	fish fillets, preferably cod
¼ teaspoon		salt
1½ tablespoons		cornflour
3floz	75ml	oil, preferably groundnut
1½ tablespoons		fresh ginger, finely shredded
1 tablespoon		chicken stock or water
½ teaspoon		salt
1 tablespoon		dry sherry or rice wine
1 teaspoon		sugar

Sprinkle the fish fillets evenly on both sides with the salt. Cut the fish into strips 1 inch (2·5 cm) wide and let these sit for 20 minutes. Then dust them with the cornflour.

Heat the oil in a wok or large frying-pan. When it is hot add the ginger and, a few seconds later, the fish. Shallow-fry the fish strips until they are crisp and brown. Remove them with a slotted spoon and drain on kitchen paper.

Pour off all the oil and discard it. Wipe the wok or pan clean and then add to it the rest of the ingredients. Bring them to the boil and then return the fish slices to the pan and coat them with the sauce. Turn the fish gently in the sauce for 1 minute, taking care not to break up the slices. Remove to a platter and serve at once.

FISH IN HOT SAUCE

Region: western
Method: shallow-frying

I like to make this quick and easy dish when I am in the mood for fish. A firm, white fish such as cod or haddock is most suitable for shallow-frying because it is meaty and holds its shape during the cooking process. (Carp would be used in China for this recipe.) Serve with plain rice and any stir-fried vegetable.

Serves 4	
12 oz 350 g	fresh fish fillets, preferably cod
½ teaspoon	salt
1–1½ tablespoons	cornflour
2	spring onions
2½ fl oz 70 ml	oil, preferably groundnut
2 teaspoons	garlic, finely chopped
1 teaspoon	fresh ginger, finely chopped
Sauce	
2½ fl oz 70 ml	chicken stock
2 teaspoons	whole yellow bean sauce
½ teaspoon	chilli bean sauce or chilli powder
1 tablespoon	dry sherry or rice wine
2 teaspoons	light soy sauce
1 teaspoon	sesame oil

Cut the fish fillets into evenly sized slices about 2 inches (5 cm) wide. Sprinkle them with the salt and then with the cornflour. Cut the spring onions into 2 inch (5 cm) diagonal slices.

Heat a wok or large frying-pan until it is hot. Add the oil and heat it until it is almost smoking. Fry the fillets on both sides until they are brown. (This should take about 5 minutes.) Then remove and drain the fish on kitchen paper. Pour off most of the oil, leaving about 1 tablespoon in the pan.

Re-heat the wok or pan and then add the spring onions, garlic and ginger. Stir-fry them for 30 seconds. Then add the sauce ingredients and bring the mixture to the boil. Turn the heat down to a simmer and return the fish to the pan. Simmer for about 2 minutes, then turn the fish and sauce onto a platter and serve.

157

FRIED FISH WITH GARLIC AND SPRING ONIONS

Region: eastern
Method: shallow-frying

This eastern fish dish is simple to make and works especially well with plaice. In coastal areas of China salt-water fish similar to sea bream or a type of red snapper would be used for this recipe. In this dish the wine, egg and spicy sauce nicely complement the taste and texture of the fish but do be careful not to overcook it. Serve this with rice and a simple stir-fried vegetable such as Chinese Leaves in Soy Sauce (page 200).

Serves 4	
12oz 350g	plaice fillets
½ teaspoon	salt
1	egg
2oz 50g	cornflour
2½floz 70ml	oil, preferably groundnut
1 tablespoon	garlic, finely chopped
1½ tablespoons	spring onions, finely chopped
1 tablespoon	dry sherry or rice wine
½ teaspoon	salt
1 teaspoon	sesame oil

Have your fishmonger remove the dark skin of the plaice or else remove it yourself with a small, sharp knife. Cut the fish fillets into 1 inch (2·5cm) strips. Sprinkle the strips with salt and let them sit for 15 minutes. Beat the egg in a small bowl. Dip the pieces of fish into the cornflour and then into the beaten egg.

Heat the oil in a wok or large frying-pan until it is hot. Shallow-fry the fish pieces on each side, in several batches, until they are golden brown. Drain them on kitchen paper. Pour off the oil and discard it. Wipe the wok or pan clean and add the rest of the ingredients. Simmer for 2 minutes. Put the fried fish fillets on a warm serving platter and pour over the hot sauce. Serve at once.

FISH IN HOT AND SOUR SAUCE

Region: western

Method: shallow-frying

The combination of hot and sour is a popular one in western China. This is a quick and simple dish which is perfect for a light family meal. Stir-fried Spinach with Garlic (page 211) is a suitable accompaniment.

Serves 4	
12 oz 350 g	fish fillets, preferably plaice
2½ fl oz 70 ml	oil, preferably groundnut
Hot & Sour Sauce	
2½ fl oz 70 ml	chicken stock
1 tablespoon	dry sherry or rice wine
1 tablespoon	dark soy sauce
2 teaspoons	tomato paste
½ teaspoon	chilli bean sauce or chilli powder
½ teaspoon	white pepper
1 tablespoon	cider vinegar or Chinese black rice vinegar
1 teaspoon	sugar
Garnish	
1 tablespoon	spring onions, finely chopped

Have your fishmonger remove the dark skin of the plaice or else remove it yourself using a small, sharp knife. Cut the fish fillets, across the width and at a slight diagonal, into 1 inch (2·5 cm) wide strips.

Heat a wok or large frying-pan until it is quite hot. Add the oil and heat it until it is almost smoking. Fry the fish strips for 2–3 minutes until they are golden brown. You may have to do this in several batches. Drain the cooked fish strips on kitchen paper.

Pour off all the oil, wipe the wok or pan clean and re-heat it. Add all the hot and sour sauce ingredients. Bring the sauce to a boil, then lower the heat to a simmer. Add the fried fish strips and simmer them in the sauce for 2 minutes. Serve garnished with the spring onions.

159

STIR-FRIED FISH WITH PEAS

Region: southern
Method: stir-frying and braising

This dish is often made in southern China with grouper, a firm, white, fleshy fish. It works equally well with cod fillets. It is important to use a firm-textured fish which will not fall apart during the stir-frying process. Serve it with Deep-fried Green Beans (page 191) and Ham and Marrow Soup (page 71).

Serves 4		
12 oz	350 g	fresh fish fillets, preferably cod
1 teaspoon		salt
2 oz	50 g	fresh or frozen peas
1 tablespoon		oil
1 oz	25 g	Parma ham or lean English smoked bacon, shredded
Sauce		
2½ fl oz	70 g	chicken stock or water
2 teaspoons		dry sherry or rice wine
2 teaspoons		light soy sauce
½ teaspoon		salt
1 teaspoon		sugar
1 teaspoon		cornflour, blended with 1 teaspoon water

Cut the fish fillets into strips 1 inch (2·5 cm) wide and sprinkle the salt evenly over them. Let them sit for 20 minutes. Cook the peas for 5 minutes in a saucepan of boiling water and then drain them in a colander.

Heat a wok or large frying-pan and, when it is hot, add the oil. Let the oil heat up and then add the fish strips. Stir-fry these gently, taking care not to break them up. Cook the strips for about 2 minutes, and then add the ham or bacon, peas and all the sauce ingredients except for the cornflour mixture. Bring the sauce to a boil, add the cornflour mixture and stir this in well. Cook for another minute and then serve at once.

BRAISED FISH

Region: eastern
Method: shallow-frying and braising

Onions in all forms are popular in Chinese cookery but shallots are especially prized for their distinctive flavour. I think they complement fish beautifully. If you can't get shallots for this recipe you can use pickling onions instead. A firm, white fish such as cod, haddock or bass will work better than delicate ones such as plaice or sole. Plain steamed rice and a fresh green vegetable would go well with this dish.

Serves 4 to 6		
1 lb	450 g	fish fillets, preferably cod or haddock
1 teaspoon		salt
5 fl oz	150 ml	oil, preferably groundnut
10 oz	275 g	small shallots or pickling onions, peeled and left whole
1 tablespoon		fresh ginger, finely chopped
1 tablespoon		light soy sauce
1 tablespoon		dark soy sauce
2 teaspoons		sugar
2 tablespoons		dry sherry or rice wine
5 fl oz	150 ml	chicken stock

Pat the fish fillets dry using kitchen paper. Rub both sides with salt and then cut them into 1½ inch (3·5 cm) wide, diagonal strips. Set the fish aside for 20 minutes, then again pat them dry with kitchen paper. The salt will have extracted some of the excess moisture from the fish.

Heat the oil in a wok or large frying-pan. Then brown the fish in two batches, draining each cooked batch on kitchen paper. Drain all but 1 tablespoon of oil from the pan and discard the rest.

Re-heat the pan and add the shallots (or pickling onions) and ginger. Stir-fry them for 1 minute, and then add the rest of the ingredients. Bring this mixture to the boil, then turn the heat down to a simmer. Return the fish to the pan, cover it and braise the fish in the sauce for 2–3 minutes. Using a slotted spoon, gently remove the fish and shallots and arrange them on a warm platter. Then pour the sauce over the top and serve at once.

161

SWEET AND SOUR FISH

Region: eastern

Method: deep-frying

A sweet and sour sauce is a perfect foil for fish. The sugar and
vinegar in the sauce contrasts well with the rich flavour of the
fish. This Chinese dish is at its most impressive when a whole
fish is used but it can be just as successfully made with fish
fillets. The best fish to use are cod, haddock or sea bass. The
sauce can be made in advance and re-heated.

		Serves 4 to 6
1 lb	450 g	whole fish or fish fillets, preferably cod, haddock or sea bass
4 oz	110 g	carrots
4 oz	110 g	peas
4 oz	110 g	mange-tout, trimmed, or 1 green pepper (about 4 oz 110 g)
2 pints	1·1 ltr	oil, preferably groundnut (see Deep-fat fryers, page 34)
4 oz	110 g	cornflour
		Sauce
2 tablespoons		spring onions, finely chopped
1 tablespoon		ginger, finely chopped
10 fl oz	300 ml	Chicken Stock (page 59)
1 tablespoon		light soy sauce
2 tablespoons		dry sherry or rice wine
1½ tablespoons		tomato paste
2 tablespoons		cider vinegar or Chinese white rice vinegar
2 tablespoons		sugar
2 teaspoons		cornflour blended with 2 teaspoons water

If you are using fish fillets, select ones which are at least 1 inch
(2·5 cm) or more thick, and remove the skin. If you are using a
whole fish it should be cleaned and gutted, and the gills
removed. Either leave the head on as the Chinese do or remove it
if you prefer. Using a sharp knife or cleaver, make criss-cross
slashes across the top of the fish or each fillet. Do not cut right
through, but keep the fish or fillets intact.

Next prepare the vegetables. Peel and dice the carrots. Blanch
the carrots, peas and mange-tout or pepper in a pot of boiling

162

water for about 4 minutes each. Now plunge them into cold water and then drain them. Put all the blanched vegetables into a pot with all the sauce ingredients. Bring the mixture to a simmer and remove the pot from the heat.

Heat the oil in a deep-fat fryer or large wok until it is almost smoking. Coat the fish fillets or whole fish well with cornflour, shaking off any excess. Then deep-fry one of the fillets (or whole fish) until it is crisp and brown. Do the same with the other fillet. Drain on kitchen paper. Bring the sauce to a simmer. Arrange the fish fillets or whole fish on a warm serving platter and pour the re-heated sauce over the top. Serve at once.

STEAMED FISH
WITH GARLIC, SPRING ONIONS AND GINGER

Region: southern
Method: steaming

Steaming fish is a great southern Chinese tradition and it is my favourite method of cooking fish. Steaming brings out the purest flavours of the fish. Because it is such a gentle cooking technique, nothing masks the fresh taste of the fish, which also remains moist and tender. Ask your fishmonger for the freshest possible fish.

Serves 4		
12oz–1lb	350–450g	firm white fish fillets, such as cod or sole, or a whole fish such as sole
1 teaspoon		coarse sea salt
1 tablespoon		fresh ginger, finely chopped
Garnish		
2 tablespoons		spring onions, finely chopped
1 tablespoon		light soy sauce
1 tablespoon		oil, preferably groundnut
1 teaspoon		sesame oil
2		garlic cloves, peeled and thinly sliced

163

If you are using a whole fish, remove the gills. Pat the fish or fish fillets dry with kitchen paper. Rub with the salt on both sides, and then set aside for 30 minutes. This helps the flesh to firm up and draws out any excess moisture.

Set up a steamer or put a rack into a wok or deep pan. Fill it with about 2 inches (5 cm) of water. Bring the water to the boil, then reduce the heat to a low simmer. Put the fish on a plate and scatter the ginger evenly over the top. Put the plate of fish into the steamer or onto the rack. Cover the pan tightly and gently steam the fish until it is just cooked. Flat fish will take about 5 minutes to cook. Thicker fish or fillets such as sea bass will take 15 minutes.

Remove the plate of cooked fish and sprinkle on the spring onions and light soy sauce. Heat the two oils together in a small saucepan. When they are hot, add the garlic slices and brown them. Pour the garlic-oil mixture over the top of the fish. Serve at once.

FISH BALLS WITH BROCCOLI

Region: eastern

Method: poaching and stir-frying

We often made this dish in our family restaurant but usually just for the Chinese customers. My uncle thought his non-Chinese diners would not enjoy it. I remember how laborious it was, mincing the fish until it was smooth and like a paste. Now, thanks to modern kitchen equipment, this dish can be easily prepared at home in minutes. And I eventually discovered how much my European friends love this dish! Serve this with plain steamed rice and Hot and Sour Soup (page 75).

164

	Serves 4 to 6	
1 lb	450 g	fish fillets, preferably cod
1		egg white
1 teaspoon		salt
2 teaspoons		cornflour
2 teaspoons		sesame oil
1 lb	450 g	broccoli
1 oz	25 g	fresh ginger
2 oz	50 g	Parma ham, or lean English smoked bacon
1½ tablespoons		oil, preferably groundnut
1 tablespoon		light soy sauce
2 tablespoons		dry sherry or rice wine
10 fl oz	300 ml	Chicken Stock (page 59)
2 teaspoons		cornflour, blended with 2 teaspoons water

Remove the skin from the fish fillets and then cut them into small pieces about 1 inch (2·5 cm) square. Combine the fish, egg white, salt, cornflour and sesame oil in an electric blender or food processor, and blend the mixture until you have a smooth paste.

Bring a large pot of water to simmering point. Take spoonfuls of the fish paste and form the mixture into balls about 1 inch (2·5 cm) in diameter. Poach the fish balls in the boiling water until they float to the top. (This should take about 3–4 minutes.) Remove them with a slotted spoon and drain them on kitchen paper.

Divide the broccoli heads into small florets. Peel the skin off the stems as it is often fibrous and stringy, and then cut them into thin slices at a slight diagonal. This will ensure that the stems cook evenly with the florets. Bring a pot of water to the boil, add the broccoli florets and stems and cook for about 5 minutes. Then drain them, plunge into cold water, and drain again. Finely shred the ginger and the ham or bacon and set them aside.

Heat a wok or large frying-pan. When it is hot, add the oil and heat it. Then add the broccoli, ginger, ham or bacon and soy sauce and stir-fry for 1 minute. Then add the sherry or rice wine, stock and the cornflour mixture. Bring to the boil and then add the poached fish balls. Stir over a high heat for 1 minute to mix, and then turn the mixture onto a serving platter. Serve at once.

165

STIR-FRIED SQUID WITH VEGETABLES

Region: southern

Method: blanching and stir-frying

Squid cooked the Chinese way is both tender and tasty. The secret is to use very hot water for blanching it and then a minimum amount of cooking time—just enough for the squid to firm up slightly. Too long will make it tough. Unlike most seafood, frozen squid can be quite good and when properly cooked it is sometimes impossible to tell it from fresh. This simple recipe can also be prepared with prawns if you find squid difficult to obtain. Serve this dish with Hot and Sour Soup (page 75) and plain rice.

Serves 4		
12 oz	350 g	squid, fresh or frozen
2 oz	50 g	red or green pepper (about ½)
1 tablespoon		oil, preferably groundnut
4 oz	110 g	mange-tout, trimmed
2½ fl oz	70 ml	chicken stock
2 teaspoons		dry sherry or rice wine
1½ tablespoons		oyster sauce
1 teaspoon		cornflour, blended with 1 teaspoon water

The edible parts of the squid are the tentacles and the body. If it has not been cleaned by your fishmonger you can do it yourself by pulling the head and tentacles away from the body. Then pull off and discard the skin. Using a small sharp knife, split the body in half. Remove the transparent bony section. Wash the halves thoroughly under cold running water and then pull off and discard the skin. Cut the tentacles from the head, cutting just above the eye. (You may also have to remove the polyp or beak from the base of the ring of tentacles.) If you are using frozen squid make sure it is properly thawed before cooking it.

Right: Stir-fried Fish with Peas (page 160) and Shredded Chicken with Sesame Seeds (page 124)

Cut the squid meat into 1½inch (3·5cm) strips. Blanch the strips and the tentacles in a large pot of boiling water for 30 seconds. The squid will firm up slightly and turn an opaque white colour. Remove and drain in a colander.

Cut the pepper into 1½inch (3·5cm) strips. Heat a wok or large frying-pan until it is hot. Then add the oil and let it get hot. Add the pepper strips and mange-tout and stir-fry for 1 minute. Then add the rest of the ingredients, except the squid, and bring the mixture to the boil. Give it a quick stir, then add the squid and mix it in well. Cook for 30 seconds more. Serve at once.

STIR-FRIED SCALLOPS WITH PIG'S KIDNEYS

Region: western

Method: stir-frying

This regional dish was a favourite in our family. My mother varied the traditional recipe a little by adding oyster sauce. Be assured that scallops and kidneys go very well together, even though they may seem an unlikely combination. If the kidneys are properly prepared their texture is quite similar to that of scallops, and their two quite different flavours blend deliciously together. The richness of this dish means that it is best for special occasions. It goes very well with plain steamed rice and Braised Cauliflower with Oyster Sauce (page 198).

Left: Sichuan Prawns in Chilli Sauce (page 174) and Stir-fried Pork with Spring Onions (page 81)

169

	Serves 4	
8oz	225g	pig's kidneys
½ teaspoon		bicarbonate of soda
1 teaspoon		cider vinegar or Chinese white rice vinegar
½ teaspoon		salt
4oz	110g	scallops, including the corals
2 tablespoons		oil, preferably groundnut
1 teaspoon		fresh ginger, finely chopped
2 teaspoons		spring onions, finely chopped
2 teaspoons		dry sherry or rice wine
1 tablespoon		light soy sauce
½ teaspoon		sugar
¼ teaspoon		salt
½ teaspoon		cornflour, blended with 2 teaspoons of stock or water

Using a sharp knife, remove the thin outer kidney membrane. Then, with a sharp cleaver or knife, split the kidney in half lengthways by cutting horizontally as described on page 39. Now cut away the small knobs of fat and any tough membrane surrounding them. Score the top surface of the kidneys in a crisscross pattern (see page 73), then cut the halved kidneys into thin slices. Toss the kidney slices in the bicarbonate of soda and let them sit for about 20 minutes. Then rinse them thoroughly with cold water and toss them in the vinegar and salt. Put them into a colander and let them drain for at least 30 minutes, preferably longer.

Cut the scallops into slices and put them in a small bowl. Blot the kidney slices dry with kitchen paper. Heat a wok or large frying-pan over high heat until it is hot. Add half of the oil and then the scallops. Stir-fry them for about 30 seconds and then add the ginger and spring onions. Stir-fry for another 30 seconds and then remove them with a slotted spoon.

Immediately re-heat the wok or pan and then add the rest of the oil. Stir-fry the kidneys for 1 minute and then add all the other ingredients except the cornflour mixture. Stir-fry for 1 minute and then return the scallops to the pan. Add the cornflour mixture and stir for a minute or so. Turn onto a warm serving platter and serve at once.

SICHUAN-STYLE SCALLOPS

Region: western
Method: stir-frying

Scallops are a favourite with the Chinese. We love them in two forms, fresh and dried. Stir-frying works especially well with scallops because if they are overcooked they become tough. Just five minutes' stir-frying, as in this recipe, is quite sufficient to cook them thoroughly without robbing them of their sweet flavour. They are particularly tasty prepared with this spicy Sichuan sauce. This dish goes well with plain rice and Ham and Bean Sprout Soup (page 64).

Serves 4	
1 tablespoon	oil, preferably groundnut
1 teaspoon	fresh ginger, finely chopped
2 teaspoons	spring onions, finely chopped
8oz 225g	scallops, including the corals
Sauce	
2 teaspoons	dry sherry or rice wine
2 teaspoons	light soy sauce
1–2 teaspoons	chilli bean sauce
2 teaspoons	tomato paste
1 teaspoon	sugar
1 teaspoon	sesame oil

Heat a wok or large frying-pan until it is hot. Add the oil and let it get hot. Add the ginger and spring onions and stir-fry quickly. Next add the scallops and stir-fry them for 30 seconds. Then add all the sauce ingredients except the sesame oil. Continue to stir-fry for 4 minutes until the scallops are firm and thoroughly coated with the sauce. Now add the sesame oil and stir-fry for another minute. Serve at once.

DEEP-FRIED OYSTERS

Region: southern
Method: deep-frying

Oysters are a favourite of the Hong Kong Chinese. The variety found in the South China Sea is quite large and they are usually cut up, dipped in batter and deep-fried. The Chinese never eat oysters raw, believing them to be unhealthy when uncooked. This dish is based on a recipe given to me by a friend who is a chef in the fishing village of Lau Fau Shan in the New Territories in Hong Kong. I have added a Western touch to it by using breadcrumbs on top of the batter. This dish makes an excellent cocktail snack.

Serves 4		
8oz	225g	oysters, shelled
1		small egg
1 tablespoon		cornflour
2 teaspoons		water
1 teaspoon		baking powder
½ teaspoon		salt
½ teaspoon		oil, preferably groundnut
1–2oz	25–50g	toasted breadcrumbs
1 pint	570ml	oil, preferably groundnut (see Deep-fat fryers, page 34)
Garnish		
		lemon wedges or
		Roasted Salt and Pepper (page 30)

Drain the oysters in a colander and then pat them dry with kitchen paper. Prepare a batter by mixing the egg, cornflour, water, baking powder, salt and ½ teaspoon of oil together in a small bowl. Let the mixture sit for about 20 minutes. Then dip some of the oysters into the batter and then in the breadcrumbs. Set them on a plate. Prepare all the oysters in this way.

Heat the oil in a deep-fat fryer or large wok. When it is almost smoking, deep-fry the coated oysters until they are golden brown. (This should take just a few minutes.) Drain them on kitchen paper and serve with Roasted Salt and Pepper (page 30) or lemon wedges.

PRAWNS

Most prawns in this country are sold cooked, either shelled or unshelled. If at all possible try to get large uncooked prawns, known as Pacific or king prawns, for Chinese cooking. Most Chinese grocers and many fishmongers and supermarkets stock them frozen and in the shell, and they are quite reasonably priced. If you can only get cooked pink prawns, buy the biggest and best you can find and cook them just long enough to heat them through.

To peel prawns
First twist off the head and pull off the tail. It should then be quite easy to peel off the shell, and with it the tiny legs. If you are using large, uncooked king prawns make a shallow cut down the back of each prawn and remove the fine digestive cord which runs the length of the prawn. Wash the prawns before you use them.

BRAISED PRAWNS

Region: northern
Method: braising

This is one of the simplest prawn recipes in Chinese cookery. It takes only minutes to prepare. If you are using cooked prawns reduce the cooking time so the prawns just heat through.

Serves 4	
8oz 225g	prawns, preferably uncooked
Sauce	
2½floz 70ml	chicken stock
2 teaspoons	dry sherry or rice wine
¼ teaspoon	salt
2 teaspoons	sugar
1 teaspoon	cider vinegar or Chinese black rice vinegar
2 tablespoons	spring onions, finely chopped
2 teaspoons	fresh ginger, finely chopped
½ teaspoon	cornflour, blended with ½ teaspoon water

173

Peel the prawns and, if you are using large uncooked ones, cut them to remove the fine digestive cord (see page 173). Wash the prawns and pat them dry with kitchen paper.

Combine the sauce ingredients in a wok or large frying-pan. Bring it to a simmer and then add the prawns. Braise the prawns slowly over a low heat for 3–4 minutes. Serve at once.

SICHUAN PRAWNS IN CHILLI SAUCE

Region: western
Method: stir-frying

Sichuan cooking is becoming increasingly popular. This is one of the best-known dishes from that area, but beware of versions which err on the side of excessive sweetness. This dish is quick and easy and makes a wholesome and delicious meal served with a stir-fried vegetable and steamed rice.

Serves 4	
8oz 225g	prawns, preferably uncooked
2 teaspoons	oil, preferably groundnut
2 teaspoons	fresh ginger, finely chopped
1 tablespoon	spring onions, finely chopped
Sauce	
2 teaspoons	tomato paste
1 teaspoon	chilli bean sauce, or ½ teaspoon chilli powder
¼ teaspoon	salt
½ teaspoon	sugar
¼ teaspoon	sesame oil

174

Peel the prawns and, if you are using large uncooked ones, cut them to remove the fine digestive cord (see page 173). Wash them and pat them dry with kitchen paper. Heat a wok or large frying-pan until it is hot. Add the oil and then the ginger and spring onions. Stir-fry quickly and then add the prawns. Stir-fry the prawns for about 30 seconds. Add the sauce ingredients and continue to stir-fry for another 5 minutes over a high heat. Serve at once.

BRAISED PRAWNS
IN SPRING ONION AND GINGER SAUCE

Region: southern

Method: braising

This method of quick braising is very simple. Street vendors or sidewalk cafes throughout southern China sell this dish because it is uncomplicated and takes only minutes to prepare. It is also excellent cold and makes a very nice dish for an exotic picnic. Serve as part of a meal with Country-style Chicken (page 122) and rice.

Serves 4	
8oz 225g	prawns, preferably uncooked
Braising sauce	
1½ tablespoons	spring onions, finely chopped
2 teaspoons	fresh ginger, finely chopped
1 tablespoon	dry sherry or rice wine
1 tablespoon	light soy sauce
2½floz 70ml	chicken stock

Peel the prawns and, if you are using large uncooked ones, cut them to remove the fine digestive cord (see page 173). Wash the prawns and pat them dry with kitchen paper.

Combine the braising sauce ingredients together in a wok or large saucepan and bring the mixture to the boil. Turn the heat down to low and simmer for 2 minutes. Then add the prawns and stir, mixing them in well. Cover the pan and braise for 2 minutes. Serve at once or allow to cool and serve cold.

175

SWEET AND SOUR PRAWNS

Region: eastern

Method: stir-frying and simmering

This is a very popular Chinese dish. The sweet and pungent flavours of the sauce combine well with the firm and succulent prawns. It is simple to make, and can be served as part of a Chinese meal or on its own as a starter for a European meal.

Serves 4		
8oz	225g	prawns, preferably uncooked
4oz	110g	waterchestnuts, tinned (drained weight) or fresh
3oz	75g	red or green pepper
2		spring onions
2 teaspoons		oil, preferably groundnut
2 teaspoons		garlic, finely chopped
Sauce		
2½floz	70ml	chicken stock
1 tablespoon		dry sherry or rice wine
2 teaspoons		light soy sauce
1 tablespoon		tomato paste
1 tablespoon		cider vinegar or Chinese white rice vinegar
1 tablespoon		sugar
2 teaspoons		cornflour blended with 2 teaspoons water

Peel the prawns and, if you are using large uncooked ones, cut them to remove the fine digestive cord (see page 173). Wash them and pat dry with kitchen paper. Slice the waterchestnuts, dice the pepper, and slice the spring onions diagonally into 1½inch (3·5cm) pieces.

Heat a wok or large frying-pan. When it is hot add the oil and stir-fry the prawns for 1 minute. Remove them with a slotted spoon and drain on kitchen paper. Add the garlic and spring onions to the pan and stir-fry them for a few seconds. Then add the pepper and the fresh waterchestnuts if you are using them. Stir-fry for 30 seconds, and then add the sauce ingredients. Bring the mixture to the boil and simmer for 4 minutes. If you are using tinned waterchestnuts, add these now. Boil over a high heat for another 30 seconds. Serve immediately with steamed rice.

STIR-FRIED PRAWNS WITH EGGS

Region: southern
Method: stir-frying

This dish is commonly known in the West as Egg Fuyung. It is very popular because it tastes delicious, is easy to make and uses familiar ingredients. You can substitute crab, fish or even minced pork or beef for the prawns. However, I think it is at its best made with good quality prawns. This distinctive dish goes well with Hot and Sour Soup (page 75) and Stir-fried Beef with Ginger (page 96).

Serves 4	
8oz 225g	prawns, preferably uncooked
1	small egg white
1 teaspoon	cornflour
2	large eggs, beaten
1 teaspoon	sesame oil
3 tablespoons	chicken stock or water
2 teaspoons	dry sherry or rice wine
½ teaspoon	salt
2 teaspoons	light soy sauce
½ teaspoon	sugar
2 tablespoons	oil, preferably groundnut
Garnish	
1 tablespoon	spring onions, finely chopped

Peel the prawns and, if you are using large, uncooked ones, cut them to remove the fine digestive cord (see page 173). Wash the prawns and pat them dry with kitchen paper. Put the prawns into a bowl, and mix in the egg white and cornflour. Let the mixture sit in the refrigerator for 20 minutes. Combine the eggs, sesame oil and the rest of the ingredients except the cooking oil in a bowl.

Heat a wok or large frying-pan and then add half the oil. When it is hot and almost smoking add the prawns and stir-fry them for 2 minutes. Remove them with a slotted spoon. Rinse the wok clean, then put the rest of the oil into the pan. Quickly add the egg mixture. Stir-fry them for 1 minute or until the egg begins to set. Return the prawns to the egg mixture and continue to stir-fry for 1 minute more. Garnish with spring onions and serve.

177

PEKING PRAWNS

Region: northern

Method: shallow-frying

This is my adaptation of a favourite northern Chinese prawn dish. The use of breadcrumbs, is, of course, a Western touch but one which works perfectly for this recipe. It is so simple to make that it presents no problem even if you are serving it at a dinner party. The shallow-frying, however, must be done at the last minute.

Serves 4		
8oz	225g	unshelled prawns, preferably uncooked
1oz	25g	plain flour
1oz	25g	toasted breadcrumbs
1		egg
½ teaspoon		sesame oil
¼ teaspoon		salt
5floz	150ml	oil, preferably groundnut
Dipping sauce		
1½ tablespoons		hoisin sauce
¼ teaspoon		sesame oil

Peel the prawns but leave the tail shell on. Using a sharp knife, split each prawn lengthways but leave it still attached at the back. Open the prawn out so that it splays out flat in a butterfly shape. If you are using large uncooked prawns, remove the fine digestive cord. Pat the prawns dry with kitchen paper.

Spread out the flour and breadcrumbs on separate plates. Beat the egg in another small bowl, add the sesame oil and salt and mix well.

Heat the oil in a wok or deep frying-pan. Dip the prawns into the flour, then into the egg mixture, and finally into the breadcrumbs, shaking off any excess. When the oil is hot, shallow-fry the prawns in two batches, and then drain them on kitchen paper.

Mix the hoisin sauce with the sesame oil in a small dish. Serve this with the hot prawns.

DEEP-FRIED PRAWNS

Region: eastern
Method: deep-frying

One of the things I most dislike about deep-fried foods in many Chinese restaurants outside China is the use of a dense batter coating. Such a thick coating soaks up the oil and makes the food very greasy. I prefer a light, almost transparent coating of batter. This way prawns will be tender and sweet and the flavour will not be obstructed. Try to obtain uncooked prawns for this recipe if you can as the flavour will be much better.

Serves 4	
8 oz 225g	prawns, preferably uncooked
1 pint 570ml	oil, preferably groundnut (see Deep-fat fryers, page 34)
Batter	
1	small egg
1 tablespoon	cornflour
2 teaspoons	cold water
1 teaspoon	sesame oil
1 teaspoon	salt
2 tablespoons	spring onions, finely chopped
Garnish	
	lemon wedges or
	Roasted Salt and Pepper (page 30)

Peel the prawns and, if you are using large uncooked ones, cut them to remove the fine digestive cord (see page 173). Wash them and pat them dry with kitchen paper. Combine the batter ingredients in a small bowl and beat them well until they are all thoroughly blended.

Put the oil into a deep-fat fryer or large wok and heat it until it almost smokes. Put the prawns into the batter. Then, using a slotted spoon, remove them from the batter leaving them with just a light coating. Now deep-fry them for about 2 minutes, and then drain on kitchen paper. Serve the cooked prawns with Roasted Salt and Pepper (page 30) or with lemon wedges.

179

SIZZLING RICE PRAWNS

Region: western
Method: stir-frying and deep-frying

This is a dramatic dish which is sure to earn you compliments. It is moderately easy to make but requires organisation and some experience of Chinese cooking. Attempt this dish after you have cooked some of the other simpler recipes in this book. I'm sure that once you have tried it, it will become a regular feature of your repertoire. The key to success is that the prawn sauce mixture and rice cake should both be fairly hot. You will then be sure to achieve a dramatic sizzle when the two are combined. Serve Sizzling Rice Prawns with Cold Marinaded Bean Sprouts (page 194) and Stir-fried Chinese Greens (page 204).

Serves 6 to 8	
1 lb 450g	prawns, preferably uncooked
2 tablespoons	oil, preferably groundnut
2 teaspoons	fresh ginger, finely chopped
1 tablespoon	garlic, finely chopped
1½ tablespoons	spring onions, finely chopped
2 pints 1·1 ltr	oil, preferably groundnut (see Deep-fat fryers, page 34)
1	rice cake, made according to the recipe on page 221, broken into pieces
Sauce	
4 oz 110g	green or red pepper (about 1), diced
1 tablespoon	cider vinegar or Chinese black rice vinegar
1 tablespoon	dark soy sauce
1 tablespoon	chilli bean sauce or 2 dried red chillis
1½ tablespoons	tomato paste
1 teaspoon	light soy sauce
1½ tablespoons	dry sherry or rice wine
1 teaspoon	sugar
10 fl oz 300 ml	Chicken Stock (page 59)
1 tablespoon	cornflour, blended with 1 tablespoon water

Peel the prawns and discard the shells. Using a small sharp knife split the prawns in half but leave them still attached at the back so that they splay out like butterflies. If you are using large uncooked

180

prawns, remove the fine digestive cord. Rinse the prawns well in cold water and blot them dry with kitchen paper.

Heat a wok or large frying-pan until it is quite hot. Add the 2 tablespoons of oil. Let it heat for a few seconds until it is almost smoking. Add the ginger and stir it quickly for a few seconds, then add the garlic and spring onions. A few seconds later add the prawns and stir-fry them quickly until they become firm. (This takes about 30 seconds.) Then add all the sauce ingredients except the cornflour mixture. Bring the mixture to the boil, remove it from the heat and add the cornflour mixture. Bring back to the boil and then reduce the heat to a very slow simmer. The prawn sauce may be cooked ahead up to this point and re-heated when required.

Now you are ready to fry the rice cake. Heat the 2 pints (1·1 litres) of oil in a deep-fat fryer or large wok until it is nearly smoking. Drop in a small piece of rice to test the heat. It should bubble all over and immediately come up to the surface. Now deep-fry the pieces of rice cake for about 1–2 minutes until they puff up and brown slightly. Remove them immediately with a slotted spoon and set them to drain on a plate lined with kitchen paper. Then quickly transfer the pieces to a platter and pour the hot prawn and sauce mixture over them. It should sizzle dramatically. Once you are skilled at preparing this dish, you can attempt to perform this trick at the dinner table. (The oil used for deep-frying the rice cake can be saved and re-used once it has cooled. Filter it through coffee filter papers before storing it.)

CRABS

Choosing a crab
Where possible the Chinese prefer to buy crabs live and cook them when they are needed. In this country most crabs are sold already cooked, so take care to buy one which is fresh and does not have a fishy smell. The heavier the crab the better.

Cooking live crabs
Bring a large pot of water to the boil, add 2 teaspoons of salt and then put in the crab. Cover the pot and cook the crab for about 5–7 minutes until it turns bright red. Remove with a slotted spoon and drain in a colander. Leave to cool.

Removing cooked crabmeat
Extracting the crabmeat is not difficult but it takes a little time and patience. Follow these steps:

181

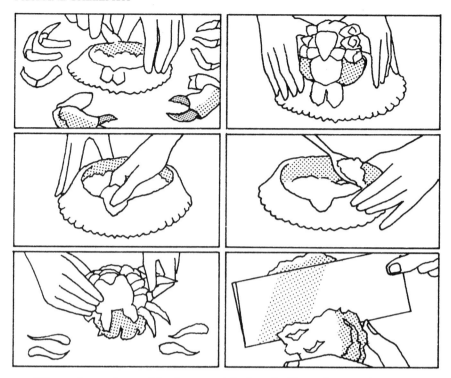

1   Place the crab upside down with the shell on the work-top. Using your fingers, twist the claws from the body. Do the same with the rest of the legs. They should come off quite easily.

2   Now twist the bony tail flap on the underside of the crab and discard it. With your fingers, prise the body from the main shell.

3   Remove and discard the small, bag-like stomach sac and its appendages which are located just behind the crab's mouth.

4   With a teaspoon, scoop out the brown crabmeat.

5   Pull the soft feathery gills, which look a little like fingers, away from the body and discard them.

6   Using a cleaver or heavy knife, split the crab body in half, and, using a knife, fork or skewer, scrape out all the white crabmeat from the body and from the claws and legs.
    Combine the brown and white crabmeat.

Tinned or frozen crabmeat

If you are using frozen crabmeat, thaw it thoroughly before you use it. Tinned crabmeat has a fishy odour. If you are forced to use it, rinse it carefully first in cold water.

CRAB IN EGG CUSTARD

Region: northern
Method: steaming

There are many delicious and meaty varieties of crab which are harvested off the coast of northern China. A favourite way to prepare them is to steam them whole and then crack them at the table and dip them in vinegar and sugar. In this northern dish, cooked crab is mixed with a light egg custard and then steamed. The result is a sort of velvet- or satin-textured custard. Although tinned or frozen crabmeat can be used I recommend using fresh cooked crabmeat for this dish. It makes a satisfying main course with rice and Curried Sweetcorn Soup with Chicken (page 68).

	Serves 4	
8oz	225g	cooked white crabmeat
	Custard	
4		eggs
10floz	300ml	Chicken Stock (page 59)
1 teaspoon		fresh ginger, finely chopped
3 tablespoons		spring onions, finely chopped
1 tablespoon		dry sherry or rice wine
½ teaspoon		freshly ground black pepper
1 teaspoon		salt
	Garnish	
2 teaspoons		dark soy sauce (optional)

Mix the custard ingredients in a bowl and then add the cooked crabmeat. Mix well to blend all the ingredients together. Put the mixture into a deep dish.

Set up a steamer or put a rack into a wok or deep pan. Pour about 1½–2 inches (3·5–5 cm) of water into the pan, and bring the water to the boil. Now place the dish of custard into the steamer or onto the rack. Cover the pan tightly and lower the heat. Gently steam for 25 minutes or until the custard has set. Remove the custard and pour the soy sauce over the top. Serve at once.

183

CRAB WITH BLACK BEAN SAUCE

Region: southern
Method: stir-frying

This recipe can only be made with fresh crabs in the shell since the shell has to protect the delicate crabmeat during the stir-frying process. If you can't get crab in the shell use prawns instead. I have added some minced pork which helps to stretch the crab which can be expensive. (Of course you can always use just crab if you are feeling extravagant.) I love to eat this dish with plain steamed rice and Braised Spicy Aubergines (page 190).

Serves 4 to 6	
3 lb 1·4 kg	freshly cooked crab in the shell
2 tablespoons	oil, preferably groundnut
2 tablespoons	black beans, coarsely chopped
2 teaspoons	garlic, finely chopped
2 teaspoons	fresh ginger, finely chopped
2 tablespoons	spring onions, finely chopped
8 oz 225 g	minced pork
1 tablespoon	dry sherry or rice wine
15 fl oz 400 ml	Chicken Stock (page 59) or water
2	eggs, beaten
1 teaspoon	sesame oil

Remove the tail-flap, stomach sac and feathery gills from the crab as described on page 182. Using a heavy knife or cleaver, cut the crab, shell included, into large pieces.

Heat the oil in a wok or large frying-pan. When it is hot, add the black beans, garlic, ginger and spring onions and stir-fry quickly. Then add the pork and stir-fry for one minute. Add the crab pieces and the rest of the ingredients except the eggs and the sesame oil. Stir-fry the mixture over a high heat for about 10 minutes. Combine the eggs with sesame oil and then mix this into the crab mixture, stirring slowly. There should be light strands of egg trailing over the crab mixture. Turn it on to a large, warm serving platter and serve. It is perfectly good manners to eat the crab with your fingers, but I suggest you have a large bowl of water decorated with lemon slices on the table so that your guests can rinse their fingers.

184

VEGETABLES

Even as a child I loved vegetables. In this regard I am certainly very much Chinese. My European friends often refuse to eat vegetables and not without reason. Many Westerners overcook them, draining them of their natural flavours and colours and rendering them limp and lifeless. In China vegetables are never overcooked. The techniques of stir-frying, blanching, deep-frying and even braising all preserve the flavours of vegetables while retaining their crispness and texture. The trick is to know when to stop cooking. Simplicity is another factor. The Chinese rarely cover their vegetables with heavy sauces, preferring the natural tastes and textures. But vegetables are rarely eaten raw unless they are pickled; even lettuce is cooked, and cold Chinese salads always consist of cooked or pickled vegetables too. All Chinese meals include one or two vegetable dishes, since apart from being highly nutritious they add colour and texture to a well balanced meal.

Westerners generally agree that vegetables cooked in the Chinese fashion are delectable. This excellence in the preparation of vegetables is, of course, based on thousands of years of culinary experience. China is also fortunate in having a vast array of native edible plants, supplemented in recent centuries by foreign imports such as tomatoes, carrots, sweet potatoes and various types of marrow.

The Buddhist–Taoist tradition is one source of the Chinese people's expertise with vegetables. Buddhists avoid meat because they abhor killing any living animal since this contradicts their doctrine of reincarnation. Taoists are vegetarian because they believe that to kill animals is to shatter the essential unity of the universe. For the past 1500 years, therefore, these minority groups have promoted vegetarianism, and their chefs have made imaginative and creative use of vegetables. They have concocted imitations of meat, fish and seafood dishes which are so realistic and delicious that people are hard-put to distinguish the replica from the real thing. Because vegetables are not good sources of protein, the soya bean, that miracle protein food which is found everywhere in China, was pressed into service. Beancurd, soyabean milk and other beancurd products became staples in the vegetarian diet. Instead of poultry or meat broths, the liquid left from soaking dried Chinese black mushrooms provided the base for sauces and soups. All of these innovations slowly spread beyond the Buddhist and Taoist groups to the much larger society of non-vegetarian Chinese.

Technique is especially important in vegetable cookery. We cook with a minimum of water or oil to obtain the best results. The use of high heat and rapid cooking seals in the flavours and nutrients but retains texture and crispness. Blanching vegetables in

186

hot water and then plunging them into cold water after brief cooking ensures that the natural flavour and colour of vegetables is retained. This process is particularly important when stir-frying harder vegetables such as carrots or broccoli which need to be partly cooked before being stir-fried.

Deep-frying is another favourite method of cooking vegetables, since hot oil seals in the flavours and gives vegetables a crunchy texture. Whatever technique you use I hope you will discover the same pleasure that the Chinese have been deriving from vegetables for centuries. Most of the vegetables used in the following recipes are well known in this country. I have, however, included some which may be less familiar.

Aubergines

Also known as eggplant. These pleasing purple-skinned vegetables range in size from the huge fat ones which are easy to find in all greengrocers, to the small thin variety which the Chinese prefer because they have a more delicate flavour.

Do not peel aubergines since the skin preserves their texture, shape and taste. Large aubergines should be cut according to the recipe, sprinkled with a little salt and left to sit for 20 minutes. They should then be rinsed and any liquid blotted dry with kitchen paper. This process extracts excess moisture from the vegetable before it is cooked.

Bean sprouts

Bean sprouts are now widely available in greengrocers, supermarkets and Chinese grocers. They are the sprouts of the green mung bean, although some Chinese grocers also stock yellow soyabean sprouts which are much larger. Bean sprouts should always be very fresh and crunchy. They will keep for several days wrapped in a plastic bag and stored in the vegetable compartment of a refrigerator. Never use tinned bean sprouts as these have been pre-cooked and are soggy and tasteless.

To grow bean sprouts

It is very easy to grow your own bean sprouts. Dried mung beans (sometimes spelt moong) are obtainable from supermarkets, Asian grocers and health food shops. You will need to obtain or devise a perforated flat surface. An old tin plate or thin metal pan punched with holes, or a bamboo steamer are all ideal. You will also need two pieces of cheesecloth and 1 oz (25 g) dried green mung beans.

187

Wash the beans several times in water. Then leave them to soak in lukewarm water for 8 hours or overnight. Once soaking is complete, rinse the beans again under warm running water until the water runs clear. Dampen the cheesecloth and spread one piece over the tin lid, pan or steamer. Spread the beans over the cloth and sprinkle them with more lukewarm water. Cover the beans with the second piece of cheesecloth and then put them in a warm, dark place. Keep them moist by sprinkling them with water over the next few days. In 3 days you should have white crisp sprouts ready for use.

Chinese broccoli

Chinese broccoli or *gai lan (Brassica oleracea capitata)* does not taste like European broccoli (calabrese). It is very crunchy and slightly bitter and is more like Swiss chard in flavour. It has deep, olive green leaves and sometimes has white flowers. It is usually only available at Chinese grocers. If you can find it, look for stems which are firm and leaves which look fresh and green. It is prepared in exactly the same way as calabrese and should be stored in a plastic bag in the vegetable compartment of the refrigerator where it will keep for several days. If you cannot find Chinese broccoli use calabrese instead.

Chinese flowering cabbage

Chinese flowering cabbage (*Brassica rapa*) is usually known by its more familiar Cantonese name, *choi sam*. It has yellowish green leaves and may have small yellow flowers which are eaten along with the leaves and stems. It is obtainable from Chinese grocers and is delicious stir-fried.

Chinese greens

Chinese greens (*Brassica chinensis*) is an attractive vegetable with a long, smooth, milky-white stem and large, crinkly, dark green leaves. It looks similar to Swiss chard, and has been grown in China for centuries where it is known as *bok choi*. In the West it is sometimes called Chinese white cabbage or Chinese chard, and it has a light fresh taste and requires little cooking. It is usually available from Chinese grocers. Swiss chard or spinach can be substituted if you cannot obtain Chinese greens.

Chinese leaves

Chinese leaves (*Brassica pekinensis*) look rather like a large, tightly packed Cos lettuce with firm, pale green, crinkled leaves. It is sometimes known as Chinese or Peking cabbage, and is widely available in greengrocers, supermarkets and Chinese grocers. This is a delicious crunchy vegetable with a distinctive but mild taste. If you cannot find it use English white cabbage instead.

Chinese white radish (*mooli*)

Chinese white radish is known better in this country as *mooli*. It is a winter radish from Asia which can withstand long cooking without disintegrating, so it absorbs the flavour of a sauce yet retains its distinctive radish taste and texture. It is long and white and rather like a carrot in shape but usually very much larger. It must be peeled before it is used. Chinese white radish can be bought in many supermarkets and greengrocers (under the name *mooli*), and in Asian and Chinese grocers. Look for ones which are firm, heavy and unblemished. They should be slightly translucent inside and not tough and fibrous. Store in a plastic bag in the vegetable compartment of your refrigerator where they will keep for over a week. If you cannot find white radish use turnips instead.

Shallots

Shallots are mild-flavoured members of the onion family. They are small—about the size of pickling onions—with copper-red skins. They have a distinctive onion taste without being as strong or overpowering as ordinary onions, and I think they are an excellent substitute for Chinese onions which are unobtainable here. They are expensive but a few go a long way. Buy them at good greengrocers, supermarkets and delicatessens. Keep them in a cool, dry place (not the refrigerator) and peel them as you would an onion. If you cannot find shallots use pickling onions or spring onions.

Spinach

European varieties of spinach are quite different from those used in China, although they make satisfactory substitutes for the real thing. Spinach is most commonly stir-fried, so frozen spinach is obviously unsuitable. Chinese water spinach (*Ipomoea aquatica*) is available in some greengrocers and in Chinese grocers. It has hollow stems and delicate, green, pointed leaves, lighter in colour than common spinach and with a milder taste. It should be cooked when it is very fresh, preferably on the day on which it is bought.

189

BRAISED SPICY AUBERGINES

Region: western

Method: stir-frying and braising

Aubergines are one of my favourite vegetables. I like their colour, taste and texture. Their subtle flavour is receptive to a good zesty sauce, such as this one from western China. It's worth trying to get the small, long thin Chinese aubergines for their sweet taste. However, this recipe also works perfectly well with the large European variety. The Chinese prefer to leave the skin on because it holds the aubergine together throughout the cooking and because the skins are tender, tasty and nutritious.

Two techniques are employed here: a quick stir-frying to blend the seasonings, and braising which cooks the aubergines and makes a sauce in which the aubergines are served. The result is a tender and distinctively flavoured vegetable dish.

Serves 4	
1 lb 450g	**aubergines**
2 teaspoons	**salt**
1 tablespoon	**oil**
1 tablespoon	**garlic, finely chopped**
1 tablespoon	**fresh ginger, finely chopped**
2 tablespoons	**spring onions, finely chopped**
2 tablespoons	**dark soy sauce**
1–2 teaspoons	**chilli bean sauce, or 1 dried red chilli**
1 tablespoon	**whole yellow bean sauce**
1 tablespoon	**sugar**
10 floz 300ml	**water**
Optional garnish	
2 tablespoons	**green spring onion tops, chopped**

Roll-cut the Chinese aubergines (see page 39), or if you are using the regular large variety, trim and cut them into 1 inch (2·5 cm) cubes. Sprinkle the cubes with salt and leave them in a sieve to drain for 20 minutes. Then rinse them under cold running water and pat them dry with kitchen paper.

190

Heat a wok or large frying-pan to a moderate heat. Add the oil and let it heat up for a few seconds. Then add the aubergines, garlic, ginger and spring onions and stir-fry them for 1 minute until they are thoroughly mixed together. Then add the rest of the ingredients. Turn the heat down and cook uncovered for 10–15 minutes until the aubergine is tender, stirring occasionally.

Return the heat to high and continue to stir until the liquid has been reduced and has thickened slightly. Turn the mixture onto a serving dish and garnish with the chopped spring onion tops.

DEEP-FRIED GREEN BEANS
Region: western
Method: deep-frying and stir-frying

This tasty dish originated in western China, as its seasonings indicate. The traditional recipe calls for Chinese asparagus or long beans but I have found runner beans equally suitable. The beans are deep-fried to transform their texture but they should remain green and not be overcooked. (Deep-frying merely gives them a chewy instead of a crunchy texture.) After deep-frying, the beans are then stir-fried in an array of spices to create a delectable dish. They should be slightly oily but if they are too oily for your taste you can blot them with kitchen paper before stir-frying them. For best results serve them as soon as they are cooked.

Serves 2 to 4	
1 pint 570ml	oil (see Deep-fat fryers, page 34)
1lb 450g	runner beans, trimmed and sliced
1 tablespoon	garlic, finely chopped
1 tablespoon	fresh ginger, finely chopped
2 tablespoons	spring onions, finely chopped
4	dried red chillis
1 tablespoon	whole yellow bean sauce
1 tablespoon	dry sherry or rice wine
1 tablespoon	dark soy sauce
1 teaspoon	sugar
1 tablespoon	water

191

Heat the oil in a deep-fat fryer or large wok until it is fairly hot. When a single bean is dropped in the oil, it should bubble all over. Deep-fry half the beans until they are slightly wrinkled, which should take about 3–4 minutes. Remove the beans and drain them. Deep-fry the second batch in the same way.

Transfer about 1 tablespoon of the oil in which you have cooked the beans to a clean wok or frying-pan. (The rest can be retained for future use in cooking vegetables.) Add the garlic, ginger and spring onions and stir-fry quickly. Add the chillis and stir-fry them for about 30 seconds until they turn black. Remove the chillis, and then add all the other ingredients. Stir-fry the mixture for a few seconds, and then add the cooked, drained beans. Mix well until all the beans are thoroughly coated with the spicy mixture. Serve as soon as the beans have heated through.

BRAISED BEANCURD WITH MUSHROOMS

Region: western
Method: deep-frying and braising

Beancurd, which is also known as *doufu* or, in Japanese, *tofu* (see page 16), is a versatile and nutritious food. It is derived from the soyabean, which is exceedingly rich in protein. Beancurd is rather bland, but this is easily remedied by recipes such as this one, in which it is deep-fried, which alters its texture, and then braised, which makes it tasty. The result is a delicious and unusual vegetable dish. An additional bonus is that it re-heats well.

Serves 2 to 4		
8oz	225g	fresh beancurd
2oz	50g	spring onions
15floz	400ml	oil (see Deep-fat fryers, page 34)
1 tablespoon		oil
1 tablespoon		garlic, finely chopped
½ teaspoon		fresh ginger, finely chopped
4oz	110g	small, whole button mushrooms, washed
1 teaspoon		chilli bean sauce, or 1 dried red chilli
1 tablespoon		dry sherry or rice wine
1 tablespoon		dark soy sauce
2 tablespoons		chicken stock or water

Cut the beancurd into 1 inch (2·5 cm) cubes. Trim the spring onions and cut them into 1 inch (2·5 cm) segments.

Heat the 15 fl oz (400 ml) oil in a deep-fat fryer or large wok until it almost smokes, and then deep-fry the beancurd cubes in 2 batches. When each batch of beancurd cubes is lightly browned, remove and drain well on kitchen paper. Let the cooking oil cool and then discard it.

Heat a clean frying-pan or wok. When it is hot, add 1 tablespoon of oil, and then add the garlic and spring onions. Stir-fry for a few seconds and then add the mushrooms. Stir-fry for 30 seconds, and add all the other ingredients. Reduce the heat to very low and then add the beancurd cubes. Cover the pan and slowly simmer the mixture for 8 minutes. It is then ready to serve.

BEANCURD WITH VEGETABLES

Region: southern
Method: shallow-frying and stir-frying

Beancurd changes its texture when it is shallow-fried from a slippery soft one to one which is light and spongy. Cooked in this way the beancurd does not absorb the oil in which it is fried but forms a sort of skin which helps to hold it together during the stir-frying stage. This is a simple, tasty dish which re-heats well.

Serves 4		
8 oz	225 g	fresh beancurd
2 oz	50 g	waterchestnuts, tinned (drained weight) or fresh
2 oz	50 g	tinned bamboo shoots
2 oz	50 g	mange-tout, trimmed
5 fl oz	150 ml	oil, preferably groundnut
Sauce		
1 tablespoon		dry sherry or rice wine
2 tablespoons		oyster sauce
1 teaspoon		sugar
2 fl oz	50 ml	chicken stock
1 teaspoon		cornflour, blended with 1 teaspoon water
2 teaspoons		sesame oil

193

Drain and rinse the beancurd in cold water. Blot it dry with kitchen paper and cut into ½inch (1cm) cubes. If you are using fresh waterchestnuts, peel and slice them. If you are using tinned waterchestnuts, rinse them in cold water and then slice them. Now slice the bamboo shoots on the diagonal into 1inch (2·5cm) pieces and trim the mange-tout.

Heat a wok or large frying-pan and then add the oil. Heat the oil until it is moderately hot. Add the beancurd cubes and shallow-fry until they are lightly brown on all sides. Remove with a slotted spoon and drain on kitchen paper.

Pour off most of the oil, leaving about 1 tablespoon in the pan. Re-heat the oil, add the vegetables and stir-fry for about 2 minutes. Then add all the sauce ingredients except for the cornflour mixture and the sesame oil. Bring the mixture to the boil, remove from the heat, and then add the cornflour mixture. Return the pan to the heat and bring it back to the boil. Return the beancurd to the pan and add the sesame oil. Give the mixture a few stirs and turn onto a warm serving platter. Serve at once.

COLD MARINADED BEAN SPROUTS

Region: northern

Method: marinading

This is a nutritious salad, easy to make and perfect either as an appetiser or as a salad course with grilled meat or fish. Always use fresh bean sprouts—never tinned ones which are soggy and tasteless. Fresh ones are widely available and are also very easy to grow (see page 187). I prefer to trim the sprouts at both ends. Although this is a bit laborious, it is well worth the effort as it makes the finished dish look more elegant. This dish may be prepared up to 4 hours in advance, and may be served cold or at room temperature. It is perfect for warm summer days.

194

Serves 4		
1 lb	450g	fresh bean sprouts
1		fresh red or green chilli, or ¼ teaspoon chilli powder
3 tablespoons		cider vinegar or Chinese white rice vinegar
2 tablespoons		light soy sauce
1 tablespoon		fresh coriander, finely chopped
½ teaspoon		garlic, finely chopped

Trim and discard both ends of the bean sprouts and put the trimmed sprouts into a glass bowl. If you are using a fresh chilli, split it in half and carefully remove and discard the seeds. Shred the chilli as finely as possible. Add it, together with all the other ingredients, to the trimmed bean sprouts. Mix well. Let the mixture marinade for at least 2–3 hours, turning the bean sprouts in the marinade from time to time. When you are ready to serve the salad, drain the bean sprouts and discard the marinade.

STIR-FRIED GINGER BROCCOLI

Region: southern
Method: stir-frying

Broccoli as it is known in the West is different from the Chinese variety. The Western variety is often considered to combine the best features of cauliflower and asparagus, and its distinctive flavour is milder than the Chinese type. It goes well with many seasonings but ginger is one of its most congenial companions. After stir-frying this dish, I let it cool and serve it at room temperature, so it is particularly suitable for summertime.

Serves 2 to 4		
1 lb	450g	fresh broccoli
1 tablespoon		oil
1 inch	2·5cm	fresh ginger, sliced and finely shredded
½ teaspoon		salt
½ teaspoon		sesame oil

195

Separate the broccoli heads into small florets, and peel and slice the stems. Blanch the broccoli pieces in a large pot of boiling salted water for several minutes, and then immerse them in cold water. Drain thoroughly.

Heat the oil in a large wok or frying-pan. When it is moderately hot, add the ginger shreds and salt. Stir-fry for a few seconds, and then add the blanched broccoli. If it seems dry, add a few tablespoons of water. Stir-fry at a moderate to high heat for 4 minutes until the broccoli is thoroughly heated through. Add the sesame oil and continue to stir-fry for 30 seconds, and the broccoli is ready to serve.

STIR-FRIED BROCCOLI WITH HOISIN SAUCE

Region: northern

Method: stir-frying

I find the sweet flavour of broccoli blends perfectly with the rich taste of hoisin sauce. This sauce gives a good colour and pleasant fragrance to the broccoli, but remember that a little goes a long way. This dish is quick and easy to make. Served hot, it makes a perfect vegetable accompaniment to any meal. (Carrots or courgettes can be used instead of broccoli.)

Serves 2 to 4	
1lb 450g	fresh broccoli
1 tablespoon	oil, preferably groundnut
2 teaspoons	garlic, finely chopped
2 tablespoons	hoisin sauce
3 tablespoons	water

Separate the broccoli heads into florets, and peel and slice the stems. Blanch all the broccoli pieces in a large pot of boiling, salted water for several minutes. Then drain them and immerse them in cold water. Drain again thoroughly in a colander.

Heat the oil in a wok or large frying-pan. When it is moderately hot, add the garlic and broccoli pieces. Stir-fry them for about 1 minute, and then add the hoisin sauce and water. Continue to stir-fry at a moderately high heat for about 5 minutes or until the broccoli pieces are thoroughly cooked. Serve at once.

196

COLD SESAME BROCCOLI

Region: northern
Method: blanching

This dish makes a good garnish for meats or a wonderful vegetable dish for summer picnics. The cold crunchiness of the broccoli goes well with the texture of the sesame seeds. For a tangy alternative, you could substitute finely chopped fresh ginger for the sesame seeds (using roughly the same amounts). Think of this dish as a cold vegetable salad with a Chinese touch, which goes well with almost any menu. It can be prepared a day in advance and actually tastes even better if you do this.

Serves 4 to 6	
1–1½lb 450–700g	broccoli
1 tablespoon	sesame seeds
1 tablespoon	oil
2 teaspoons	sesame oil
1 teaspoon	garlic, finely chopped
1½ tablespoons	light soy sauce
2 tablespoons	spring onions, finely chopped

Cut off the broccoli heads and break them into small florets. Peel and slice the broccoli stems. Blanch the broccoli heads and stems in a large pot of boiling salted water for 4–5 minutes. Then plunge them into cold water. Next, drain the broccoli dry in a colander or a salad spinner, and put it into a clean bowl.

Roast the sesame seeds in a pre-heated oven, gas mark 5, 375°F (190°C), or under a grill, until they are brown. In a small glass bowl combine the roasted sesame seeds with all the rest of the ingredients and mix them together well. Then pour the mixture into the bowl of broccoli and toss well. If you are serving this dish the next day, tightly cover the bowl with clingfilm and keep it in the refrigerator until it is needed.

197

BRAISED CAULIFLOWER WITH OYSTER SAUCE

Region: southern

Method: braising

I find cauliflower a versatile vegetable which is both delicious and easy to prepare. It has a distinct but rather mild taste which goes very well with oyster sauce. It needs a longish cooking time so stir-frying is not the most appropriate cooking technique. I prefer to braise it in oyster sauce.

Serves 4	
1½lb 700g	cauliflower
1 tablespoon	oil, preferably groundnut
2	garlic cloves, crushed
2 slices	fresh ginger
½ teaspoon	salt
3 tablespoons	oyster sauce
15 floz 400 ml	Chicken Stock (page 59) or water
Garnish	
2 tablespoons	spring onion, finely chopped

Cut the cauliflower into small florets about 1–1½ inches (3·5 cm) wide.

Heat a wok or large frying-pan over a moderate heat. Add the oil and then add the garlic and ginger. Stir-fry for about 20 seconds to flavour the oil. Then remove the garlic and ginger and discard them. Add the cauliflower florets and stir-fry them for a few seconds. Next add the salt, oyster sauce and the stock or water. Bring the mixture to a simmer and cook for 5–10 minutes or until the cauliflower is tender. Turn onto a warm serving platter and sprinkle with the spring onions. Serve at once.

SPICED CHINESE LEAVES

Region: western
Method: braising

Unlike the more familiar green and red cabbage, Chinese leaves (sometimes known as Chinese cabbage) have a bland, sweet flavour which is delicate, rather like lettuce. Cooking is needed to make it palatable, and because it is so light, it calls for a robust sauce. I like to serve it with this spicy sauce. For a variation you could substitute curry powder for the chilli.

Serves 2 to 4	
1½lb 700g	Chinese leaves or white cabbage
1 tablespoon	oil
2 teaspoons	fresh ginger, finely chopped
2 teaspoons	garlic, finely chopped
1	dried red chilli, or 1 teaspoon chilli powder
1 tablespoon	dry sherry or rice wine
2 tablespoons	dark soy sauce
2 teaspoons	sugar
2floz 50ml	water
2 teaspoons	sesame oil

Separate the Chinese leaves or cabbage and wash the leaves well. Cut them into 1 inch (2·5cm) strips.

Heat a large wok or frying-pan. When it is hot, add the oil. A few seconds later add the ginger and stir-fry it quickly. Then add the garlic and dried chilli if you are using it. Toss them well for a few seconds and then add the sherry or rice wine, soy sauce, sugar, water and the chilli powder if you are using it. Bring the mixture to a simmer and then add the Chinese leaves or cabbage. Boil over a high heat for 5 minutes until it is thoroughly cooked, stirring occasionally. Just before you serve it, add the sesame oil and stir it in well.

199

CHINESE LEAVES IN SOY SAUCE

Region: southern
Method: blanching

This simple dish is one of my favourite ways of preparing Chinese leaves. The blanching preserves its sweetness while the hot oil imparts a richy nutty flavour to the vegetable. It is quick and easy to make. You can also use white cabbage or any other leafy green vegetable for this dish.

Serves 2 to 3	
1lb 450g	Chinese leaves
1 tablespoon	oil, preferably groundnut
1 tablespoon	light soy sauce

Cut the Chinese leaves into 1½ inch (3·5 cm) strips and blanch them in a pot of boiling, salted water for about 1 minute. Drain thoroughly, and put the blanched leaves onto a platter. Dribble the soy sauce over them.

Heat the oil in a wok or frying-pan until it is almost smoking and then pour the hot oil over the leaves. Serve at once. For a spicy taste, try using Chilli Oil (page 28) instead of groundnut oil.

COLD SWEET AND SOUR CHINESE LEAVES

Region: northern
Method: blanching and pickling

In northern China, with its short growing season and long cold winters, fresh vegetables are available for only a few months of the year. In the absence of modern refrigeration, other means of

Right: Potsticker Dumplings (page 239) and Fried Stuffed Cucumbers (page 206)

preserving foods are necessary. Some of the most common methods are pickling in brine, in salt and wine, in a mixture of sugar and salt, or by inducing fermentation.

In this recipe from the north, Chinese leaves or cabbage undergo what is essentially a sweet and sour pickling process. It can be eaten at once or stored for later use. Dishes like this are served at room temperature at the beginning of a meal, and their sweet and sour flavours are designed to stimulate the palate and whet the appetite.

Serves 4 to 6		
1½lb	700g	**Chinese leaves, or white cabbage, cut into 2inch 5cm strips**
3floz	75ml	**groundnut oil**
1 tablespoon		**sesame oil**
5		**dried red chillis**
2 tablespoons		**whole roasted Sichuan peppercorns (page 25)**
4oz	110g	**sugar**
5floz	150ml	**cider vinegar or Chinese white rice vinegar**
1½ tablespoons		**salt**
1 tablespoon		**fresh ginger, finely chopped**
2 tablespoons		**garlic, finely chopped**

Blanch the Chinese leaves or cabbage strips in hot water for a few seconds until they wilt. Drain them and put them to one side in a glass bowl. Heat the two oils in a pan or wok until they are hot. Add the chillis and whole roasted peppercorns. When the chillis and peppercorns turn dark, turn the heat off. Pour the flavoured oil through a strainer and then over the leaves or cabbage strips. Wrap the chillis and peppercorns in cheesecloth and tie into a bag like a bouquet garni, so that it can be removed later. Place it among the vegetable strips.

Now add the sugar and vinegar to the leaves and mix well. Add the salt, ginger and garlic and make sure that all the ingredients are mixed in well. Let the mixture sit at room temperature for several hours. It is now ready to be refrigerated overnight and then served. This dish will keep for up to 1 week in the refrigerator. Before you serve it, drain off all the marinade and remove the chilli–peppercorn bouquet garni.

Left: (from the top) Stir-fried Rice Noodles with Vegetables (page 231), Bean Sauce Noodles (page 228) and Beef Noodle Soup (page 230)

STIR-FRIED CHINESE GREENS

Region: southern

Method: stir-frying

Chinese greens are also known by their Cantonese name, *bok choi*. They were a staple food in my childhood as they were inexpensive, nutritious and readily available. Even today I look forward to this simple stir-fried dish. Sometimes the greens are merely blanched but I think they are delicious stir-fried with oil and garlic or with a little soy sauce and stock. They make a delicious dish to serve with meat and fish and are excellent in vegetarian menus. You can get Chinese greens at Chinese grocers, but Swiss chard or mange-tout work equally well.

Serves 2 to 4	
1 tablespoon	oil
1½lb 700 g	Chinese greens
1 tablespoon	light soy sauce
1 teaspoon	salt
2 tablespoons	chicken stock or water

Heat a wok or large frying-pan to a moderate heat. Add the oil and then the Chinese greens. Stir-fry for 3–4 minutes until the greens have wilted a little. Then add the soy sauce, salt and chicken stock or water. Continue to stir-fry for a few more minutes until the greens are done but are still slightly crisp.

204

STIR-FRIED CUCUMBERS WITH HOT SPICES

Region: western
Method: stir-frying

It always mystified me when I was a child to see Americans eating cucumbers raw. We Chinese never eat them like this. If they are not pickled then they must be cooked. We prefer them when they are in season, young, tender and bursting with juice. This is a simple stir-fried cucumber dish from western China. Once the ingredients are assembled, it is very quick to cook. The chilli and garlic contrast well with the cool, crisp cucumber.

Serves 4 to 6		
1½lb	700g	cucumbers (about 1½)
2 teaspoons		salt
1 tablespoon		oil
¼ teaspoon		chilli bean sauce or chilli powder
1½ tablespoons		garlic, finely chopped
1½ tablespoons		black beans, coarsely chopped
4 floz	110ml	water
1 teaspoon		sesame oil

Peel the cucumbers, slice them in half lengthways and, using a teaspoon, remove the seeds. Then cut the cucumber halves into 1 inch (2·5cm) cubes. Sprinkle them with the salt and mix well. Put the mixture into a colander and let it sit for 20 minutes to drain. This rids the cucumber of any excess liquid. When the cucumber cubes have drained, rinse them in water and then blot them dry with kitchen paper.

Heat a wok or large frying-pan until it is hot. Add the oil, and when it is almost smoking add the chilli bean sauce or chilli powder, garlic and black beans and stir for about 30 seconds. Then add the cucumbers and stir for a few seconds until they are coated with the spices and flavourings. Add the water and continue to stir-fry over a high heat for 3–4 minutes until most of the water has evaporated and the cucumbers are cooked. At this point, add the sesame oil and serve immediately.

FRIED STUFFED CUCUMBERS

Region: eastern

Method: shallow-frying

There are countless Chinese recipes for all kinds of stuffed vegetables. Even beancurd can be filled. Cucumbers, in particular, lend themselves to stuffing because their tender, succulent flesh is complemented by a savoury filling. The stuffing in this recipe uses seasoned minced pork, but you can use minced beef instead if you prefer. Thick cucumber slices are stuffed and then shallow-fried; this seals in the flavours of the stuffing. Then the cucumbers are simmered to create the sauce. I think you will agree that cucumbers have never tasted so good!

		Serves 4 to 6
1½	700g	cucumbers (about 1½lb)
2 tablespoons		cornflour
1 tablespoon		oil, more if needed
		Stuffing
8oz	225g	fatty pork, finely minced
1 tablespoon		spring onions, finely chopped
2 teaspoons		fresh ginger, finely chopped
2 teaspoons		dry sherry or rice wine
2 teaspoons		light soy sauce
2 teaspoons		sugar
½ teaspoon		salt
1		small egg
		Sauce
10floz	300ml	Chicken Stock (page 59)
2 tablespoons		dry sherry or rice wine
2 tablespoons		light soy sauce
2 teaspoons		sugar
		Garnish
1 teaspoon		sesame oil
1 tablespoon		fresh coriander, finely chopped

Cut the cucumbers into 1 inch (2·5cm) slices without peeling them. Remove the seeds and pulp from the centre of each cucumber slice using a small sharp knife. Lightly dust the hollow interior of the cucumber slices with a little cornflour. Mix all the stuffing ingredients together in a large bowl. Then stuff each cucumber ring with this mixture.

Heat a wok or large frying-pan and add the oil. When it is moderately hot, add the stuffed cucumber rings and cook them slowly until they are lightly browned. Turn them over and brown the other side, adding more oil if necessary. You may have to do this in several batches. When the cucumber rings are brown, remove them from the oil and put them on a plate. When you have fried all the cucumber rings, wipe the wok or pan clean.

Mix the sauce ingredients and put them into a re-heated wok or pan. Bring the liquid to a simmer, and then add the stuffed cucumber rings. Cover the pan with a lid and simmer slowly for 7 minutes or until the cucumbers are completely cooked. Transfer them to a serving platter, lifting them out of the sauce with a slotted spoon.

Reduce the sauce by a third over a high heat. Then add the sesame oil and fresh coriander. Pour the sauce over the stuffed cucumbers and serve at once.

LETTUCE WITH OYSTER SAUCE

Region: southern

Method: blanching

Here is lettuce prepared in a very familiar Chinese way— blanched and served with oyster sauce. Lettuce prepared like this retains a crispy texture and its delicate flavour is unimpaired by cooking. The combination makes a simple, quickly prepared, tasty vegetable dish.

207

Serves 2 to 4	
1½lb 700g	Cos lettuce
3 tablespoons	oyster sauce
1 tablespoon	oil

Separate the lettuce leaves and blanch them in a pot of boiling, salted water for about 30 seconds, or until they have wilted slightly. Remove them and drain well. Mix the oyster sauce with the oil. Arrange the lettuce leaves on a serving dish, pour the oyster sauce mixture over it, and serve it immediately.

STIR-FRIED MANGE-TOUT WITH WATERCHESTNUTS

Region: eastern and southern
Method: stir-frying

Fresh waterchestnuts are cultivated between rows of rice plants. You can sometimes buy them fresh, but tinned ones are easier to obtain. Fresh waterchestnuts are often dipped into a sugar syrup and eaten as a snack. Cooked, they have a sweet taste and a crunchy texture. This is a straightforward recipe which should be made with the freshest mange-tout you can find. Asparagus, when in season, makes a delightful alternative.

Serves 2 to 4	
8oz 225g	waterchestnuts, tinned (drained weight) or fresh
1 tablespoon	oil, preferably groundnut
3 tablespoons	spring onions, finely chopped
8oz 225g	mange-tout, trimmed
1 tablespoon	light soy sauce
2 tablespoons	water
½ teaspoon	salt
½ teaspoon	sugar
1 teaspoon	sesame oil

If you are using fresh waterchestnuts, peel them. If you are using tinned waterchestnuts, drain them well and rinse in cold water. Thinly slice the waterchestnuts.

Heat a wok or large frying-pan over a medium heat. Add the oil, and when it is hot, add the spring onions. A few seconds later, add the mange-tout and fresh waterchestnuts if you are using them, and stir-fry for 1 minute. Make sure you coat them thoroughly with the oil. Then add the rest of the ingredients and continue to stir-fry for another 3 minutes. If you are using tinned waterchestnuts add these now and cook for a further 2 minutes or until the vegetables are cooked. Serve at once.

SPICY STIR-FRIED MUSHROOMS

Region: western
Method: stir-frying

Although button mushrooms are common in Europe and America they were virtually unknown in China until quite recently. They are now increasingly popular there. Their mild, subtle flavour makes them perfect for stir-frying with Chinese spices. This dish is simple to make and re-heats well. Serve it with Braised Duck (page 145) and plain steamed rice. It also goes perfectly with English grills.

Serves 4	
1 tablespoon	oil, preferably groundnut
1 teaspoon	fresh ginger, finely chopped
2 teaspoons	spring onions, finely chopped
1 teaspoon	garlic, finely chopped
8oz 450g	small button mushrooms, whole
1 teaspoon	chilli bean sauce
2 teaspoons	dry sherry or rice wine
2 teaspoons	dark soy sauce
1 tablespoon	chicken stock or water
½ teaspoon	sugar
¼ teaspoon	salt
1 teaspoon	sesame oil

Heat a wok or large frying-pan over a high heat until it is hot. Add the oil and then the ginger, spring onions and garlic. Stir-fry for about 20 seconds. Then add the mushrooms and stir-fry them for about 30 seconds. Quickly add the rest of the ingredients except the sesame oil. Continue to stir-fry for about 5 minutes or until the mushrooms are cooked through and have absorbed all the spices and seasonings. Just before serving, add the sesame oil and give the mixture a couple of quick stirs. Turn it onto a warm serving dish and serve at once.

THREE MUSHROOMS BRAISED

Region: southern

Method: stir-frying and braising

Mushrooms are very popular in China, especially in the south where the warm, moist climate is ideal for fungi. The varieties of mushrooms are endless. The three used in this recipe have very different characteristics: straw mushrooms have a musky scent and meaty texture; Chinese dried mushrooms are smoky-flavoured and densely textured; button mushrooms are mild and soft. Combining all three in a substantial and rich sauce transforms the mushroom from a supporting ingredient to a vegetable dish in its own right. Straw and dried mushrooms can be bought at Chinese grocers but if you can't get them, this recipe is nearly as delicious made entirely with button ones. (Use 12 oz (350g) button mushrooms.)

Serves 4 to 6		
1 oz	25 g	Chinese dried mushrooms
8 oz	225 g	tinned Chinese straw mushrooms
3 oz	75 g	button mushrooms
1 tablespoon		oil
1 tablespoon		light soy sauce
2 tablespoons		dry sherry or rice wine
3 tablespoons		oyster sauce
2 teaspoons		sugar
2 teaspoons		garlic, finely chopped
2½ floz	70 ml	chicken stock
2 tablespoons		spring onions, finely chopped

If you are using Chinese dried mushrooms, soak them in warm water for 20 minutes, and then drain them. Rinse them well and squeeze out any excess liquid. Discard the tough stem, then shred the caps and put them aside. If you are using tinned straw mushrooms, drain and rinse them but leave them whole. Wash and slice the button mushrooms.

Heat a wok or large frying-pan, then add the oil. Now add all the mushrooms and stir-fry them, mixing them well, for a few seconds. Then quickly add the soy sauce, sherry or rice wine, oyster sauce, sugar, garlic and chicken stock. Turn the heat down and cook for about 7 minutes, stirring continually, until the fresh mushrooms are thoroughly cooked. Then mix in the spring onions, stirring for a few seconds, and serve at once.

STIR-FRIED SPINACH WITH GARLIC

Region: southern
Method: stir-frying

Spinach has often been regarded with disdain in the West, probably because it is usually overcooked. This is a time-honoured, delicious southern Chinese recipe. The spinach is quickly stir-fried and then seasoned. It is very simple to prepare and may be served hot or cold.

Serves 4	
1½lb 700g	fresh spinach
1 tablespoon	oil
½ teaspoon	salt
1 teaspoon	sugar
2 teaspoons	garlic, finely chopped

Wash the spinach thoroughly. Remove all the stems, leaving just the leaves. Heat a large wok or pan to a moderate heat. Add the oil, and then add the salt and spinach. Stir-fry for about 2 minutes to coat the spinach leaves thoroughly with the oil and salt. When the spinach has wilted to about one-third of its original size, add the sugar and garlic and continue to stir-fry for another 4 minutes. Transfer the spinach to a plate and pour off any excess liquid. Serve hot or cold.

BUDDHIST CASSEROLE

Region: eastern
Method: deep-frying and braising

This is my adaptation of a famous Buddhist dish. The original recipe calls for many obscure, dried Chinese vegetables but my version uses vegetables which are readily available. I like to add a little coriander which Buddhists do not eat. A deeply satisfying dish, this casserole is suitable for both summer and winter. I prefer to cook it in a Chinese clay pot (see page 36) but you can also use a good, small cast-iron pot. Take care not to overcook the vegetables. The casserole may be made in advance and re-heated very slowly. It is delicious with rice, noodles or even with fresh bread.

Serves 4 to 6		
8oz	225g	fresh beancurd
4oz	110g	broccoli
4oz	110g	Chinese leaves or white cabbage
4oz	110g	small courgettes
4oz	110g	red pepper (about 1), sliced
4oz	110g	mange-tout, washed and trimmed
15fl oz	400ml	oil (see Deep-fat fryers, page 34)
1½pts	900ml	Chicken Stock (page 59)
2 tablespoons		light soy sauce
3 tablespoons		hoisin sauce
2 tablespoons		whole yellow bean sauce
1 tablespoon		fresh coriander, finely chopped

Cut the beancurd into 1inch (2·5cm) cubes. Next prepare all the vegetables. Separate the broccoli heads and break them into small florets. Peel and slice the broccoli stems. Cut the Chinese leaves or cabbage into 1inch (2·5cm) chunks. Slice the courgettes into rounds ¼inch (0·5cm) thick or roll cut them (see page 39). Thinly slice the pepper. Leave the mange-tout whole, but trim the ends.

Heat the oil in a deep-fat fryer or large wok. When the oil is almost smoking deep-fry the beancurd cubes in two batches. Drain each cooked batch on kitchen paper.

Put the chicken stock, soy sauce, hoisin sauce and whole yellow bean sauce into a large, cast-iron enamel pot or Chinese clay pot and bring it to the boil. Next add the broccoli and stir in the Chinese leaves or cabbage. Boil for 2 minutes. Then add the courgettes and pepper and cook for another 2 minutes. Finally add the mange-tout and beancurd cubes. Cook for 1 minute more then stir in the fresh coriander and the dish is ready to serve. (The dish should be quite liquid.) To re-heat, bring to a simmer on a very low heat until all the vegetables are hot.

PICKLED VEGETABLES

Region: northern and western

Method: pickling

Pickled vegetables were much more common in Western households before the advent of the domestic refrigerator. Now they are usually only available sold in jars and full of preservatives. This I regard as one of the losses we incur with progress. Even today pickled vegetables, fruits and ginger are still very popular with the Chinese, and deservedly so. I remember watching my mother pickling vegetables for use the following week. She often used to pickle carrots and turnips but my favourite was pickled young fresh ginger. Pickled vegetables make delicious snacks and appetisers and can also be used to garnish cold platters. They are easy to make and may be prepared well ahead. They should rest in the brine mixture for at least 3 to 4 days; thereafter, they will keep in the refrigerator for up to 2 weeks.

This recipe makes 2 lb 900g pickled vegetables		
8oz	225g	carrots, peeled
1lb	450g	white radish (*mooli*) or turnips, peeled
8oz	225g	Chinese leaves or white cabbage
2		fresh red or green chillis
Pickling brine		
2oz	50g	salt
4 pints	2·3ltr	water
3floz	75ml	dry sherry or rice wine
3oz	75g	sugar
2 tablespoons		fresh ginger, finely chopped
2 tablespoons		garlic, finely chopped

213

First prepare all the vegetables. Cut the peeled carrots, white radish or turnips and the washed Chinese leaves or cabbage into chunks 1 inch (2·5 cm) × ½ inch (0·5 cm). Thinly slice the fresh chillis, retaining the seeds.

Now mix all the pickling brine ingredients together in a glass bowl and stir them to make sure the salt and sugar have dissolved. Put the vegetables into the brine and let them sit in the refrigerator for 3 or 4 days. Drain the vegetables and rinse them well in cold water before storing them in a covered glass bowl in the refrigerator. They will keep for 2 weeks. Discard the drained brine before serving the vegetables, and remember that the longer you leave them in the brine, the stronger and saltier they will be.

RICE,
NOODLES AND
DOUGHS

All Chinese meals must be composed of two parts: the *cai* or meat, fish, poultry and vegetable dishes, and the *fan* or staple. Both parts are important. As one Chinese sage put it, 'Without the *cai* the meal is less tasteful, but without the *fan* one's hunger cannot be satisfied'. Most Westerners think that rice is the only Chinese staple food, but in the northern parts of China where it is too cold to grow it, wheat takes precedence and so noodles, dumplings and pancakes are eaten more often than rice. This chapter is divided into three sections: rice; noodles; and doughs which include dumplings, buns and pancakes. I have given detailed information on different types of rice, noodles and flour in the appropriate sections.

RICE

There are many types of rice, including long-grain, short-grain and glutinous varieties, and all are made into flour, noodles, wines and vinegars as well as being used in cooking. Brown rice, which is a popular wholefood in the West, is not used by the Chinese who dislike its texture. Plain boiled or steamed white rice is eaten with meals. Fried rice, now popular in Chinese restaurants all over the world, is served in China as a snack or as the last course at a banquet, and never with other *cai* dishes.

Long-grain rice
This is the most popular rice for cooking in southern China and it is my favourite too. It needs to be washed before it is cooked. Do not confuse it with the 'easy-cook' and pre-cooked varieties which are now widely available as these are unsuitable for Chinese cooking. They lack the starchy flavour, texture and clean white colour which is so essential to Chinese cuisine.

Short-grain rice
This rice is not to be confused with pudding rice. Short-grain rice is usually used in Chinese cooking for making congee and is more popular outside southern China. Varieties known as 'American Rose' or 'Japanese Rose' are very suitable and can be found in many Chinese grocers. If you cannot find short-grain rice, use long-grain instead.

Glutinous rice
Glutinous rice is also known as sweet rice or sticky rice. It is short, round and pearl-like, and is not to be confused with regular short-grain rice or pudding rice. It has more gluten than ordinary rice, and when cooked is stickier and sweeter. It is used mainly for stuffings and desserts and for making Chinese rice wine and vinegar. Most Chinese grocers stock it. Glutinous rice must be washed and soaked for at least 2 hours before cooking. You may cook it in the same way as long-grain rice (see page 218) or by steaming. If you want to steam it, soak the rice for at least 8 hours or overnight. Then line a bamboo steamer with cheesecloth and spread the rice over it. Steam it for about 40 minutes or until the rice is cooked.

To wash rice
Put the required amount of rice into a large bowl. Fill the bowl with cold water and swish the rice around with a spoon or with your hands. Carefully pour off the cloudy water keeping the rice in the bowl. Repeat this process several times until the water is clear.

STEAMED RICE
Region: all
Method: steaming

Steaming rice the Chinese way is quite easy. I prefer to use long-grain white rice which is drier and fluffier when cooked. Don't use pre-cooked or 'easy-cook' rice for Chinese cookery as both these types of rice have insufficient flavour and lack the texture and starchy taste which is fundamental to Chinese rice.

The secret of preparing rice without it being sticky is to cook it first at a high heat until most of the water has evaporated. Then the heat should be turned very low, the pot covered and the rice cooked slowly in the remaining steam. As a child I was always instructed never to peek into the rice pot during this stage or else precious steam would escape and the rice would not be cooked properly, bringing bad luck.

Here is a good trick to remember: if you make sure that you cover the rice with about 1 inch of water it should always cook

217

properly without sticking. Many packet recipes for rice use too much water and result in a gluey mess. Follow my method and you will have perfect steamed rice, the easy Chinese way.

Most Chinese eat quite large quantities of rice (about 5oz (150g) per head which is more than many Westerners are able to manage). This recipe and that for Fried Rice allows about 13oz (375g) (dried weight) of rice for 4 people. If you want more than that just increase the quantity of rice, but remember to add enough water so that the level of water is about 1 inch (2·5cm) above the top of the rice.

Serves 4		
	Enough long-grain rice to fill a glass measuring jug to 15 floz 400ml level	
1½ pts	**900 ml**	**water**

Put the rice into a large bowl and wash it in several changes of water until the water becomes clear. Drain the rice and put it into a heavy pot with 1½ pints (900ml) water and bring it to the boil. Continue boiling until most of the surface liquid has evaporated. This should take about 15–20 minutes. The surface of the rice should have small indentations like a pitted crater. At this point, cover the pot with a very tight-fitting lid, turn the heat as low as possible and let the rice cook undisturbed for 15–20 minutes. There is no need to 'fluff' the rice before serving it.

FRIED RICE

Region: eastern
Method: stir-frying

In China fried rice is eaten as a 'filler' at the end of a dinner party. It is not eaten with other dishes in place of steamed rice, though many Westerners do so. Although fried rice is common in Chinese restaurants, it is frequently incorrectly cooked. Often the rice is sticky and coloured with soy sauce. Here are a few important points to remember when making authentic fried rice.

● The cooked rice should be thoroughly cool, preferably cold. Once cooled, much of the moisture in the rice evaporates, allowing the oil to coat the dry grains and keep them from sticking. (For hygiene reasons, always store cooked rice in the refrigerator, never at room temperature, and only remove it when you are ready to cook it.)

● Never put any soy sauce into fried rice. This not only colours the rice unnaturally but makes it too salty.

● Some recipes for fried rice involve cooking the eggs ahead of time and then adding them to the fried rice. Never do this as the eggs will get tough and dry.

● Always be sure the oil is hot enough to avoid saturating the rice. Saturated rice is greasy and heavy.

If you follow these simple guidelines, you will be rewarded with fried rice as it should be. Fried rice goes with almost any dish, but in China it is usually served at the end of a dinner to clean the palate.

	Serves 4	
2oz	50g	**Parma ham or lean English smoked bacon**
4oz	110g	**fresh or frozen peas**
		long-grain rice measured to the 15 fl oz 400ml level in a measuring jug and cooked according to the method given on page 217
2 tablespoons		**oil, preferably groundnut**
1 teaspoon		**salt**
2		**eggs, beaten**
4oz	110g	**fresh bean sprouts**
	Garnish	
2 tablespoons		**spring onions, finely chopped**

Cut the Parma ham or bacon into fine dice. Blanch the peas in a saucepan of boiling water for about 5 minutes if they are fresh and 2 minutes if they are frozen. Drain them in a colander.

Heat a wok or large frying-pan until it is hot. Then add the oil and wait until it is almost smoking. Add the cooked rice and stir-fry it for 1 minute, and then add the ham or bacon, peas and salt. Continue to stir-fry the mixture for 5 minutes over a high heat. Next add the beaten egg and bean sprouts and continue to stir-fry for 2 minutes or until the eggs have set. Turn the mixture onto a plate and garnish it with the spring onions. Serve at once, or let it cool and serve as a cold rice salad.

219

RAINBOW RICE

Region: southern

Method: stir-frying

This is a popular rice dish in the south. At first glance the recipe may seem similar to that for Fried Rice (page 218) but it is really quite different since the rice and the other ingredients all have to be cooked separately, and then combined. It is a substantial dish, beautifully coloured and ideal for a special dinner.

Serves 4 to 6		
		Long-grain rice measured to the 15 fl oz 400 ml level in a measuring jug and cooked according to the method on page 217
2 oz	50 g	Chinese dried mushrooms
2 oz	50 g	red pepper (about ½)
2 oz	50 g	carrot
4 oz	110 g	Chinese sausages or Parma ham
2 oz	50 g	green peas
2 tablespoons		oil, preferably groundnut
3 tablespoons		spring onions, finely chopped
1 tablespoon		light soy sauce
2 teaspoons		sesame oil

Prepare the rice as instructed in the recipe on page 217. Soak the dried mushrooms in warm water for about 20 minutes until they are soft. Meanwhile cut the red pepper, carrot and sausages or ham into small dice. Squeeze the excess liquid from the mushrooms and remove and discard their stems. Cut the caps into small dice. If you are using frozen peas make sure they are thoroughly thawed.

Heat a wok or large frying-pan. Add the oil and spring onions and stir-fry for about 30 seconds. Then add all the vegetables and the sausages or ham. Stir-fry the mixture for about 2 minutes and then add the soy sauce. Give the mixture a few stirs and then add the sesame oil. Remove the pan from the heat and let the mixture cool.

When the rice is almost ready, pour the cooked mixture over it to cover the rice. Let the rice and the stir-fried mixture cook for a further 5 minutes. Then stir to mix well. Turn onto a serving platter and serve at once.

RICE CAKE

Region: all
Method: steaming

Rice cakes were probably invented by a thrifty Chinese cook centuries ago in order to make use of that thin layer of rice which sometimes gets stuck at the bottom of the pot. This crispy leftover has evolved into an accompaniment to many dishes. Its taste and crunchy texture go deliciously with Sizzling Rice Prawns (page 180) for example. My mother often used to serve rice cakes with hot chicken broth for a sizzling rice soup. We also ate them as a snack with just a touch of oil and salt. After trying them you will never discard your leftover rice crust again.

Do not use 'easy-cook' rice for this dish because it does not have enough starch to form any crust; use long-grain white rice. Basically the method is the same as for steamed rice but the cooking time is longer.

Makes a 9inch 23cm rice cake	
8 oz 225g	long-grain, white rice
1 pint 570ml	water
2 teaspoons	oil, preferably groundnut

Wash the rice and put it, with the water, in a 9–9½inch (23–24cm) wide, heavy pot. Bring the water to the boil over a high heat. Then turn the heat down as low as possible, cover and let the rice cook for about 45 minutes. The rice should form a heavy crust on the bottom. Remove all the loose surface rice, leaving the heavy crust. This loose rice can be used for making Fried Rice (page 218).

Dribble the oil evenly over the top of the crust and let it cook over a very low heat for 5 minutes. The crust should lift off easily at this point. If it is still sticky, add another teaspoon of oil and continue to cook until the whole thing comes loose. Put the crust onto a plate until it is ready for use. Once it has been cooked, it can be left out at room temperature for several days. Do not cover it, as moisture will form and make the cake soggy. Let the rice cake dry out, and it is then ready to be deep-fried and put into hot chicken stock to make a soup or used for Sizzling Rice Prawns (page 180). As a simple snack, break it into chunks and eat it hot with a sprinkling of salt.

RICE CONGEE

Region: southern
Method: simmering

Rice congee is what many Chinese eat for breakfast; it is simply a boiled rice porridge. In various areas of China, fried dough bread, fermented beancurd, pickles, preserved salt or spicy mustard greens may be added to the congee. In the south, meat, chicken, roast duck, peanuts or fermented eggs are added. Interestingly enough, the word congee is a Hindi word and this perhaps indicates the origin of the dish.

The technique used in making congee is to boil the rice and then simmer it slowly. The starch is released gradually, thickening the porridge without the rice grains disintegrating. I find short-grain rice best for making congee, but you can use long-grain. In this recipe the rice needs no washing as all the starch is needed to thicken the porridge.

Serves 4	
4oz 110g	Chinese sausages (or any flavouring of your choice, such as Sichuan preserved vegetable, or diced cooked chicken or duck)
1¼ pts 700ml	water
	Enough short-grain rice to fill a glass measuring jug to the 5floz 150ml level, unwashed
½ teaspoon	salt
2 tablespoons	spring onions, finely chopped
1 tablespoon	fresh coriander, finely chopped

Cut the Chinese sausages, or whatever flavouring you are using into fine dice and set aside.

Bring the water to the boil in a large pot and add the rice and salt. Let the mixture come back to the boil and give it several good stirs. Then turn the heat down to low and cover the pot. Let the mixture simmer for about 35 minutes, stirring occasionally. Then add the Chinese sausages or your chosen flavouring and simmer for a further 5 minutes with the pot uncovered. Just before serving, add the spring onions and fresh coriander. Serve it at once. If you like, congee can be made in advance. In this case re-heat it slowly and add some more water if the porridge is too thick.

CHICKEN, SAUSAGE AND RICE CASSEROLE

Region: southern
Method: steaming

I have many pleasant memories of this dish. Even though I grew up in America, I often went to school with a typically Chinese lunch. Very early in the morning, my mother would steam chicken and sausage with rice and put it in a thermos flask to keep it warm. I would often exchange bits of my hot lunch for portions of my classmates' sandwiches! This dish is easy to make and is a simple but fully satisfying meal in itself.

It is well worth the effort to try and get authentic Chinese sausages from a Chinese food shop. Pork sausages could be substituted, but they should be browned first to rid them of their excess fat, and, of course, the taste will be quite different.

Serves 4 to 6		
2lb	900g	boneless chicken pieces, skinned
1 tablespoon		dry sherry or rice wine
1 tablespoon		light soy sauce
2 teaspoons		sugar
1 teaspoon		sesame oil
1oz	25g	Chinese dried mushrooms (optional)
6oz	175g	Chinese sausages or pork sausages
14oz	400g	long-grain rice, washed
1½pts	900ml	Chicken Stock (page 59) or water
1½ tablespoons		fresh ginger, finely chopped
2 tablespoons		spring onions, finely chopped

Cut the chicken into 2 inch (5 cm) pieces. Put these into a bowl and combine them with the dry sherry or rice wine, soy sauce, sugar and sesame oil. Let the mixture sit for at least 20 minutes. If you are using the dried mushrooms, soak them in warm water for 20 minutes. Then drain them, squeeze out any excess liquid, cut off and discard the stems and coarsely chop the mushroom caps. Slice the Chinese sausages thinly into 2 inch (5 cm) pieces at a slight diagonal. If you are using pork sausages, grill them for 3 minutes to partially cook them, and then slice them into 2 inch (5 cm) rounds.

223

Combine the rice and stock together in a large pot and bring to the boil. Continue to boil until most of the surface liquid above the rice has evaporated. Then mix in the chicken, mushrooms, ginger, spring onions and sausages. Turn the heat down low, cover, and cook for about 25 minutes until the rice, chicken and pork are cooked. Serve at once. You might serve this with Braised Spicy Aubergines (page 190) or Spiced Chinese Leaves (page 199).

NOODLES

There has always been an argument about whether the Chinese invented noodles before the Italians discovered spaghetti. Chinese noodles are more varied than Italian ones. They come in all shapes and sizes and are made from a variety of flours. They are most commonly made from wheat or rice flour and water, and in the south from wheat flour, water and eggs. There is also a type which is made from mung beans although this is strictly speaking not a noodle but a vegetable.

To see an expert noodlemaker at work is a real treat. Hand-made noodles are formed by an elaborate but rapid process of kneading, pulling, tossing and twisting of the dough into a cascade of fine long noodles. This spectacular skill takes four to five years to acquire and is a delight to watch.

Noodles play an important part in Chinese tradition since they are a symbol of longevity. For this reason they are often served at Chinese New Year and at birthday dinners and it is considered bad luck to cut them since this might shorten one's life! Noodles can be boiled and eaten plain instead of rice, with sauces, cold as salads, or in soups. Alternatively, fried with meat and vegetables they make a delicious and sustaining light meal. Here are some of the most common types of noodles.

Wheat noodles and egg noodles
These are made from hard or soft wheat flour and water. If egg has been added the noodles are usually labelled as egg noodles. They can be bought dried or fresh from Chinese grocers, and many supermarkets and delicatessens also stock the dried variety. Flat noodles are usually used in soups and rounded noodles are best for stir-frying. If you can't get Chinese noodles you can use Italian egg noodles (dried or fresh) instead.

224

To cook wheat and egg noodles

Noodles are very good boiled and served with main dishes instead of plain rice. I think dried wheat or fresh egg noodles are best for this.

Serves 2 to 4		
8oz	225g	**fresh or dried noodles**

If you are using fresh noodles, immerse them in a pot of boiling water and cook them for 3–5 minutes until they are soft. If you are using dried noodles, either cook them according to the instructions on the packet, or cook them in boiling water for 4–5 minutes. Then drain and serve.

If you are cooking noodles ahead of time before using them in another dish or before stir-frying them, toss the cooked drained noodles in 2 teaspoons of sesame oil and put them into a bowl. Cover this with clingfilm and put it in the refrigerator. The cooked noodles will keep like this for about 2 hours.

Rice noodles

Rice noodles are popular in southern China, especially with seafood. They are usually dried and can be found in Chinese grocers. They are white and come in a variety of shapes. One of the most common is rice stick noodles which are flat and about the length of a chopstick. Rice noodles are very easy to use. Simply soak them in warm water for 15 minutes until they are soft. Drain them in a colander or a sieve and they are then ready to be used in soups or to be stir-fried.

Cellophane (bean thread) noodles

These noodles, also called transparent noodles, are made from ground mung beans and not from a grain. They are available dried, and are very fine and white. Easy to recognise, packed in their neat, plastic-wrapped bundles, they are stocked by most Chinese grocers and some supermarkets. They are never served on their own but are added to soups or braised dishes or are deep-fried as a garnish. They must be soaked in warm water for about 5 minutes before use. As they are rather long you might find it easier to cut them into shorter lengths after soaking.

CHOW MEIN

Region: southern

Method: stir-frying

Chow Mein literally means 'stir-fried noodles' and this dish is as popular outside China as it is in southern China. It is a quick and delicious way to prepare egg noodles. Almost any ingredient you like, such as fish, meat, poultry or vegetables, can be added to it. It is a popular lunch dish, either served at the end of the meal or eaten by itself. It also makes a tasty noodle salad if served cold.

		Serves 4
8oz	225g	dried or fresh egg noodles
4oz	110g	chicken breasts, skinned
2 teaspoons		light soy sauce
2 teaspoons		dry sherry or rice wine
2 teaspoons		oil, preferably groundnut
1 tablespoon		oil, preferably groundnut
1 teaspoon		garlic, finely chopped
2oz	50g	mange-tout, trimmed
1oz	25g	Parma ham or lean English smoked bacon, finely shredded
1 teaspoon		light soy sauce
½ teaspoon		sugar
1 tablespoon		spring onions, finely chopped
1 teaspoon		sesame oil

If you are using dried noodles, cook them according to the instructions on the packet or else boil them for 4–5 minutes. Then cool them in cold water until you are ready to use them. If you are using fresh Chinese noodles, boil them for 3–5 minutes and then immerse them in cold water.

Using a cleaver or sharp knife, slice the chicken breasts into fine shreds 2 inches (5 cm) long. Combine the chicken shreds with the 2 teaspoons of light soy and sherry or rice wine in a small bowl. Mix well together and let the chicken marinade for about 10 minutes.

Heat a wok or large frying-pan, add the 2 teaspoons of oil and then the chicken shreds. Stir-fry the mixture for about 2 minutes and then transfer to a plate. Clean the wok or pan.

Drain the noodles, shaking off as much excess water as possible. Re-heat the pan and add the 1 tablespoon of oil and then the garlic. Stir-fry for 10 seconds and then add the mange-tout and ham or bacon. Stir-fry for about 1 minute, and then add the noodles, 1 teaspoon of soy sauce, sugar and spring onions. Continue to stir-fry for about 2 minutes and then return the chicken to the noodle mixture. Continue to stir-fry for about 3–4 minutes or until the chicken is cooked. Next add the sesame oil and give the mixture a few final stirs. Turn it on to a warm platter and serve at once.

NOODLES WITH BEAN SPROUTS AND HAM

Region: eastern

Method: stir-frying

Like many Chinese noodle dishes this one is very easy to make. It is very suitable for a simple lunch or for a picnic. Serve the noodles with snacks such as Stuffed Peppers (page 250) or Steamed Buns (page 234).

		Serves 4 to 6
1 lb	450g	dried or fresh egg noodles
12 oz	350g	fresh bean sprouts
2 oz	50g	Parma ham or lean English smoked bacon, shredded
		Sauce
10 fl oz	300ml	Chicken Stock (page 59)
2 tablespoons		dark soy sauce
1 tablespoon		light soy sauce
2 tablespoons		dry sherry or rice wine
1 tablespoon		garlic, finely chopped
3 tablespoons		spring onions, finely chopped
2 teaspoons		sesame oil

Cook the fresh or dried noodles for 3–5 minutes in a pot of boiling water. Then immerse them in cold water until you are ready to use them. (They can be left in the cold water for up to 1 hour.)

Now prepare the bean sprouts. I prefer to remove both ends of the bean sprouts as I think this gives them a cleaner look and taste. Shred the ham or bacon into 2 inch (5 cm) lengths.

227

Heat a wok or large pot. Add all the sauce ingredients, except the sesame oil, and bring the liquid to a simmer. Add the cooked noodles and stir-fry them to mix them in well with the sauce. Then turn the heat back to high and add the bean sprouts, sesame oil and ham or bacon. Continue to stir-fry for about 3 minutes until the noodles are thoroughly heated. Turn them onto a warm serving platter and serve at once.

BEAN SAUCE NOODLES

Region: northern

Method: stir-frying and simmering

Noodles are so popular in northern China that they are even eaten for breakfast, usually in soup. They are also a common snack. This recipe is an adaptation of a common noodle dish on which there are hundreds of variations. Once you have mastered this recipe you can add your own touches, just as the Chinese do. Serve with snacks such as Spring Rolls (page 245) and Fried Wuntun (page 248).

Serves 4		
1lb	450g	dried or fresh egg noodles
1½ tablespoons		sesame oil
Sauce		
1 tablespoon		oil, preferably groundnut
1½ tablespoons		garlic, finely chopped
2 tablespoons		spring onions, finely chopped
1lb	450g	minced pork
3 tablespoons		whole yellow bean sauce
1–2 teaspoons		chilli bean sauce (optional)
1 tablespoon		dry sherry or rice wine
2 tablespoons		dark soy sauce
2 teaspoons		salt
1 teaspoon		Chilli Oil (page 28), or 2 teaspoons chilli powder
2 teaspoons		sugar
10floz	300ml	Chicken Stock (page 59) or water
Garnish		
2 tablespoons		spring onions, coarsely chopped

228

If you are using fresh noodles, blanch them first by boiling them for 3–5 minutes in a pot of boiling water. If you are using dried noodles, cook them in boiling water for 4 or 5 minutes. Drain the noodles, toss them in the sesame oil and put them aside until you are ready to use them. They can be kept in this state, if tightly covered with clingfilm, for up to 2 hours in the refrigerator.

Heat a wok or large frying-pan until it is hot. Then add the oil and when it is hot add the garlic and spring onions. A few seconds later add the pork. Stir well to break up all the pieces and continue to stir-fry for about 1 minute or more until it loses its pink colour. Then add the rest of the sauce ingredients, stirring all the time. Bring the mixture to the boil, turn the heat down to low and simmer for 5 minutes. Plunge the noodles into boiling water for 20 seconds and then drain them well in a colander or sieve. Then quickly tip the noodles into a large bowl and pour the hot sauce over the top. Sprinkle on the spring onions, mix everything together well and serve at once.

COLD SPICY NOODLES

Region: western

Method: blanching

These savoury noodles are perfect for summertime, and I enjoy making them because much of the work can be done ahead of time. Most people enjoy the fragrance of the sesame paste in this recipe, but if you can't get it you can use peanut butter instead. Cold Spicy Noodles can be served with that very British dish—a mixed grill.

	Serves 4	
1lb	450g	dried or fresh egg noodles
1 tablespoon		sesame oil
	Sauce	
3 tablespoons		sesame paste or peanut butter
2 teaspoons		chilli powder
1½ tablespoons		garlic, finely chopped
2 teaspoons		Chilli Oil (page 28)
2 tablespoons		light soy sauce
1 teaspoon		salt
2 teaspoons		sugar
3 tablespoons		spring onions, finely chopped

229

Cook the noodles by boiling them for 3–5 minutes in a pot of boiling water, and then put them into cold water until you are ready to use them.

Mix the sauce ingredients together in a bowl or in an electric blender. This can be done in advance and kept refrigerated, as the sauce is meant to be cold.

Drain the cooked noodles, and toss them with the sesame oil to make sure none of the noodles stick together. Arrange the noodles on a platter or in a large bowl. Pour the sauce over the top and sprinkle on the spring onions. Toss the noodles well with the sauce before serving.

BEEF NOODLE SOUP

Region: northern

Method: blanching and braising

This is a warming, satisfying dish, rich in beefy flavour—one of my favourite northern Chinese dishes. It re-heats wonderfully and is especially delicious on cold winter nights. Don't use an expensive cut of meat for this recipe. Even stewing steak is too extravagant as it has insufficient flavour and will be too dry. Use a coarse, gristly cut of beef, such as chuck or shin.

Serves 4 to 6		
2lb	900g	boneless shin or chuck beef
1		whole cinnamon stick or Chinese cinnamon bark
2		star anise (optional)
2 tablespoons		light soy sauce
6		dried red chillis
2		dried citrus peels, soaked and finely chopped (page 18) (optional)
1 teaspoon		salt
2 pints	1·1 ltr	Chicken Stock (page 59)
12oz	350g	egg noodles, fresh or dried

Cut the meat into 2inch (5cm) cubes. Combine the meat cubes with all the other ingredients except the noodles in a large pot. Bring the mixture to the boil and then lower the heat to a simmer. Skim any scum or fat off the surface for the first 15 minutes. Then cover the pot and simmer gently for 2–2½ hours or until the meat is tender.

Cook the noodles for 3–5 minutes in a pot of boiling hot water. Then put them in cold water until you are ready to use them. When the meat is tender, drain the noodles, put them into the pot and let them warm through. Ladle some meat, broth and noodles into individual serving bowls. (This dish re-heats well.)

STIR-FRIED RICE NOODLES WITH VEGETABLES

Region: eastern and southern
Method: stir-frying

My mother often used to cook rice noodles as an alternative to egg noodles. I like the drier texture of the rice noodles and the way they absorb the flavour of a sauce. I think my mother liked them because they needed little cooking! Instead of blanching the noodles before stir-frying all she had to do was to soak them. She often cooked them with small dried shrimps, but they are equally good with vegetables as in this recipe. Rice noodles can be found in Chinese grocers, but if you can't get them, this recipe can be made with egg noodles. As with most noodles, this dish is best served with snacks such as Steamed Spareribs with Black Beans (page 244) or Sesame Prawn Toast (page 247).

Serves 3 to 4		
8oz	225g	rice noodles, rice vermicelli or rice sticks
8oz	225g	fresh bean sprouts
4oz	110g	red or green pepper (about 1)
8oz	225g	waterchestnuts, tinned (drained weight) or fresh
2 tablespoons		oil, preferably groundnut
6		spring onions, shredded
1 teaspoon		salt
2 tablespoons		light soy sauce
2 tablespoons		dry sherry or rice wine
2½ tablespoons		tomato paste
5 tablespoons		chicken stock or water

Soak the rice noodles in a bowl of warm water for 25 minutes. Then drain them in a colander or sieve. If you are using dried egg noodles, cook them for 3–5 minutes in boiling water, drain and immerse in cold water until you are ready to use them.

If you prefer (and have the time), trim the bean sprouts at both ends. Finely shred the pepper. If you are using fresh waterchestnuts, peel them, then slice and finely shred them. If you are using tinned waterchestnuts, drain them and rinse them well in cold water before shredding them finely.

Heat a wok or large pot over a high heat. Add the oil and when it is almost smoking add the spring onions. After a few seconds add the bean sprouts, shredded pepper and shredded waterchestnuts and stir-fry for about 1 minute. Then put in the rest of the ingredients and the drained noodles. Stir-fry the mixture for about 3 minutes until it is well mixed and heated through. Serve at once.

HOT BEAN THREAD NOODLES

Region: western

Method: stir-frying

Bean thread or cellophane noodles are delightfully light noodles. They are very fine, white and almost transparent and can be easily obtained from Chinese grocers and some supermarkets. They are quite easy to prepare and go well with almost any kind of sauce. Unlike other types of noodle, they can be very successfully re-heated. The spicy sauce in this recipe gives the noodles body and character, and I think it makes an excellent dish for lunch or a light supper.

Serves 4		
4oz	110g	bean thread (transparent) noodles
1 tablespoon		oil
3 tablespoons		spring onions, finely chopped
2 tablespoons		garlic, finely chopped
1lb	450g	minced beef

Sauce	
15 floz 400 ml	Chicken Stock (page 59)
1½ tablespoons	chilli bean sauce
1 tablespoon	whole yellow bean sauce
1	dried red chilli, or 1 teaspoon chilli powder
2 tablespoons	light soy sauce
1 teaspoon	sesame oil

Soak the noodles in a large bowl of warm water for 15 minutes. When they are soft, drain them and discard the water. Cut them into 3 inch (7·5 cm) lengths using scissors or a knife.

Put 1 tablespoon of oil into a hot wok or pot. Then add the spring onions and garlic and stir-fry quickly for a few seconds. Add the meat and stir-fry until it is cooked. (This should take between 5 and 10 minutes.) Then add all the sauce ingredients except the sesame oil and cook the mixture over a gentle heat for about 5 minutes. Now add the drained noodles and sesame oil and cook the mixture for a further 5 minutes. Ladle some noodles and sauce into individual bowls or into one large serving bowl, and serve at once.

DUMPLINGS, BUNS AND PANCAKES

Many types of flour are used in China to make dough for pancakes, buns and dumplings. Rice flour, especially that made from glutinous rice, is particularly favoured for desserts and pastries. I have used two types of flour in the recipes in this book. Neither of them are Chinese flours but both work very satisfactorily and they are easy to handle and to obtain.

Plain white flour

Plain white wheat flour is a soft flour which is ideal for making Chinese pancakes. It contains relatively little gluten and can be quickly mixed and rolled out. Wholewheat flour is not suitable for Chinese cookery.

Self-raising flour

This is not at all Chinese but I find it works well for buns and dumplings, and it is easier and quicker to use since it avoids the need for yeast. (Of course your buns will be slightly heavier than the authentic Chinese ones.)

STEAMED BUNS

Region: all

Method: steaming

Steamed buns are popular throughout all of China. Being steamed they have no crust. Their texture is soft and light, fluffy yet firm. They make a pleasing foil for savoury dishes. In the south they are often stuffed with savoury meats or sweet bean paste and served as *dim sum* snacks. In the north and west they are served with Smoked Tea Duck or Crispy Sichuan Duck (page 142). The Chinese would use plain flour and yeast to make these buns but I find self-raising flour is easier and quicker to use. Steamed buns re-heat well and can also be frozen and, once thawed, re-steamed. They make a delightful alternative to rice.

Serves 6 to 8		
1lb	450g	**self-raising flour**
6oz	175g	**sugar**
8oz	225g	**warm water or milk**
1oz	25g	**lard**
		parchment or greaseproof paper

Combine all the ingredients in a large bowl and mix them well into a smooth dough. Knead the mixture for about 5 minutes on a board floured with self-raising flour. Then cover the dough with a damp tea-towel and let it rest for about 1 hour in a warm place. After this period the dough should have risen a little. Meanwhile, cut the sheets of parchment or greaseproof paper into 16 pieces, 2½inches (6cm) square.

Right: Marbled Tea Eggs (page 253), Stuffed Peppers (page 250) and Sesame Prawn Toast (page 247)

Take the risen dough out of the bowl and knead it again for about 5 minutes on a floured board. If it is still sticky, dust lightly with a few tablespoons of flour. Then form it into a roll about 18 inches (45·5 cm) long and about 2 inches (5 cm) wide. Take a sharp knife and cut the roll into equal segments. There should be about 18 pieces. Take a segment of dough and work it in the palm of your hand until it forms a smooth ball. Put the ball onto a paper square. Do the same with all the rest of the pieces, and put them, together with their paper bases, onto a heatproof plate.

Set up a steamer or put a rack into a wok or deep pan and fill it with 2 inches (5 cm) of water. Bring the water to the boil and then put the plate of dough balls into the steamer or onto the stand. Cover the pan tightly and turn the heat to low. Steam the buns for about 25 minutes. (You may have to do this in two batches.)

The steamed buns are now ready to be served with Crispy Sichuan Duck (page 142) or Peking Duck (page 143). Alternatively you can let them cool and then pack them into a plastic bag and freeze them. Be sure to thaw them completely before re-heating. The best way of re-heating them is by re-steaming, as above, for 10–15 minutes, until they are thoroughly hot.

CHINESE PANCAKES
Region: northern

These pancakes are the classic accompaniment to Peking Duck (page 143) and reflect the northern Chinese use of wheat instead of rice. The pancakes are easy to make once you get the knack, which comes with practice. The unusual method of rolling 'double' pancakes is designed to ensure thinner, moister pancakes with less risk of overcooking them. Since they can be frozen it is possible to make them weeks ahead. They can also be used with other dishes, such as Stir-fried Minced Pork (page 82) or instead of the lettuce leaves in Rainbow Beef in Lettuce Leaves (page 98).

Serves 6 to 8		
10 oz	275 g	plain flour
8–9 fl oz	225–250 ml	very hot water
2 tablespoons		sesame oil

Left: Toffee Apples and Bananas (page 260)

Put the flour into a large bowl. Stir the hot water gradually into the flour, mixing all the while with chopsticks or a fork until the water is fully incorporated. Add more water if the mixture seems dry. Then remove the mixture from the bowl and knead it with your hands until it is smooth. This should take about 8 minutes. Put the dough back into the bowl, cover it with a clean, damp towel and let it rest for about 30 minutes.

After the resting period take the dough out of the bowl and knead it again for about 5 minutes, dusting with a little flour if it is sticky. Once the dough is smooth, form it into a roll about 18 inches (45·5 cm) long and about 1 inch (2·5 cm) in diameter. Take a knife and cut the roll into equal segments. There should be about 18. Roll each segment into a ball.

Take two of the dough balls. Dip one side of one ball into the sesame oil and place the oiled side on top of the other ball. Take a rolling pin, and roll the two simultaneously into a circle about 6 inches (15 cm) in diameter. It is important to roll double pancakes in this way because the resulting dough will remain moist inside and you will be able to roll them thinner but avoid the risk of overcooking them later.

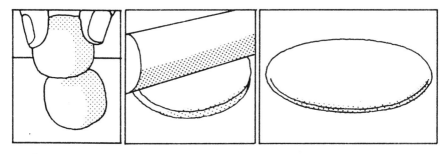

Heat a frying-pan or wok over a very low flame. Put the double pancake into the wok or pan and cook it until it has dried on one side. Flip it over and cook the other side. Remove from the pan, peel the 2 pancakes apart and set them aside. Repeat this process until all the dough balls have been cooked. (There should be about 18 pancakes in all.)

Steam the pancakes to re-heat them, or alternatively you could wrap them tightly in a double sheet of foil and put them into a pan containing 1 inch (2·5 cm) of boiling water. Cover the pan, turn the heat down very low and simmer until they are re-heated. Don't be tempted to re-heat them in the oven as this will dry them out too much. If you want to freeze the cooked pancakes, wrap them tightly in clingfilm first. When using pancakes which have been frozen, let them thaw in the refrigerator first before re-heating them.

POTSTICKER DUMPLINGS

Region: northern
Method: shallow-frying

This is a popular and rather substantial snack from northern China where, during the harsh cold winter, the dumplings are often frozen outside until they are needed. At Chinese New Year whole families gather round and stuff the dumplings together. The dumplings can be shallow-fried, boiled or steamed, but I find shallow-frying to be the tastiest way of cooking them. Shallow-fried dumplings are called potstickers because once they have been fried they are covered with liquid and cooked until they literally stick to the pan. They should be crispy on the bottom, soft on the top, and juicy inside. A dipping sauce made from Chilli Oil (page 28), vinegar and soy sauce is generally served with the potstickers. Potsticker dumplings can be made in advance and then frozen, uncooked. If you do this you don't need to thaw them before cooking them, but you will need to cook them for a little longer.

This recipe makes about 18 dumplings		
5oz	150g	plain flour
4floz	110ml	very hot water
2 tablespoons		oil, preferably groundnut
5floz	150ml	water
Stuffing		
3oz	75g	minced pork
1oz	25g	Chinese leaves or spinach, finely chopped
1 teaspoon		fresh ginger, finely chopped
1 tablespoon		dry sherry or rice wine
1 tablespoon		dark soy sauce
½ teaspoon		salt
1 tablespoon		spring onions, finely chopped
1 teaspoon		sesame oil
½ teaspoon		sugar
1 tablespoon		chicken stock or water

First make the dough. Put the flour into a large bowl and stir the hot water gradually into it, mixing it all the while with a fork or with chopsticks until most of the water is incorporated. Add more water if the mixture seems dry. Then remove the mixture from the bowl and knead it with your hands until it is smooth. This should take

239

about 8 minutes. Put the dough back into the bowl, cover it with a clean damp towel and let it rest for about 20 minutes. While the dough is resting, combine the stuffing ingredients in a large bowl and mix them together thoroughly.

After the resting period, take the dough out of the bowl and knead it again for about 5 minutes, dusting with a little flour if it is sticky. Once the dough is smooth, form it into a roll about 9 inches (23 cm) long and about 1 inch (2·5 cm) in diameter. Take a knife and cut the roll into equal segments. There should be about 18.

Roll each of the dough segments into a small ball. Then roll each ball into a small, round, flat 'pancake' about 2½ inches (6 cm) in diameter. Arrange the round skins on a lightly floured tray and cover them with a damp kitchen towel to keep them from drying out until you are ready to use them.

Put about 1 teaspoon of filling in the centre of each 'pancake' and then fold in half. Moisten the edges with water and pinch together with your fingers. Pleat around the edge, pinching to seal well. (The dumpling should look like a small Cornish pasty with a flat base and a rounded top.) Transfer the finished dumpling to the floured tray and keep it covered until you have stuffed all the dumplings in this way.

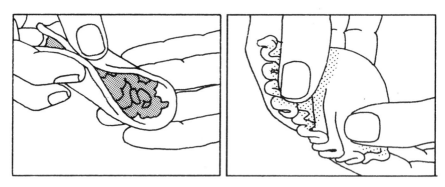

Heat a frying-pan (preferably a non-stick pan) over a high heat until it is hot. Add 1 tablespoon of oil and place the dumplings flat-side down into the pan. Turn down the heat and cook for about 2 minutes until they are lightly browned. (You may need to cook the dumplings in two batches.) Add the 5 floz (150 ml) of water, cover the pan tightly and cook for about 12 minutes or until most of the liquid is absorbed. Uncover the pan and continue to cook for a further 2 minutes. Remove the dumplings and serve.

Provide each person with three small bowls each containing some Chinese white rice vinegar, Chilli Oil (page 28), and light soy sauce. The idea is to concoct your own dipping sauce by mixing these three things exactly to your taste.

240

SNACKS
AND
SWEETS

There is an enormous variety of Chinese savoury and sweet snacks which are eaten between meals and during banquets. Such treats have been savoured by the Chinese for hundreds of years. Originally they were enjoyed only by members of the Imperial household whose chefs concocted savoury delicacies such as minced pheasant dumplings and sweet ones made from steamed milk and sweet bean sauce. Over the centuries these and many less expensive versions have found their way into the diet of the ordinary Chinese. By 1900, Cantonese restaurants were the acknowledged masters of this speciality. Appropriately, the Cantonese term for such snacks is *dim sum* which means 'eating snacks for pleasure' or 'order what you fancy'. Today, Hong Kong's Cantonese restaurants are some of the best places to enjoy *dim sum* because there the range of snacks is both wide and adventurous.

Dim sum are eaten between mid-morning and late afternoon, and most usually as a light, inexpensive lunch. Many *dim sum* restaurants in Hong Kong are enormous, consisting of a number of cavernous rooms which are jam-packed at lunchtime as family and friends meet to gossip or discuss business. The noise is deafening.

In many restaurants no menu is presented. Diners are provided with a pot of tea, cups, small plates and chopsticks. Waiters and waitresses circulate around the huge rooms pushing trolleys containing various *dim sum*. Diners stop the trolleys and select whatever appeals to them, sometimes accumulating as many as 3 dozen different small dishes. Tea is drunk throughout the meal, which is why *dim sum* is sometimes referred to as *yam cha*—the Cantonese words for drinking tea. At the end of the meal the bill is calculated by counting up the number of small plates or steamers on the table. It is all great fun.

Dim sum come in all flavours and can be hot, sour, sweet or spicy. They are prepared in many different ways, although some of the most popular are cooked in attractive little round bamboo steamers which are then transported in stacks on *dim sum* trolleys. Some of the most popular *dim sum* snacks are:

● Spring roll (*chun guen*): the familiar deep-fried pastry filled with vegetables and meat.

● Barbecued pork bun: (*cha siu bau*): steamed or baked buns filled with delicious pieces of roasted pork.

● Pork dumplings (*siu mai*): dumplings filled with minced pork and steamed.

● Steamed spareribs (*pai gwat*): spareribs cut into short pieces and steamed with black bean sauce.

242

● Shrimp dumplings (*har gau*): delicate light dumplings filled with shrimp and pork, and steamed.

● Fried taro dumplings (*woo kok*): mashed taro root filled with pork and deep-fried.

There are dozens of other simple and exotic varieties. In this chapter I have included recipes for some of the simpler *dim sum* which can be successfully made at home. If you have never tried *dim sum*, do seek out a Chinese restaurant which serves them. (You will find not every Chinese restaurant offers them as they require the expertise of special *dim sum* chefs.)

As for desserts, I knew nothing of them as a child. In authentic Chinese tradition my mother served fresh fruit at the end of a family meal, usually fresh oranges cut into wedges. Puddings, ice-cream and sweets were unknown to me until I ventured out into the non-Chinese world. Of course Chinese desserts do exist although they are not a feature of the cuisine as they are in the West. They usually come in the form of sweet *dim sum*, but I find most of them overpoweringly sweet. I have therefore included recipes for some of the simpler and less sickly Chinese desserts. Of course, one may serve European-style desserts at the end of a Chinese meal, but my experience is that the subtle and complex tastes and flavours of Chinese dishes are best appreciated when followed by a simple dessert of fresh fruit.

PRAWN CRACKERS

Region: southern
Method: deep-frying

I have always had a fondness for crispy snacks, especially prawn crackers. They are made from a combination of prawn meat, starch, salt and sugar which is pounded into a paste and then dried into hard, round crisps. They are sold in many supermarkets and Chinese grocers and need only to be deep-fried. They are terrific for serving with drinks.

Serves 4 to 6		
1 pint	570ml	**oil, preferably groundnut (see Deep-fat fryers, page 34)**
3½oz	100g	**prawn crackers**

243

Heat the oil in a deep-fat fryer or large wok until it is hot. Test the oil to see if it is hot enough by dropping in one prawn cracker. If it puffs up and floats immediately to the top then the oil is ready. If not, wait a few minutes more and test again.

Deep-fry a handful of the prawn crackers. Once they have puffed up, scoop them out immediately with a slotted spoon and drain them on kitchen paper. Then deep-fry the rest, a handful at a time.

STEAMED SPARERIBS WITH BLACK BEANS

Region: southern

Method: steaming

This is a popular *dim sum* snack. The spareribs are steamed until they are so tender they melt in your mouth. The steaming process ensures that the meat is permeated by the pungent flavour and smell of the black beans.

Serves 2 to 4	
1½lb 700g	pork spareribs
1 teaspoon	salt
4floz 110ml	chicken stock
1 tablespoon	light soy sauce
1 teaspoon	sesame oil
1 teaspoon	fresh ginger, finely chopped
1½ tablespoons	black beans, coarsely chopped
2 teaspoons	garlic, finely chopped
½ teaspoon	salt
1 teaspoon	sugar
1 tablespoon	dry sherry or rice wine

If possible, ask your butcher to cut the spareribs into individual ribs and then into 2 inch (5 cm) segments. Otherwise do this yourself with a cleaver or a sharp, heavy knife (see illustration page 92). Rub the spareribs with salt and let them sit in a bowl for about 20–25 minutes. Fill a large saucepan with water and bring it to the boil. Turn the heat to low, add the spareribs and simmer them for 10 minutes. Drain them and discard the water.

Mix the other ingredients together in a large bowl and stir in the spareribs, coating them well with the mixture. Transfer the mixture to a deep plate or dish.

Set up a steamer or put a rack into a wok or large, deep pot. Pour in 2 inches (5 cm) water. Bring the water to the boil, and then reduce the heat. Lower the plate of spareribs carefully into the steamer or onto the rack. Cover it with a lid and steam gently for 1 hour or until the spareribs are very tender. Remember to keep a careful watch on the water level, and replenish it with hot water when necessary. Skim off any surface fat and serve.

You can make this dish ahead of time and re-heat the ribs by steaming for 20 minutes or until they are hot.

SPRING ROLLS

Region: all
Method: deep-frying

Spring rolls are among the best-known Chinese snacks. They are not difficult to make and are a perfect starter for any meal. Spring rolls should be crisp, light and delicate. Avoid all greasy, bulky imitations which are sometimes called egg rolls. The skins for spring rolls can be obtained fresh or frozen from Chinese grocers. Be sure to let them thaw thoroughly if they are frozen.

This recipe makes about 12–15 spring rolls		
1 packet		spring roll skins
6oz	175g	Parma ham or lean English smoked bacon
4oz	110g	mange-tout, trimmed
4oz	110g	red or green pepper (about 1)
4oz	110g	waterchestnuts, tinned (drained weight) or fresh
1 tablespoon		oil, preferably groundnut
4oz	110g	fresh bean sprouts
4		spring onions, finely shredded
1 teaspoon		salt
1 teaspoon		sugar
1 teaspoon		light soy sauce
1 teaspoon		dark soy sauce

1 teaspoon	sesame oil
1½ tablespoons	dry sherry or rice wine
2 pints 1·1 ltr	oil, preferably groundnut, for deep-frying (see Deep-fat fryers, page 34)

Flour paste seal

3 tablespoons	plain flour blended with 1½ tablespoons water

Finely shred the ham or bacon, mange-tout and pepper into very thin slices using a sharp knife or cleaver. If you are using fresh waterchestnuts, peel them and then thinly slice them. If you are using tinned waterchestnuts, rinse them well in cold water, drain and then slice them finely.

Heat a wok or large frying-pan, add the oil and, when it is hot, stir-fry the ham or bacon and all the vegetables for 1 minute. Add the salt, sugar, soy sauces, sesame oil and sherry or rice wine. Stir-fry this mixture for 3 minutes and then turn it into a colander to drain and cool.

Mix the flour paste seal in a small bowl. Put about 3 table-spoons of the cooled filling on each spring roll skin. Fold in each side and then roll it up tightly. Use the flour paste to seal the open end by brushing a small amount on the edge. Then press the edge onto the roll. You should have a roll about 4 inches (10 cm) long, a little like an oversized cigar.

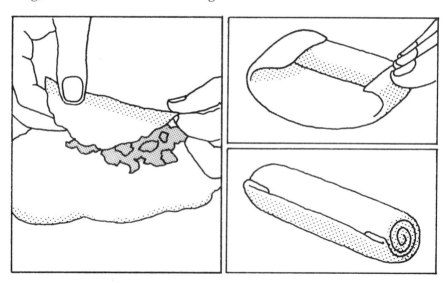

Heat the 2 pints (1·1 ltr) oil in a deep-fat fryer or large wok until it is hot and almost smoking. Deep-fry the spring rolls in several batches until they are golden brown. Drain them on kitchen paper. Serve at once with your choice of dipping sauces (pages 27 to 30).

246

SESAME PRAWN TOAST

Region: southern
Method: deep-frying

Sesame Prawn Toast is a savoury snack which is often served in *dim sum* restaurants outside China. Its origins are rather obscure, but I suspect it is a variation on the prawn paste used widely in southern China for stuffings or for deep-frying into crispy balls. Whatever its origin it is delicious and easy to make.

Makes about 30 pieces	
10 slices	bread, very thinly sliced
3 tablespoons	white sesame seeds
15 floz 400 ml	oil, preferably groundnut (see Deep-fat fryers, page 34)
Prawn paste	
1 lb 450 g	peeled prawns, preferably uncooked
1 teaspoon	salt
1	egg
2 tablespoons	spring onions, finely chopped
2 teaspoons	fresh ginger, finely chopped
1 tablespoon	light soy sauce
1 teaspoon	sesame oil

Using a cleaver or sharp knife, chop the prawns coarsely and then mince them finely into a paste. Put the paste into a bowl and mix in the rest of the ingredients. (You could do this in a food processor.) This step can be done hours in advance, but you should then wrap the paste well in clingfilm and put it into the refrigerator until you need it.

If the bread is fresh, place it in a warm oven to dry out. (Dried bread will absorb less oil.) Remove the crusts and cut the bread into rectangles about 3 inches (7·5 cm) × 1 inch (2·5 cm). (You should have about 3 pieces per slice.) Spread the prawn paste thickly on each piece of bread. The paste should form a mound about ⅛ inch (0·3 cm) deep, although you can spread it more thinly if you prefer. Sprinkle the toasts with the sesame seeds.

Heat the oil in a deep-fat fryer or wok to a moderate heat. Deep-fry several prawn toasts at a time, paste-side down for 2–3 minutes. Then turn them over and deep-fry for about 2 minutes, or until they are golden brown. Repeat the process until they are all done. Remove with a slotted spoon, drain on kitchen paper and serve.

247

FRIED WUNTUN

Region: southern
Method: deep-frying

Although I have rarely seen fried wuntun in China, they are common in Chinese restaurants in the West. This is perhaps because they are easily prepared and their crisp, dry texture goes well with drinks. Wuntun skins can be bought fresh or frozen from Chinese grocers. (Be sure to thaw them thoroughly if they are frozen.) Filled, uncooked wuntun can be frozen successfully.

	Serves 6
1 packet	**wuntun skins (about 30–35 skins)**
1 pint 570ml	**oil, preferably groundnut (see Deep-fat fryers, page 34)**
	Filling
12oz 350g	**minced pork**
2 tablespoons	**Parma ham or lean English smoked bacon, finely chopped**
1 tablespoon	**dark soy sauce**
1 tablespoon	**dry sherry or rice wine**
1½ tablespoons	**spring onions, finely chopped**
2 teaspoons	**fresh ginger, finely chopped**
1 teaspoon	**sesame oil**
1	**egg, beaten**
½ teaspoon	**cornflour**
1 teaspoon	**sugar**

Combine the filling ingredients together in a large bowl and mix well. Then, using a teaspoon, put a small amount of filling in the

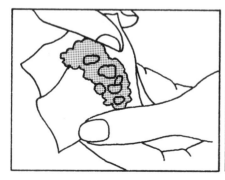
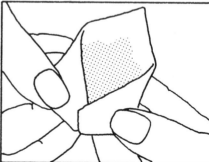

centre of each wuntun skin. Bring up two sides, dampen the edges with a little water and pinch them together to make a triangle. Fold over the bottom two corners and press together. The filling should be well sealed in.

Heat the oil in a deep-fat fryer or large wok until it is very hot. It should almost smoke. Deep-fry the filled wuntun in several batches and drain each batch on kitchen paper. Serve them at once with your choice of dipping sauces (pages 27 to 30).
'

STEAMED OPEN DUMPLINGS

Region: southern
Method: steaming

This is a favourite snack in many *dim sum* teahouses throughout southern China. It is merely a wuntun or egg dough dumpling which is filled and steamed instead of being poached and deep-fried. The steamed dumpling has a character wholly different to pan-fried or boiled dumplings. The texture and taste of the steamed dumpling filling is more pronounced, yet delicate and subtle at the same time. The skin, once steamed, retains a slightly chewy texture. Wuntun skins can be obtained fresh or frozen from Chinese grocers, and filled wuntun can be frozen successfully and thawed when required. This dish can be made ahead of time and re-heated by re-steaming when you are ready to serve it.

Serves 4 to 6	
1 packet	wuntun skins (about 30–35 skins)
Filling	
12oz 350g	minced pork
2 tablespoons	Parma ham or lean English smoked bacon, finely chopped
1 tablespoon	light soy sauce
2 teaspoons	dry sherry or rice wine
1½ tablespoons	spring onions, finely chopped
1 teaspoon	fresh ginger, finely chopped
1 teaspoon	sesame oil
1	egg, beaten
1 teaspoon	sugar

Combine the filling ingredients and mix them together well. Spoon a generous portion of filling onto each wuntun skin. Bring up the sides and press them down over the top of the filling mixture. Tap the dumpling on the bottom to make a flat base. The top should be wide open, exposing the meat filling.

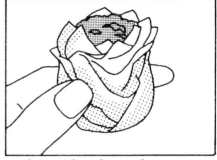

Set up a steamer or put a rack inside a wok or large, deep pot. Pour in about 2 inches (5 cm) of water and bring it to the boil. Put the dumplings on a plate and place this into the steamer or onto the rack.

Cover the pot tightly, turn the heat low, and steam gently for about 20 minutes. (You may have to do this in several batches.) Serve the dumplings hot with your choice of dipping sauce (see pages 27 to 30). Keep the first batch warm by covering them with foil and placing them in a warm but switched-off oven until all the dumplings are ready to serve.

STUFFED PEPPERS

Region: southern

Method: steaming and shallow-frying

Red or green sweet peppers are delicious when they are stuffed. These snacks feature on many *dim sum* menus in southern China. Easy to make, they also re-heat well. The quick pan-frying before serving gives the snacks a crusty brownish top. They make an attractive dish for a light luncheon.

Serves 4 to 6		
1 lb	450 g	**red or green peppers**
3 tablespoons		**cornflour**
1½ tablespoons		**oil, preferably groundnut**

Filling		
4 oz	110 g	waterchestnuts, tinned (drained weight) or fresh
8 oz	225 g	prawns, preferably uncooked, or white fish fillets, skinned
8 oz	225 g	minced pork
1		egg white
1 teaspoon		cornflour
1 teaspoon		salt
1½ tablespoons		light soy sauce
2 teaspoons		sesame oil
1 tablespoon		dry sherry or rice wine
1 teaspoon		sugar
2 tablespoons		spring onions, finely chopped

Halve the peppers and remove the seeds and pulp. Next prepare the stuffing. If you are using fresh waterchestnuts, peel and chop them finely. If you are using tinned waterchestnuts, first rinse them well in cold water. Drain in a colander and then chop them finely. Shell the prawns and, if you are using the large uncooked ones, remove the fine digestive cord. Coarsely chop the prawns or fish. Put the waterchestnuts and prawns or fish into a bowl with the rest of the filling ingredients and mix them together very well. Dust the pepper halves lightly with cornflour and stuff them with the filling mixture. Now cut each stuffed pepper half into 2 or 4 chunks and arrange them on a plate.

Set up a steamer or put a rack into a wok or deep pan and pour in 2 inches (5 cm) of water. Bring the water to the boil and then carefully put the plate of stuffed peppers into the steamer or onto the rack. Cover the wok or pan tightly and steam gently for 20 minutes. (You may have to do this in two batches.) The snacks may be prepared in advance up to this point.

When you are ready to serve the peppers, heat the oil in a wok or large frying-pan until it is moderately hot. Fry the peppers, stuffing-side down, until they are lightly brown and heated through. Serve immediately.

CARAMEL WALNUTS

Region: northern
Method: deep-frying

The first time I had this delicious snack was at a Beijing restaurant in Hong Kong and I was determined to learn how to make them. As it turned out they were surprisingly easy. The shelled walnuts must be blanched first to rid them of any bitterness. They are then rolled in sugar, left to dry for several hours, then deep-fried to caramelise the sugar coating. Finally they are rolled in sesame seeds. The result is a classic contrast of tastes and textures. They can be served cold or hot and they are perfect with drinks.

Serves 4		
8oz	225g	walnuts, shelled
4oz	110g	sugar
15floz	400ml	oil, preferably groundnut (see Deep-fat fryers, page 34)
3 tablespoons		white sesame seeds

Bring a pot of water to the boil. Add the walnuts and cook for about 10 minutes to blanch them. Drain the nuts in a colander or sieve, and then pat dry with kitchen paper and spread them on a baking tray. Sprinkle the sugar over the walnuts and roll them around in the sugar to cover them completely. Put the tray of sugared walnuts into an oven which has been heated to a low temperature and switched off. Let them dry for at least 2 hours.

Heat the oil in a deep-fat fryer or wok to a moderate heat. Fry a batch of the walnuts for about 2 minutes or until the sugar melts and the walnuts turn golden. (Watch the heat to prevent burning.) Remove the walnuts from the oil with a slotted spoon or strainer. Sprinkle them with some of the sesame seeds and lay them on a cake rack to cool. (Do not drain them on kitchen paper as the sugar will stick to it when it dries.) Deep-fry and drain the rest of the walnuts in the same way. Once cooled, the caramel walnuts can be kept in a sealed glass jar for about 2 weeks. Serve them warm or cold.

MARBLED TEA EGGS

Region: southern
Method: simmering

This unique method of cooking eggs in spiced tea derives its name from the marbled texture and web of cracks which appear on the surface of the eggs when they are shelled. Traditionally, tea eggs are served cold and they make a wonderful and easy garnish for cold platters. Not only are they delicious but they are also beautiful to look at. Once the eggs have cooled they can be kept in the tea liquid and stored in the refrigerator for up to 2 days.

Serves 4 to 6	
6	eggs
3 pints 1·7ltr	water
Tea mixture	
3 tablespoons	black tea, preferably Chinese
2 tablespoons	dark soy sauce
1 teaspoon	salt
1	cinnamon stick or Chinese cinnamon bark
1	star anise (optional)

If you keep your eggs in the refrigerator, take them out and let them warm to room temperature. (This will help prevent premature cracking of the egg shells when they are boiled.)

Fill a large pot with the water and bring to the boil. Using a spoon, lower the eggs into the pot and turn the heat down to a simmer. Cook the eggs for 10 minutes, then remove them and place in a bowl of cold water. (Do not discard the water in which you have cooked them.) In about 10 minutes, when the eggs have cooled, gently crack each shell with the back of a spoon until the entire shell is a network of cracks.

Take the pot of water in which you have cooked the eggs and combine it with the tea mixture. Bring the mixture to a boil and return the cracked eggs to the pot. Reduce the heat to a simmer and cook them for about 25 minutes. Remove the pot from the heat and allow the eggs to cool in the liquid.

Remove the eggs from the cooled liquid and gently peel off the cracked shells. You should have a beautiful marble-like web on each egg. Serve them cut in half or quarters as a snack with other cold dishes or use them as garnish. They are also a glamorous dish for a picnic.

253

COLD MARINADED PEANUTS

Region: northern

Method: marinading

Peanuts were only introduced into China in the sixteenth century, but they quickly won an important place in Chinese agriculture. The peanut plant replenishes the soil as it grows and the nuts themselves are a nutritious supplement to the diet both in their natural form and as groundnut oil. This dish may be made a day or two in advance and can be served cold or at room temperature.

Serves 6 to 8		
1 lb	450 g	raw peanuts
3 tablespoons		light soy sauce
3 tablespoons		dark soy sauce
1 tablespoon		garlic, finely chopped
5 fl oz	150 ml	cider vinegar or Chinese white rice vinegar
3 fl oz	75 ml	dry sherry or rice wine

First blanch the peanuts by immersing them in a pot of boiling water for about 2 minutes. Drain them and let them cool and the skins should come off easily.

Put the blanched peanuts in a bowl. Mix in all the other ingredients. Let the peanuts marinade in this mixture for at least 2 or 3 hours, stirring from time to time to ensure an even distribution of the marinade. Most of it will be absorbed by the peanuts. Serve with Pickled Vegetables (page 213) as snacks or appetisers. We Chinese eat them one by one using chopsticks!

FRESH FRUIT
Region: all

Our family meals always ended with a plate of fresh oranges sliced into wedges. Occasionally during the summer we had special treats such as wedges of watermelon or honeydew melon instead. It has always struck me how appropriate simple fresh fruits are after a Chinese meal. They are invariably refreshing, cleansing the palate and adding a final sweet note to the end of a meal. I think it is probably one of the most pleasing and sensible desserts for a Chinese or any other meal and it is easy!

FRUIT COMPOTE
Region: southern

Southern China is fortunate in having a bountiful supply of fruits, some of which are very exotic such as lychees, loquats and kumquats. Lychees were so sought after by the Imperial Court that, once picked, they were rushed to the Court by special fast horse relays. Some of these special fruits are now available in tins. They are acceptable but should be served without their sickly sweet syrup. A mixed compote of fresh and tinned fruits is a delicious and most appropriate dessert for any dinner party.

	Serves 4 to 6	
2		apples
2		oranges
6oz	175g	cantaloupe melon
14oz	400g	tinned lychees, drained

Using a sharp knife, peel, core and slice the apples into thin wedges. Peel and slice the oranges into segments. Cut the melon in half, scoop out and discard the pulp and seeds. Cut the melon flesh into 1inch (2·5cm) cubes. Combine all the fruits together in a large bowl. Mix them gently together. Wrap the bowl tightly in clingfilm until you are ready to serve the compote.

ALMOND JELLY WITH FRESH ORANGES

Region: southern

This is my version of a classic Chinese dessert. In the original version, agar-agar (a type of seaweed) is used instead of gelatine, ground almond juice is used instead of almond extract, and a sugar syrup is served with it instead of orange juice. The original version involves a long and laborious process which requires obscure ingredients. I think this recipe, although it departs from the original, is nevertheless a delicious and refreshing variation.

Serves 4		
1 tablespoon		gelatine
10 fl oz	300 ml	water
10 fl oz	300 ml	milk
3 tablespoons		sugar
1 teaspoon		almond extract
10 fl oz	300 ml	fresh orange juice
2		oranges

Put the gelatine into a small bowl. Add half the water to dissolve the gelatine and bring the other half to a boil in a small pot. Pour the hot water into the gelatine and cold water and stir until the gelatine has completely dissolved. Combine this with the milk, sugar and almond extract in a large bowl. Pour the mixture into a pyrex dish or square baking tin about 7 inches (18 cm) square and 1½ inches (3·5 cm) deep. Put it in the refrigerator for about 2 hours or until it has completely set.

Peel the oranges and remove all the white pith. Separate them into segments. When the almond jelly is ready, cut it into 1 inch (2·5 cm) cubes. Put some orange segments into individual bowls. Add some almond jelly cubes, and then pour a little orange juice over each portion.

PEACHES IN HONEY SYRUP

Region: western
Method: simmering

Any list of the classical fruits of China should begin with the peach which figures prominently in folklore, traditional religion, literature and popular affection. New exotic varieties were introduced into China from Central Asia during the Tang dynasty (618–907 AD). In this recipe, peaches are poached in a sugar syrup and then the liquid reduced to a honey-like consistency. The dish can be served warm or cold and makes a simple, light, sweet dessert.

Serves 4	
2	large firm peaches
4 tablespoons	sugar, preferably Chinese rock sugar
5 floz 150ml	water

Bring a pot of water to the boil and quickly blanch the peaches in it for a few seconds. Remove them with a slotted spoon. With a sharp knife, peel the skin off the peaches and split each one in half, discarding the stone.

Combine the sugar and water in a small pot and boil the mixture together until the sugar dissolves. Then add the peach halves and turn the heat down to a low simmer. Simmer the peach mixture for about 15 minutes or until the peaches are tender. Gently remove them with a slotted spoon. Turn the heat to high and reduce the liquid to about half the amount—it should become a sweet syrup. If you are serving the dish hot, pour the liquid over the peaches and serve at once. If you are serving it cold, let the liquid cool, pour it over the peaches and refrigerate until you are ready to serve it.

STEAMED PEARS

Region: northern
Method: steaming

Pears are a northern Chinese fruit which are eaten fresh, cooked in soups, deep-fried, and are especially delicious when steamed. The steaming process cooks the pears without drying them out. The Chinese traditionally serve this dish hot, but I find it equally good cold.

Serves 4	
4	firm pears
3 tablespoons	sugar, preferably Chinese rock sugar
3 fl oz 75 ml	water
2	cinnamon sticks or Chinese cinnamon bark

Peel the pears and cut them in half. Remove the core and seeds. Combine the sugar and water together in a small pot and boil it until the sugar has completely dissolved. Allow it to cool slightly.

Put the pears, sugar-water and cinnamon together into a shallow bowl. Set up a steamer or put a rack into a wok or pan. Add about 2 inches (5 cm) of water and bring to the boil. Put the bowl of pears into the steamer or on to the rack, turn the heat down to a simmer and cover the wok or pot tightly with a lid. Slowly steam the pears for about 15–25 minutes until they are tender. (The cooking time will depend on the ripeness of the pears.)

When the pears are cooked, drain all the liquid and cinnamon stick or bark into a small saucepan and reduce the liquid to a syrup by boiling it fast. Remove and discard the cinnamon stick. Pour the syrup over the pears and serve at once. Alternatively you can let the mixture cool, cover it with clingfilm and refrigerate until you are ready to serve it.

EGG CUSTARD

Region: southern

Method: steaming

One of the delights I have enjoyed since childhood, whether at a formal dinner or at a casual *dim sum* lunch, is egg custard. I love egg custard served on its own in a cup or as a filling for little pastry tartlets. The secret of this light, velvety and satin-textured custard lies in both the addition of sugar-water to lighten the eggs and in the steaming technique. I have added my own touch of crystallised ginger or you could use fresh orange zest. It can be served hot or cold.

Serves 4 to 6		
15 floz	400 ml	water
4 oz	110 g	sugar
6		eggs, beaten
¼ teaspoon		almond or vanilla extract
2 tablespoons		crystallised ginger or fresh orange zest, finely chopped

Combine the water and sugar together in a large pot and bring it to the boil. Continue to boil the mixture until the sugar has entirely dissolved. Let the mixture cool completely.

In a large bowl combine the eggs, almond or vanilla extract and ginger or orange. Mix them thoroughly and add the cooled sugar-water mixture. Pour the mixture into a heatproof shallow bowl. Cut a round piece of waxed paper or parchment paper to cover the top of the bowl. (This will prevent the top of the custard from drying out.)

Set up a steamer or put a rack into a wok or pan. Add 2 inches (5 cm) of water and bring to a simmer. Put the bowl of custard into the steamer or onto the rack and cover the wok or pan tightly. Gently steam for about 20 minutes or until the custard has set. Remove the cooked custard and allow it to cool slightly before serving it. Alternatively let it cool completely. Then wrap it in clingfilm and put it in the refrigerator until you are ready to serve it.

TOFFEE APPLES AND BANANAS

Region: northern
Method: deep-frying

Although apples and bananas are most often associated with southern China, they are glazed with honey or sugar and eaten as snacks throughout the country. The dish requires some dexterity which will come with experience. Make it for yourself a few times before you attempt it for guests.

Serves 4		
2		large firm apples
2		firm bananas
1oz	25g	plain flour
1oz	25g	cornflour
1		large egg
1 teaspoon		sesame oil
10floz	300ml	oil, preferably groundnut (see Deep-fat fryers, page 34)
2 teaspoons		sesame oil
6oz	175g	sugar
2 tablespoons		white sesame seeds

Peel and core the apples and cut each into 8 large thick wedges. Peel the bananas and cut them into 1½inch (3·5cm) chunks. Combine the flour, cornflour, egg and 1 teaspoon of sesame oil in a small bowl. Mix them well to form a smooth, very thick batter.

Combine the groundnut oil and 2 teaspoons of sesame oil in a deep-fat fryer or wok and heat the mixture until it is moderately hot. Put the fruit into the batter mixture. Then lift out several pieces of fruit at a time using a slotted spoon and drain off any excess batter. Deep-fry for about 2 minutes until they are golden. Remove with a slotted spoon and drain on kitchen paper. Repeat the process until you have deep-fried all the fruit.

Just before serving, prepare a bowl of iced water filled with ice cubes. Re-heat the oil to a moderate heat and deep-fry the fruit a second time for about 2 minutes. Drain again on kitchen paper. Put the sugar, sesame seeds and 2 tablespoons of oil from the deep-frying oil into a pot. Heat the mixture until the sugar melts and begins to caramelise. (Watch the heat to prevent it from burning.) When the caramel is light brown, add the fruit sections. Stir them gently in the caramel syrup to coat them. Then take them out and put them into the iced water to harden. Do a few at a time to prevent them from sticking together. Remove them from the water and place on a serving platter. Serve at once.

WALNUT BISCUITS

Region: southern

Method: baking

Although baking is not a common Chinese method of cooking, biscuits of all kinds are quite popular in the south. The most famous is the almond biscuit, but walnut biscuits are equally delicious. They can be served alone or with fresh fruit.

Makes about 12 biscuits		
12		walnut halves
1½oz	40g	lard
4oz	110g	self-raising flour
1 teaspoon		baking powder
4oz	110g	sugar
2		eggs

Immerse the walnut pieces in a pot of boiling water for about 5 minutes. Remove them with a slotted spoon, pat dry with kitchen paper and set aside.

Pre-heat the oven to gas mark 6, 400°F, 200°C. In a large bowl rub the lard into the flour and baking powder until it is well mixed. Next mix in the sugar and 1 egg to form a thick paste. Divide the mixture into 12 balls of dough and press them into flattish, biscuit shapes about 2 inches (5 cm) in diameter. Put them on a non-stick baking tray or use a plain baking sheet greased with 1 teaspoon of oil. Press a piece of walnut on the top of each biscuit. Using a pastry brush, glaze the top of each biscuit with 1 beaten egg. Put them in the oven and bake them for about 20 minutes. Remove the cooked biscuits and set them on a cooling rack. Once cooled, the biscuits can be stored in a tightly covered jar where they will keep for about a week.

Mail-order sources of Chinese ingredients and cooking equipment

There are now many Chinese grocers throughout the UK. Here is a list of those which offer a mail-order service.

Greater London

Cheong-Leen Supermarket
4–10 Tower Street
Cambridge Circus
London W2 9NR
01–836 5378/9

Wah Fung Chinese
 Supermarket
146 Camden High Street
London NW1 0NE
01–485 6156

Maysun Markets
869 Finchley Road
London NW11
01–455 4773

Ken Lo's Kitchen
14 Eccleston Street
London SW1W 0NZ
01–730 7734

Matahari Impex (Far East) Ltd
11 & 12 Hogarth Place
Earl's Court
London SW5
01–370 1041

and at:

328 Balham High Road
Tooting Bec
London SW17
01–767 3107

Chinese Food Centre Ltd
156 Balham High Road
London SW12 9BN
01–675 3120

S.W. Trading
283 Water Road
Alperton, Middlesex HA0 1HX
01–998 2248/9

Sheen Road Food Stores
116 Sheen Road
Richmond
Surrey
01–948 6805

South and East England

Eastern Stores
214–216 Kingston Road
Portsmouth PO2 7LR
0705 662816

Man's Cafe
30 Spring Street
Portsmouth
Hants PO1 4AA
0705 822504

Continental Food Centre
148 Cornwall Street
Plymouth PL1 1NJ
0752 669073

The Delicatessen
164 Old Christchurch Road
Bournemouth
Dorset
0202 295979

Kam Cheung Chinese
 Supermarket
28–30 Burleigh Street
Cambridge CB1 1DG
0223 316429

Jason's Oriental Shop
16 Milton Road
Cambridge CB4 1JY
0223 68735

Midlands

Janson Hong Chinese
  Supermarket
17–18 St Martin's House
Bull Ring
Birmingham B5 5DD
021–643 4681

P.K.M. Chinese Co. Ltd
5 Melton Street
Leicester LE1 3NA
0533 29656

North-west and North-east England

Man Cheong Hong
99 Fishergate Hill
Preston
Lancs
0772 22509

Quality Foods Cash and Carry
Quality House
Edderthorpe Street (off Leeds
  Road)
Bradford BD3 9JX
0274 393328/663944

Chung Wah Trading Co.
31–32 Great George Square
Liverpool L1 5DZ
051–709 2637

Hondo Trading Co. Ltd
149–153 Duke Street
Liverpool L1 4JR
051–708 5409

Tai Sun Chinese Supermarket
49 College Road
Balby
Doncaster
South Yorkshire
0302 4360

Scotland

Jim's Chinese Supermarket
7A Bath Street
Glasgow G2
041–342 4492

The BBC would like to thank the following for the loan of equipment and accessories for the photographs: William Mehornay, 52 Worple Way, Richmond, Surrey: George Horan (Oriental Antiques), 38a Kensington Church Street, London W8: Neal Street East, 5 Neal Street, London WC2: Craftsmen Potters Association, William Blake House, Marshall Street, London W1.

INDEX

264